BE A VOICE
NOT AN ECHO

BE A VOICE
NOT AN ECHO

PAT REGAN

To Kelly.
every blessing to you kelly
on your journey of life

26th February
2021

Published by Zaccmedia
www.zaccmedia.com
info@zaccmedia.com

Published June 2020

ISBN: 978-1-911211-94-5 (paperback)
         978-1-911211-95-2 (hardback)
         Also available as a Kindle eBook

British Library Cataloguing-in-Publication Data.
A catalogue record for this book is available from the British Library.

Typesetting & Cover Design by Zaccmedia.com

CONTENTS

Part Two

ACKNOWLEDGEMENTS AND DEDICATION

I acknowledge the Father of all who sent His son Jesus to bring me into a relationship with Him, that stands the test of time.

For my dear wife Daph, and family, who have been instruments of God to bring change in my life.

I am indebted to the Reverend D W Anthony, and the Reverend John Barr who watched over me in the wilderness experience. Also, Bill and Molly Worboys who taught me and demonstrated a love that affected me greatly.

For Jean Darnell and Dr Sharon Stone, whose prophetic words came to me that brought such life and encouragement when I wanted to give up.

I also acknowledge those that have spent hours helping me in ministry: Diane Bailey, Allyson Osborn and Patricia Biddulph, and all those that I have ministered with.

I acknowledge Alison Gray, for her great patience in the preparation of this book. Also, for Janet and Selwyn Goodacre, for their encouragement and all the work they also have put into this book.

I am a welder by trade: a very practical person. But I know this wouldn't have been possible to write down all the lessons of life and watching so many life changes, without His presence. My prayer is that my story will encourage you to trust and obey the Lord. He is alive today, with a passion in His heart for you to fulfil your calling and destiny in life with Him.

I dedicate this book to those who have much and those who have little, and all those in between, who are honest with themselves, who seek real life and the answers to living.

FOREWORD

By Daphne Regan (Pat's wife)

When Pat mentioned that he felt God was calling him to write a book, I knew immediately I wanted to write the "Foreword". Probably I am the person who knows him best, his strengths and weakness, victories and struggles – the man he is, but always a man who totally "lives what he preaches" and believes.

Many people easily say one thing but totally live another. Pat is one of those rare people who totally lives what he says. If he says 'trust God in the situation' you know he has lived it and proved it for himself. His commitment to God is total.

Never over 50 years have I heard him say anything negative about his relationship with God or doubt Gods' ability to heal, restore and bless His children. What Pat says is what he lives!

Over 50 years of marriage my judgement on Pat is that "here is a man of God".

His faith is simple, doesn't complicate it with current beliefs and attitudes or fashionable thinking. Gods' Word is always the plumb line for his life.

This book has been produced from a lifetime of trusting God and allowing Him to work in his life, make mistakes, get it wrong but always learn and submit to the Lordship of Christ. Even when it is hard, against the norm and goes against what he wants to do, or people's expectations. Not a perfect man but one who loves with all his heart a perfect God.

As his wife it has been an honour and a privilege to stand with him although I may not totally understand Gods' dealing with Pat, to totally respect him and his relationship to God.

His concern and love for me, his precious children, Patrick, Matthew, Becky, Diane and John and grandchildren, Keziah, Daniel, Abigail, Caleb, David and Esther, results in many long hours of fasting and prayer and "being there" if needed.

Pat has a big heart to see his family and Gods' family come into the fulness of knowing God, the reality of Him in their lives and will totally "lay down his life" in order for others to be healed, set free and living life as God intended.

This book is the story of one man who simply found God to be a "living reality". The words of a song came to mind "I'm everything I am because you loved me". I can echo these words as Pat's wife and I know Pat would say:

"Lord I'm everything I am because you love me".

PREFACE

My wife came into my prayer cabin in our back garden and asked what I was doing. I said, "I am going to write a book".

Daph responded, "This is a miracle!"

I knew what she meant. Daph knows I don't like writing as I am a very practical person. But I am now convicted. During my life, so many people have said I should write a book, but when the Lord tells you to do it, not once but three times, you know it's right. I can't make any more excuses.

My heart is to see ordinary people have such a relationship with the Lord our God that their whole being is passionate about loving Him, and out of this to have relationship with Him; to want to please Him by doing His Will. The Lord wants to be involved in our lives. I have seen Him heal and deliver people in Costa, Starbucks, bus stations, on planes, trains, in their homes, on the streets, across Eastern Europe and many parts of the world. Why is this? Even as I began writing, in these last few days, I have had 7 divine appointments, with God bringing people to me from across the world. I can't thank God enough that today we can experience a living relationship with our Father in Heaven through Jesus Christ, the Son of the Living God. I believe it's God's main objective that we move from being ordinary and insignificant and unqualified to do the works of Jesus, to being Jesus to a world of people that are separate from God, but have desperate needs to have a purpose in life, to have a sense of fulfilment as well as a relief from their pain, whether it be rejection, great loss or any kind of bondage or sickness.

There is a reason to get up in the morning that is bigger than our world and all its needs.

This is my story – how I found a life that is eternal, or should I say, how God found me and by his foreknowledge gave me His grace that enables me to walk and live this journey in life.

Part One

Chapter 1

EARLIEST DAYS

To be honest, I don't have a lot of memories of the earliest years of my life when we lived in Norfolk. My parents got married just after the Second World War. It wasn't a brilliant start. There was very little choice where to live. My first home was a railway carriage situated just by Wroxham Broads. It was damp, with rats being our companions.

My grandfather, who had alcohol problems, died while my mother was pregnant with me. Perhaps this was part of the problem of fear and anxiety becoming part of who I am, being transferred while I was in the womb. If so, it was certainly compounded by the fact I was nearly born in a taxi as my mother headed for North Walsham Nursing Home.

Just after a year or so my brother Kevin came along, which enabled the council to rehouse us in a very small terraced house in West Earlham, which is in Norwich City. We had a small wood at the rear of our garden, which at the time I thought was huge. It is still there to this day. It was normal for everyone in those days to keep chickens – anything to help with lowering the household bills helped. My mother told me when I first started school I wouldn't go without my brother Kevin as I was so insecure.

We had trouble with our neighbours who lived just a few doors away from us. I can recall a very large lady with a short sleeve dress on, with what appeared to be bulging muscles on her arms. Apparently she had a reputation in the road of being rather loud and bossy. Early one morning she came round to the back of our house and just walked into our tiny kitchen and started punching my mother. I felt the fear and shock and trauma of the situation. Instinctively I jumped on her back to try and grab her hands to stop them from hitting my mother. Meanwhile my brother Kevin took the biscuits off the table and hid under the table. My dad, who was mowing the grass at the time, heard all the commotion, came in, got hold of her and pulled her away. She fell and broke her arm. It wasn't long before she arrived again to show us her plaster and threaten us.

We were taken to court. We had very little money as Dad had a lot of mental health issues. He had been in hospital a number of times to receive electric shock treatment on his brain. He had also had an operation on his lungs; despite this he still rolled his own fags. Sun Valley was his favourite brand. Dad was always in and out of work; he just couldn't hold a job down for any length of time. Dad defended himself when we got to court. It was out of the question to hire a solicitor.

Looking back, I can't remember any time of happiness. At

six, I had German Measles with complications and had to keep going back to hospital for some sort of ray treatment. I lost a stone in weight.

Everything was getting too much for my mother. She was alone in her relationship with my dad. Then her mother had a perforated appendix, but nobody believed her. The GP kept saying it was indigestion, however, my mother knew it was more than that. That fateful day arrived when the appendix burst and it wasn't long before she died. I was still in nappies at the time and she was only 56 years of age. My mother's world was falling apart. The person that she loved with all her heart, and it seemed the only person mother felt loved by, had gone and sadly it could have been avoided.

I knew that the pain of this loss within my mother was there for years. Only later on in life could I pray with her to forgive the GP and the hospital who had never listened to her concerns.

It was in 1954 when my mother heard that Billy Graham was holding a large crusade at Haringey. It was at this crusade that my mother responded to an appeal to surrender her life to Jesus Christ. She walked down to the front of the auditorium to the song, 'Just as I am, without one plea', and through her brokenness gave her life to Jesus.

It wasn't long after Mum had taken that decision to follow Jesus that an exchange council house in Chelmsford, Essex, became available for Mum and Dad, with the promise of a job with Gestener, a company that sold and repaired typewriters. For my dad, the decision to move wasn't going to be too difficult. It was an opportunity to start afresh and create a new life.

So, at the age of seven, I sat in the front of a very large removal van late one night as my mother, conscious of our

Norfolk accents, impressed on us that we were moving to a more up-market people who spoke and pronounced their words with greater clarity, that is rather than our country dialect of the Norfolk Broads where people spoke too fast without any pauses. It did seem, looking back, that after mother taking the decision to follow Christ, things started moving.

But, life for us didn't start well in Chelmsford. Dad had a thing about concrete houses; he didn't like them and always said that they are prone to cracking and that he would never live in one.

When daylight came the next day, we discovered it was a concrete house. Apparently, Dad had viewed the property sometime earlier, but he only saw it in the dark. Needless to say, he wasn't happy. My mother saw the funny side of it and said, 'Isn't that typical? Never mind, we will make the best of it,' and it was that attitude that impregnated my personality. That no matter how bad things look, and how things are and you can't change it, keep positive. There are always people worse off than you.

Home life didn't improve. Dad's angry outbursts seemed to increase; no matter what I did, I could never please him. I was often taken to his bedroom where I would hear those dreaded words that sent fear, and my nerves into shock, 'Bend over and touch your toes'. No explanation. No communication. He would just hit me as hard as he could. It was usually three whacks on the backside. I used to feel the injustice of it all, as something within me was asking "why?"

Dad was home a lot as he was always in and out of work. He just couldn't hold a job down for any length of time. To keep out of debt, Mum used to work at the local sweet shop as an assistant during the day, and in the evening she would go and clean at Crompton's in Writtle Road.

It was at this time, I was transferred to Moulsham Junior School, as apparently I wasn't doing very well in my education.

Mother decided to get myself and my brother Kevin to join the local Church of England, which was then in Waterhouse Lane. It was an opportunity to get us out of my dad's way as it seemed we were always upsetting him.

Mum kept to her word to follow Jesus, and taught us to kneel down by our bunk beds every night and pray with our hands together and eyes closed. And every time we had a meal we were not allowed to start until we said grace as a family. To me it was just a ritual. I had no personal relationship with God. I didn't even know if there was such a person called God.

I found church very boring. At least I could have a bit of fun at choir practice. I would take my matchstick cannon and fire it at the girls in the opposite pew, and at least I wasn't verbally or emotionally abused. I joined the local boy scouts at Chelmsford, Widford, and really enjoyed that until we went on a backwoodsman course at Danbury where I was left alone with some older senior scouts who bullied me, as I was very small for my age. They would start shoving me around and giving me verbal abuse. They humiliated me by making me kiss the ground in front of the other boys.

It seemed my world consisted of being a victim. Junior School was no different. When I stood up for myself in the classroom against some of the bullies' one of the teachers came in and picked on me to make an example of me. I was called to the front of the classroom, in front of over 20 boys, and those dreaded words came again: "Bend over and touch your toes".

His slipper was enormous – a size 12. He used to bend it in front of you just to increase the fear. My bottom, by the time of impact, was like jelly. It felt like it was stinging for hours. I would just retreat in a cave of quietness. It just seemed I wasn't of value to anyone. What was the point of speaking?

Tension at home now was going from bad to worse. We had a very small kitchen. Dad would sit as head of the table at one end, I would sit opposite. My brother Kevin to the left, and my mother to the right. It was a little yellow Formica steel table. We would be enjoying our Sunday roast, conversation would start, then it seemed Dad would get angry and without any warning he would tip the table up into the air with all our hot dinners and plates and cutlery just flying and crashing everywhere. Most of it landed on me because I sat opposite. Mum and Dad would be shouting. We would all be crying. This happened so frequently, I would once again be paralysed in anxiety and fear as it was like living with a time bomb. Life was so unpredictable. The after effect and long-term effect was, it seemed, that my emotions and body was just going numb. I had a tightness in my gums that seemed permanent.

The whole experience, once again, left me questioning – why? It all felt so wrong and unjust. I just felt picked on, but at the same time, being the eldest, I had to protect my brother Kevin.

Surely life couldn't get any worse? It all seemed so unfair. We were a good family, obeyed the laws of the land. Something was wrong. I watched other children at school and everyone seemed so happy. I just carried on life pretending that everything was ok, because I didn't want anyone finding out what my life was like. I hid behind a cloak of shame. Then at ten, just before my third brother Melvin arrived, I was sitting in my usual place at the kitchen table. Mum and Kevin were out. Dad was wiping up the dishes. I noticed he was using the towel instead of the tea towel, so I said to Dad, "Do you know you are using the towel?" With that, the dish he had in his hand was thrown at me with lightning speed. It hit me so hard in the chest I nearly fainted with shock. He then pulled me off the chair and started beating me. I fell to the ground as he kicked me. My whole body was not only filled with physical pain, but the emotional pain of being rejected. I didn't understand why. My nerves were all over the place. I had no control of anything in my body; I wee'd all over the floor. When Dad calmed down, my eyes were so sore and red with so much crying. I was then sent to bed early and told not to say anything to Mum when she came in; otherwise, there would be trouble.

I heard the doorbell go. I went under the covers in my bunk bed and was still shaking with so much fear. I dreaded Mum coming into the room to say goodnight as I knew I wouldn't be able to hide my feelings from her; the tears were still flowing out of me. I was still out of control. I just couldn't stop. As you can guess, mums do what mums do, and Mum checked on me. I heard World War 3 break out between them while I was lying in bed. The time came when Mum and myself would go to the telephone box at the end of our road and ring a solicitor to find out about divorce, but nothing came of it.

I remember having a conversation with myself 'that no matter what I did it seemed to be wrong so something must be wrong with me'.

That day, not realising the implication of the power of words spoken or thought, I made what we know today as an inner vow. I said I would try to be perfect. I wouldn't be controlled by my emotions. I would be strong and always try to do the right thing. Perhaps that would please everyone, as I was sick of being a victim and being abused. No longer would I have to hide my bruises so I couldn't do PE.

I didn't realise by agreeing with these thoughts that this decision would open me up to become a controller of myself. That I would champion any cause of injustice and stand up so nobody could hurt me again. I learned to overcome – to become stronger in spirit. To become independent as I felt all the people I had trusted had hurt me and this was just not going to happen again. I would seek to control by doing the right thing. Otherwise, the alternative would be to give in and become depressed, and possibly have a breakdown.

I really would have loved to have had somebody in my life at that time to talk to and guide me, but there was no-one. The world I lived in was very lonely and isolating, but it was the world I believed at the time would protect me and keep me safe.

I didn't have a faith. I didn't believe in God. I had never seen any miracles. I didn't know the bible.

The only person I could trust at that time was myself.

Chapter 2

MY INTRODUCTION TO CHURCH WORLD

Life didn't get any easier now I had two younger brothers, Kevin and Melvin. I felt being the eldest son I would look after them when things go wrong. Instinctively I would protect them as I didn't want them to go through what I had to. Looking back now I can see at times I made things a lot worse. Arguments and rows it now seemed were every day. As I was getting older I started to stand up to Dad. On one occasion he threw a pot of tea at me that Mum had just made. The top was off and boiling hot tea scalded all my back. I had no shirt on, only short trousers as it was a lovely sunny day. I ran out of the kitchen into the back garden screaming and crying. The pain seemed unbearable. I didn't know what to do. I was running up and down the lawn. Fortunately, we had a very high privet hedge all around our back garden, so nobody else could see into it. Mum did her best and covered me with a damp towel.

I just couldn't understand why I was not allowed to speak and have my own view. I got used to no explanation and no apology. Experiences like this caused me to bury all the shock and trauma and just carry on with life as if nothing had happened, not realising that I was becoming harder and emotionally numb. This was my culture: living with the unpredictable, never knowing if the table would be thrown, or another war of abuse.

I looked forward to Sunday morning, as it was church time. It was boring, but at least it was safe. It wasn't long before we had the opportunity to attend the Pentecostal Church on Sunday afternoon. A double-decker bus would come round the estate and pick us up. Mum's logic was that I would be out of Dad's way which meant more peace for the rest of the family.

My first impressions of this church were there seemed to be so much joy and happiness. People were actually smiling and enjoying church, and wasn't looking like expressionless blocks of concrete.

Sundays now looked a lot better with C of E Sunday morning service and Sunday afternoon, Sunday School. That was all right for a while till the day came in the C of E calendar that all the male choir boys had to go through some special ceremony. I remember standing in a row with all the other choir boys with our white gowns on and this tall Bishop came round laying his hands on people's heads and praying. When he came to me he asked me a question – did I still go to the other Sunday School? I replied, 'yes'. With that, he just passed me by and started praying for the next boy. I thought at the time – how strange was that? What's so different about me? It just made me feel odd.

It wasn't long before my parents were paid a visit from the vicar. He let it be known that the Pentecostal doctrine was pagan, according to him. We then decided to ask for a visit from the Sunday School Superintendent from the Pentecostal church. He was so nice and really had a very different spirit. The vicar made it clear I couldn't be part of the choir if I continued going to the other Sunday School. My parents gave me the choice whether to go to the C of E or Pentecostal Church. What was it to be?

I didn't like the Vicar saying such bad things about the people he had never met, but taking decisions was not easy for me in case I was wrong, because whenever I thought I was right at home, I was always wrong.

It was with fear that I decided to leave the C of E and go to the Pentecostal Church, hoping it would work out. Because of my decision, Mum felt she too, could no longer attend the C of E, so as a family we would all attend the Pentecostal Church.

It didn't take us long to realise after attending the Pentecostal Church that everything seemed well structured. Sunday morning was communion, Sunday afternoon was Sunday School and Sunday evening was called the Gospel Service, with prayer meeting on Tuesdays and Bible Studies on Thursday.

In those days, in the sixties, there seemed to be an unwritten dress code with most of the men wearing suits and the ladies, even young teenagers, would all be wearing hats. At least nobody was wearing robes and looked unapproachable. That was till I saw the Pastor. He was a short, Welsh man who had a white collar on with a black vest and glasses. At first, I didn't like him. He did most of the preaching. Looking around it seemed everyone was middle class and fairly well off and respectable and had 'got it all together', but we managed to fit in despite our appearance and background.

The people were lovely. Most Sundays there would be approximately 150 people in attendance. It wasn't long before church became a place we began to enjoy. The hymns were rousing, people were raising their hands up in the air – not so bad after all.

I loved the Sunday morning communion service – breaking bread and wine in remembrance of what Jesus has done for us – as this wasn't controlled by those on the platform, the pastor and deacons. There was an open time to worship as these services were about God, not about us and trying to disciple us. The whole service was to have communion in the communion service – a place of intimacy with God and his people. The people could stand up and just worship God from the depth of their hearts. I felt there was such a presence there – a sense of holiness and reverence, yet a freedom to be yourself and still be loved.

The first time in a communion service I heard someone speaking in another language, then another person stood up and gave the interpretation. They called this one of the gifts of the Spirit being manifested as found in 1 Corinthians 12 in the bible. This really touched me. I did feel a little scared at first. I thought – is it possible God could communicate with us?

Some of the people used to shake a lot. It looked as if they had grabbed hold of an electric cable and couldn't let go.

These people, I found out, were known as the Peculiar People. They were the foundation of the Pentecostal Church in Chelmsford. It wasn't long before I started to get more involved with this church. I joined what was known then as the Crusaders. This was only for teens and twenties; they met every Wednesday evening.

Church now was becoming a big part of my life. I was very keen. I felt accepted and not abused. Home life was much more bearable. Very little violence, just the verbal and emotional abuse. I think we were all getting that much older and could stand up for ourselves.

There came a time I had John 3:16 (NKJV) explained to me:

> *"For God so loved the world that He gave His only begotten Son, that whoever believes in Him should not perish but have everlasting life"*.

They asked me – 'who is the world? 'Of course, I said 'me'. So it read if God loves Pat, and if Pat believes, now that it has been identified that Christ died for me, would I like to pray the sinner's prayer? This would be to confess and repent of my sins and ask Jesus in my life? I felt a little uneasy as they were asking me to open my heart to someone I could not see. I had never opened my heart to those I could see, as I had become so used to wearing a mask, and now this seemed a bit too personal.

I didn't want to upset them or feel odd or different, because I had learnt it was safer to be one of the crowd as it was too dangerous to be different and have a voice with a different view. I couldn't risk it as I felt I could be abused again. So I went along with it and said this sinner's prayer.

Once that had happened, it seemed everyone was really happy. I had now joined the Christian Church. I had now got my ticket to heaven. Now I am a new person, so I was told. All the old has gone and there is a new me, as I believe in Jesus. It wasn't long before I had to tell my youth group I was now a Christian. I did feel a bit like a trophy on display at times, but it kept everyone happy so I thought, let's run with it. At last, I have fitted in somewhere, so it would seem. I have started a new journey in my life.

I continued going to church, singing the hymns and choruses, and getting really involved in all the activities that seemed to be centred around church.

The problem I found I had was that I didn't feel any different. My mouth was saying all the right things. I got used to church language. 'I am saved'. 'I am born again'. Yet within the deep recesses of my heart, I knew something wasn't right. I could sing the happy choruses, get excited, clap my hands, and enjoy the atmosphere which was full of emotion and joy. I could get carried away with it all. But if there was one thing that I had learned, it was to be honest with myself. I had come from a culture of living behind a mask of being unreal. I knew I couldn't keep this pretence up for too long, and I didn't want to anyway. What value is there to give my identity away, for what it is worth, to anyone? But I could have the dignity of being honest and true to myself. By doing so I have kept safe on the inside of me, from any more harm.

It must have been almost a year after praying that sinner's prayer. I was lying on my bunk bed. I was probably about 14 ½ years old, thinking about my future, as I was expected to leave school at 15. I had no qualifications; I had failed the 11+. I didn't like school (I just couldn't remember anything). I think my mind was always so tight and under pressure with all the emotional trauma I lived in. I thought, what am I going to do with my life?

I thought of Mum and Dad and how they had always struggled in so many ways. I knew deep down they were good people, but life had been hard for them, always trying to make ends meet. People from the church would often drop off bags of shopping to help us. Yet we had experienced so little happiness. I really didn't want to live like them. There must be a better way.

By this time, I believed there was a God and He had a son called Jesus who died on a cross for me and had taken the punishment for all my wrongdoing. But then I thought – **the devils believe that and they are not going to heaven.**

If you had asked me at that moment the question: 'if I was to die, would I go to heaven?' all I would have said was, 'I hope so'.

For some reason I started to cry. Looking back I believe the Holy Spirit was calling me to Himself. I started to feel undone, very vulnerable and transparent, before a Holy God. I knew I was in a bad shape. I just cried out to God with tears streaming down my face. 'Lord, I give you my life. Please forgive me'. Somehow I pushed through that barrier of unbelief believing God would answer me. At that moment, pure love of the Heavenly Father filled my whole being. It seemed all my emotions were so caught up in the moment. I didn't know what love felt like before. This love was so undefiled, without any demands. Somehow I felt that this God, who before was so distant and unreachable, was in the room. Now I was basking in this presence of pure love and glory. Light had come into my dark world and given me a reason for living, a purpose in life. This was so real to me.

I felt humbled to think the God of Heaven who created all things and sustains all things in the galaxies and should come to planet earth into this room on a council estate, with all its issues, no carpets, just cheap lino on the floor, to bring a new value to me and put eternity in my heart. Now I definitely knew, without a shadow of a doubt, that Jesus Christ is the son of the Living God, and that He emptied Himself of all His divinity, and was born of the Virgin Mary, by the seed of God's life being planted by the Holy Spirit, and He became the Son of Man, who lived and dwelt among us. He knows us so well. He is not remote. He does understand us and He does listen to us and has a plan for our lives, but needs our permission to have access to our hearts, unlike the arch-enemy of God, Satan, who brought slavery and control and death into this wonderful creation.

I went to school the next day with such a peace, even the world looked so much brighter. I had a new appreciation of life. I didn't really have a lot of theology. I had the experience. Now I understand that my spirit had been dead to God and when I invited Jesus in, my spirit became alive. No wonder we use the term 'Born Again'. It's just like when a baby is born the baby comes out of darkness into a new world and breathes life. That day I can honestly say the breath of life filled me and I began to experience not only a new life, but I was being led into a new way of living.

This pattern of having the experience first, then the theology, it appears, is the way God was going to teach me. Otherwise, I would be following the doctrine and trying to make it work.

I realise now, looking back, praying the sinner's prayer was just on a mental level, not a spiritual level that demanded my heart. If we are going to walk with God, He is Spirit and the only way to worship and to communicate is by the Spirit which then can enlarge our understanding by revelation, not just information.

Prayer

Dear Lord Jesus,

I am not quite sure how to say this but I don't want to keep living my life my way. I do believe you died on the cross for me and rose from the dead to take the punishment for my sins. I ask you to forgive me for my sins (whatever God shows you specifically). I ask you now to come into my heart and change me. I surrender to you and receive you now.

Amen

Chapter 3

A PLAN UNFOLDING

Leaving school at 15 wasn't easy. I didn't feel I was capable of doing much. Being a postman looked like an easy job; probably the only job I could do as I found studying and reading difficult. I thought it was possible I could do that, and it would mean I could be by myself, outside in the fresh air, delivering the mail. I knew I couldn't work inside a factory. I needed to be in open spaces, not confined spaces.

I took the entrance test so that I could work in the Post Office, and I was told that I would have to wait until October, which was 3 months away, to see if I had passed. In the meantime, I decided to help my mum and go with her apple picking, then potato and strawberry picking. It was a bit strange as I was the only boy among a group of women, all trying to earn some money, but it filled the time in. October came around. I couldn't wait for the mail to arrive. At last, the day came when the letter was delivered from the Post Office with the news – I wasn't accepted. It felt like an electric shock had gone through my body and paralysed me. My mind was reeling. All I could think was that all my friends had jobs, and now after waiting 3 months (that I now felt had been wasted), I had nothing. I just felt I had no hope, with no future. I had given my best taking the test and I couldn't even be accepted. It was like living in a bubble of abandonment and rejection, and all I could see around this bubble was everyone getting on with their lives, going to work with smiles on their faces. They had purpose. Even my dad felt sorry for me which to me at the time, felt really strange. I didn't understand that.

Dad then took me down to the Youth Employment Office, and all they could offer me was work at a butchers, or becoming a cobbler, somebody that would repair shoes. With my face in my hands, I just cried in despair. It felt that my whole world had just fallen apart.

I can't remember having any faith as I was mentally and emotionally all over the place with the trauma of the situation. I didn't realise that my mum had been praying for her boys every day.

My dad paid another visit to the Youth Employment Office and insisted he wasn't leaving the office until they found me a job. The guy in charge opened his filing cabinet and opened a drawer with all his files and said there was nothing he could offer me. We were about to leave the office when he noticed, and was surprised himself to see, a card with an advert on it, wanting an apprentice welder to work for a plant hire company. "I can't understand", he said. "It must have been here all the time but had fallen down behind the other cards". Was this the job that would be the answer to my mum's prayers? Anyway, an interview was arranged and I went to visit this company with my dad.

For the first time, I saw huge cranes and massive earth-moving diggers and lots of sparks flying everywhere, as the welder worked on a crane. That freaked me out. It looked so dangerous. Once again my nerves went into play. I looked at the men, who looked quite rough and dirty, but this was the end of the road. It was this job or nothing. With much trepidation, I started a 6-month trial with the view of a 6-month apprenticeship – working a 52 hour week with a starting wage packet of £3.09.

I passed the trial period and became the first-ever apprentice welder. I didn't know at the time that the boss was a Christian. I actually started to enjoy the work as I could travel all around Essex repairing broken machinery on building sites and farms.

I remember one morning, while in the washroom thinking, "This isn't such a bad job after all. But why are my gums so white and numb that everything feels so tight on my face? I am now a Christian. I am supposed to be different".

Church World was going well. I couldn't wait for Sunday morning, for the communion service. After a hard week at work, I really needed to spend some quality time thinking and praying and focussing on God.

The Holy Spirit would move every Sunday. These services were so unpredictable. There were so many times I would be just sitting on my chair listening to everyone else, then the Spirit of God would start to well up within me and I just couldn't keep to my seat any longer. I would just have to stand. I would only just have a few words, but as soon as I started to worship it was like a dam had burst and a flow of words would just pour out of me. I would become so passionate as I knew this wasn't me, this was God. In these times of worship my faith just increased. I would see certain pictures in my imagination and describe them in such power. They call this prophecy today, but in those days we didn't box things up. Our whole focus in the meeting was God, as we, His people, were worshipping and having fellowship with our spirit to His Spirit.

I realise now that God had given us a pattern of worship in the Old Covenant (Testament) of the tabernacle; God's people would enter His gates with thanksgiving, and then go through the outer court with praise into a holy place, then through a veil into the Holy of Holies where the glory of God's presence was. Now as a young believing teenager, I was experiencing this wonderful glory of His presence along with a family of people who were a lot more mature than me. Just being one with God was the entirety of our focus. There wasn't any teaching or doctrine – it felt like nothing was between God and us as His people. The weariness we often brought along to church, with so many issues going on in our lives, faded into insignificance only as we were just lost in His presence. The strength we received in our spirit and bodies was, it seemed, revitalising. The Lord was among us, as if He was walking down each aisle ministering to us, yet we were all so different; young and old, rich and poor. We felt like this was our family and we felt as one, completed. Despite all the other activities that were going on this was the highlight of the week. We came to this communion service with excitement and anticipation that we were going to meet with God, and God was going to meet with us. There was no control and no spiritual template. It was the

Fear of God that kept us free from imposing our agendas and traditions on Him. Looking now in the book of Acts, it said of the early church that they moved in the Fear of God and the comfort of the Holy Spirit – what a wonderful balance. I am so grateful to God that despite my world being one of shock and trauma, He provided this oasis to establish a foundation in me with the Lord Himself being the foundation He would build upon. It felt great to belong and just be accepted without having to perform or do anything.

I found out later that Pastor Anthony and his wife Millie used to pray for the congregation by name early every morning. They had not been able to have children, so we were their family.

I was so keen to follow Jesus that I soon followed His teaching on baptism. It was expected when one had repented of one's sins and committed their life to God as an outward sign of the inward experience: being baptised in water – which means being fully immersed in water. Thankfully the church had a tank under the platform. On the night of my baptism, the deacons of the church read out a text from the bible they had all prayed about. It was:

> *"I will instruct you and teach you in the way you should go; I will guide you with My eye."*   (Psalm 32:8 NKJV)

I didn't realise at the time how important that verse would be to me in later life.

Once you are baptized the next experience is to be baptised in the Holy Spirit, like the early church in Acts 2.

In those days, we had what was called waiting meetings

after the evening meeting where we would all sit and wait for the Holy Spirit to move upon us. When that happened, we would speak in another language. I lost count of the number of meetings my mother and I went to receive the experience. I even went to the Royal Albert Hall on Easter Monday when the Pentecostal church family went to celebrate the resurrection of Jesus from the dead.

Between afternoon and evening services we would all go down to what seemed a very long passage, with chairs either side. We would sit on these chairs and a number of Pastors would come round and lay hands on us to receive the baptism of the Holy Spirit. Well, I have never had my head shaken so many times in all my life. I came away very disappointed after 4 years of seeking the experience and nothing happening. All I did was get frustrated and down on myself thinking something was wrong with me, as nothing was working. I decided to go to a Christian youth camp at Felixstowe. It was the year England won the World Cup when we beat Germany in the finals. I was earning my own money now and wanted to be in fashion. I used to wear blue hipsters with brown platform shoes with a black polo neck t-shirt, under a denim blue shirt. My hair was down to my shoulders. I stood out a mile from the other young people. I suppose on the inside of me I was trying to draw attention to myself to feed my rejection. I also used to walk around the campsite with a very large red radio which I had painted silver on the front with the words written in black, my name 'PAT' in black capitals, listening to the sixties music. I used to love the Hollies song, 'I am Alive'. Such unusual sound. I loved The Beatles and Dave Clark Five.

There would be a couple of hundred young people there. It

was expected we would go to the meetings. I used to watch people go to these waiting meetings to receive the baptism of the Holy Spirit but by this time I had almost given up. I didn't know what more I could do. While walking through the campsite one evening I looked up into the heavens. It was a clear evening. The stars looked radiant. Then a word came to me by the Spirit of God – that I would receive the baptism of the Holy Spirit tonight. I just knew at that moment, when I would walk into that tent with all the other young people, I would receive. It's a job to explain but I just had an inward assurance within myself this was going to happen, even after 4 years of frustration and self-inflicted mental torture.

I walked into that waiting meeting, just sat down and worshipped God from my innermost being, started to speak in faith, and as I did the Spirit of God just overwhelmed me and I spoke in another tongue, as if I had known this all my life. The overwhelming power and presence of God was just flowing through my body and a peace and assurance that I really did belong to Him, the Lord God.

Being a welding engineer, I needed to know why I had to wait so long. I felt the Lord saying, "Nothing to do with me. I have already given the Holy Spirit, but you have been waiting instead of receiving". I realised that everything I was to receive from God would be in my faith first before it became my experience. When I got home from camp, I told my mum I had received the baptism of the Holy Spirit, as we had gone on this journey together, and that all she had to do was return back to simplicity – not trying to complicate things, and just receive like a child. But all it did to Mum was make her feel worse. She, too, had tried so hard to receive.

Life was changing for the better. I had grown in spirit and physically and was now 5'10" – still quite thin at 9 stone. I was part of the Crusader Youth Group as well as part of the Church Choir. I used to sit in the front of the choir as my voice hadn't broken, as part of the soprano section. The choir didn't have a dress code, unless we went out visiting or special occasions like the annual choir festival.

The choir used to sit in the first 4 rows of the congregation, and when it was our turn to sing in the service we would all turn round and face the congregation. One Sunday, I had a massive blood blister on the inside of my cheek where we had another smashing session at home and I got hit by something. The whole sense of shame went through me as I tried to hide my face. My eyes were stained with tears, the embarrassment was almost too much to bear as so many people would be looking at me and I was the only boy in the front row singing soprano. I thought it might get found out that I didn't have this wonderful life that everyone else seemed to have. I used to put puff powder over my eyes to hide the tearstains. I don't know how I sang the song that evening with so much emotion in my voice. That was one of the few times I was getting close to exposure and I felt I wouldn't put myself in that position again.

At 17 years of age, I bought myself my first car, a 1954 Hillman Minx, with a long bench seat in the front of the car and a 4-speed column changer. It was great to be able to get out of the house and be a little bit more independent. I said to Mum one evening, as we were all so bored and needed cheering up, let's go out for a drive. We were driving around, and while driving through the council estate the thought came to me it would be good to pay a surprise visit to my mum's best friend

Bertha Hobbs whom she worked with at Woolworths in Chelmsford. I knew Mum's best friend had a daughter and between them, they had been trying to get us together, but I didn't want to know as she wasn't a Christian, and I wasn't interested in a non-Christian girl, but I thought 'let's check this out, then this will put an end to matters while we are in the area'.

We knocked at the door, and I followed my mum into the lounge, and was introduced to her daughter, Daphne, who was mightily embarrassed as she had just taken her make-up off and was going to have an early night. Little did she know I wasn't too keen on heavily made-up people as I liked the more natural look, as you can see what you are getting.

The mums chattered away while I tried to talk to Daph, who appeared very shy. I really quite fancied her so I asked her out. I didn't know anything of her background, but it turned out that 3 weeks previously she had the police round her house and had put a lot of fear in her saying 'the way she was going she was going to be just like her dad' who had been in prison a few times. That was the last thing she ever wanted to do as her dad was very abusive to her and her mum, to the point of being physical and violent. On the day of the local carnival in Chelmsford, Daph's name was called out over the tannoy that Daphne Hobbs needed to go home urgently. Daph arrived home to find her mother was covered in bruises and had had her arm broken by her husband. It was at the age of 12 her parents divorced. Daph became a mod in the days of mods and rockers. The mods were the smart ones who rode on scooters like the Vespa and Lambretta, and the rockers rode motorbikes and wore black leathers. Daph stayed all night at a friend's party in Hornchurch which was why the police were called. Nobody knew where she was. It was after that experience with the police, that Daph, for some reason, started to pray that someone would help her as she too, like myself, had nobody. But now I was in a different place in my experience. I had someone I could call on and talk to and that was Jesus Christ. I didn't realise that day would be really significant in my life as 4 years later I would be marrying her!

Once again, it seemed as if I was walking into a plan already prepared for me before I was born. My dear Pastor Anthony wasn't too pleased with me as I brought Daph to church and she wasn't a Christian. It seemed I was breaking all the unwritten rules about dating a non-Christian.

One thing I had learnt was to respect my Pastor. He never used to control me. There were times as I was growing up he would take me for a long walk down the road where the church was at the time and give me Godly council. I had so much respect and love for him it seemed, as my dad was unable to represent the Father God to me, which is a role the father is meant to do. But this dear Pastor watched over me, guided me and was always there for me, despite him being so popular in the Elim movement as a conference speaker. He had such revelation knowledge and experience of what the bible teaches.

I used to go on my bicycle and with my mum. I used to cycle in all weathers for 2 years every Thursday evening to hear Pastor Anthony teach the book of Revelation, verse by verse. I so admired his insight and the sheer grace and love he showed to everyone. I believe he was one of Christ's gifts to the church. One of the 5 fold ministry. He held the office of Pastor given to him by God. He certainly was God's provision for me, as my own father was unable to represent the father heart of God in the way that God intended fathers to behave. I love that wonderful passage of John 10 as Jesus as the Good Shepherd, which is a pattern for all pastors to be; one who loves and knows his sheep and would die for them.

My dad did put in an appearance at church from time to time, but like everything else in his life, found it hard to commit.

It was one quiet evening while I was sitting in the kitchen that the silence was broken by the mother of all rows. I could hear voices rising to a crescendo. It was so loud. It was accompanied by the familiar sound of things being slung up the wall. The door opened. Mum was in tears and very angry. Dad had picked up the brand new 22" television which we had only bought a few days ago and thrown it across the room, smashing the screen (It had replaced our small 12" black and white television). I saw the tall lampstand on its side along with broken ornaments and pictures. Mum was very frightened. I had never seen Dad as bad as this. Mum shouted at me to go and get the Pastor. I ran outside trembling with shock. Once again, I would go numb with fear and anxiety. I got on my bicycle and cycled as fast as I could with tears streaming down my face and knocked on my Pastor's door, which was over 3 miles away. The Pastor opened the door. It was dark and quite late in the evening. Pastor Anthony listened to my story as I stuttered between breaths and tears. I just couldn't stop shaking. He went to the back of the house leaving me with his wife, Millie. It seemed he had been gone ages. I suppose he was in the back praying. Then the decision was taken. He would take me back to see my dad and mum. When we arrived home, my mum opened the door. I followed my Pastor into the living room. It looked like a bomb had hit it and there, sitting on an armchair, was my dear Dad, crying like a baby regretting his actions. I left the room and left the Pastor and my dad to talk. I still couldn't stop shaking. All the time I was thinking – why? What a waste! We had been looking forward to watching a bigger screen television. Now it is all smashed up. I suppose it still had to be paid for.

The shame on my family and myself was that we couldn't tell anyone else. Nobody knew, only the Pastor. This was our culture of living.

I felt comfortable getting to know Daph as I didn't have to hide my home life from her as her own background was so similar to my own. Introducing her to the church on what I thought was her first visit, but it appeared, when she was a little girl, she had got the bus to Sunday School, so when she came to the church it was like coming home.

An amazing series of events – who could plan such things?

Chapter 4

AGAINST ALL ODDS

It was great having a car, although it was an old banger, but after cycling everywhere in all weathers it was such a blessing. That was, until I put it in for the M.O.T. and it failed with the chassis being so rotten. It wasn't fit to drive and my welding skills at the time weren't good enough to repair it. Scrapping it was the only realistic option.

Back to cycling! This attitude I adopted once again. I had learned from living in so much shock and trauma – "Well, there is nothing I can do about it, so no use crying over spilled milk" – the phrase my mother used to say to me, so get on with life.

I didn't realise at the time once again I would just push down my true feelings, only just to become harder again to the events of life. This was to affect my spirit as I became stronger but emotionally, I was getting out of touch with my true feelings.

This attitude didn't really help in my relationship with Daph, as I would always see the bright side and the positive side to life, not realising Daph dealt with her shame and abuse differently to me. I would go into fight mode and stand up for the injustice happening around me, and Daph would go into flight mode, retreat to her inner cave, and shut everyone out to save herself from being hurt any further.

They say opposites attract. I can honestly say I still don't quite understand that statement, but I do know a lot of people who are married to someone with a temperament and personality that are opposite.

My life seemed to be improving slowly. I wasn't spending so much time at home. I would cycle over to the council estate most nights to see Daph. During the day I was working and travelling to college for day release, as well as 2 nights a week studying to pass my City of Guilds certificate in welding. I was desperate for Daph to come to know the wonderful Father God who had won my heart and find that this Heavenly Father would accept her as she was, turn her life around and give her a real purpose in life, instead of living life feeling so empty. I grew to love her as she was very honest, had respect and was different.

One Sunday evening we had a visiting speaker come to the church and he spoke on sin and the power of sin, the consequences of our sin and our need of a saviour. I was used to the gospel message so I wasn't really affected by it but as we walked back to Daph's home, Daph was so convicted she said she really needed to go back and talk to somebody. It was in the little minor hall at the back of the church that my dear Pastor explained to Daph the gospel message of Jesus dying on the cross, rising from the dead and taking the penalty of her sin. That evening, after everyone had gone home, Daph gave her life to the Lord by opening up her heart to receive the Lord Jesus Christ as her Saviour. I was so grateful to God for answered prayer.

It wasn't an easy start for Daph as she wasn't used to church world. I had got quite established in the church. I obeyed what was expected of me as I had so much respect for Pastor Anthony. I often questioned why going to the cinema and taking part in raffles was looked upon as inappropriate behaviour. From the church perspective, this was all part of the world and we must be separate from the world. That was okay, I could live with that until I wanted to go to a football match. Rather than get out of line, I thought I had better ask the Pastor. With such love, he explained the church's view but gave me the freedom to choose. From that day, I never went to a football match while he was alive out of love and respect for him, and I didn't want to offend God in case I was wrong. Yet I still wasn't convinced. I can see now that football has become very tribal as each team competes against each other with so much passion and life.

For Daph to understand church rules and what seemed very politically correct, was like another planet to her. But one thing Daph does enjoy is fashion and it did give her the opportunity to go somewhere dressed up, but I wasn't sure being a teenager wearing hats was her thing. It was very different from riding on the back of a scooter as a mod with a long parkey coat on.

We were now a couple who were opposite yet blinded by the love of the day.

After cycling from Daph's home on a lovely sunny day feeling so happy, I knocked on my front door at home to be greeted by my dad. He didn't look very happy. I thought, I wonder who has upset him. It can't be me – I haven't been here. I got as far as the hall when I could feel someone punching me in my back and head. My nerves automatically came into play. I turned around to go back the way I came in but Dad was standing right in front of the door and I had nowhere to go, so I managed to get to the stairs with him still punching me. I got to the second step to realise I was now taller than him and without giving it a thought, I smashed him in the face with a good right-hand punch. He fell to the ground. This was my opportunity to run. I was surprised as much as he was that I could do that. I managed to open the front door, trembling, thinking, when he gets up he'll kill me. I ran down the road so fast it felt as if my feet weren't touching the ground. I turned my head when I reached the bottom of the road which was about 50 yards away and looked round and saw Dad, who looked like he had the strength of 10 men, with my bicycle above his head, with his arms fully stretched, chasing me. My legs turned to jelly. I just legged it so fast. I was numb with fear. I ran back to Daph's house, which must have been about 4 miles. I was in total shock. Not only for what I had done as I was a Christian, but I knew the fourth commandment which had a condition attached to it:

> *"Honour your father and your mother, as the Lord your God has commanded you, so that you may live long and that it may go well with you in the land the Lord your God is giving you".* (Deuteronomy 5:16 NIV)

I now hadn't met the condition for that promise of God's to be mine. I had dishonoured my dad. I knew I couldn't go home so I stayed the night round at Daph's house, trembling all night. To be honest, I thought I would feel better after the way he had treated me, but that couldn't be further from the truth. I felt so guilty. I had hit my dad and it was wrong. Despite all the provocation, as my mum used to say – two wrongs don't make it right. I also didn't realise at the time I would put myself under a curse as found in Deuteronomy 27:16 (NIV):

"Cursed is anyone who dishonours their father or mother".

What does that all mean? To honour means to raise up, to lift up. Yet I had floored Dad. I understood later that he had to go to hospital with a suspected broken nose.

That was the last time Dad ever hit me. Not only did I feel ashamed and regret my action, but I felt guilty for weeks.

After a few days, I did manage to go home. I gingerly opened the front door, not really knowing what to expect. By now, I was quite used to living with unpredictability. I walked into the lounge and there was Dad sitting on the sofa looking very sorry for himself. As soon as he saw me, he got up, muttered a few words and retreated into a little box room by the kitchen. He always called the room his workshop. No one was allowed in there, not even Mum.

Mum's life was never easy bringing up 3 boys. She also had 2 miscarriages. She desperately would have loved a little girl in the family, but it seemed God had other ideas, and in her early forties, my mother gave birth to my youngest brother Terence. There would be 20 years between myself and Terence. It was good for Mum to be able to give and receive love without any hassle. I tried to keep out of the house as much as possible. I felt it would be better for everyone in the family.

I didn't realise at that time what a deep thinker I was, being so young. I would reflect on Mum and Dad's lifestyle, and how we lived so often from hand to mouth, depending if Dad had any work. We never wasted anything, and I really wanted to break this cycle of poverty. I didn't want to struggle like them and I had this desire in me – to buy a house. I was a very practical person. I had to be, being a welding engineer. I remember before I met Daph, the Lord gave me a promise and it came while I was reading my daily reading from a little book called 'Daily Light'. It was a combination of different scriptures for each day. The word was "*Whatever I put my hand to, I would prosper and also He had anointed me with a gift of joy*", which would explain how I could recover so fast with so much shock and trauma in my life. I can't explain it, but I just believed it, and knew this was God. I didn't know how that would work out in my life, but that word came into my spirit and wasn't just some more information to process. This word brought change within me. I would say today that the word became flesh.

I spoke to Daph about saving as I could see she liked nice clothes and seemed to be spending all her wages as soon as she got them. I remember saying, be practical, whoever you marry. In life you will need money as our parents didn't have any. We both saved regularly and at the age of 19 started looking for a property. The Building Society was very strict in lending in those days and would only give us £3000 over 25 years.

We didn't have a clue how much the house would cost, but we were really excited to be looking at properties. It didn't take very long for our bubble to burst. The only property we could afford was a 2-bedroom terrace house that needed a lot of money spent on it. We just got tired of looking, and realised that despite all our efforts trying to find a suitable property, we had come to a dead end.

I started to pray and seek God for an answer and gradually within me, God gave me a word and said, "You must build your own house." I thought that must be God as the mere concept of building a house, I wouldn't ever consider. But with such assurance in myself that this was God, and being practical, I thought, well, first things first. You need land. I never thought about how much it would cost. I felt I didn't need to. I would just trust God.

In those days we only had 2 weeks holiday a year, so I asked my employers for a week off. We hired a MK2 Escort car and travelled over 1,000 miles in that week looking for land within a 10-mile radius of Chelmsford, as I didn't want to move too far from the church.

We went to almost every estate agent in the town and district. Even the plots we did manage to find the owners were keeping the land in the family. We didn't leave a stone unturned, even the most obscure places right off the beaten track. We couldn't find anywhere. We kept hearing the saying – it's like gold dust trying to find land.

After the week, feeling mentally and emotionally tired and disappointed despite all our efforts, thinking what more can we do, doubt started to hit me and suggested I had heard God wrong. It was foolish to think a 19-year-old welder, not even a builder, could take such a project on, especially with my limited educational abilities. I refused to listen to those thoughts, but to be honest, in the natural, I had to conclude it did seem impossible. It was only a few weeks later that the Pastor was visiting a lady who lived in Broomfield. In the middle of a conversation she asked him resolutely, "*I don't suppose you know anyone who wants to buy a plot of ground as we have a plot for sale because, being older, we can't look after it?"*

As soon as she asked this question, my name popped into the Pastor's head. The following Sunday, after the service, Pastor Anthony approached me and asked, *"was I looking for a piece of land to purchase?"* and if so, would I like to view it. I couldn't believe what I was hearing. This plot of land was behind their garden and was an orchard. It was quite small. Of course, I said yes. We couldn't get up there quick enough. Daph and myself arrived at the house. As soon as I saw this piece of land I felt God say to me – *"this is yours"*. Wow God! You are such a great Father. The couple then explained why they wanted to offload the small piece of land. Before they could get any further in the conversation I said I would buy it. Bless their hearts, they were very up-front and honest. They too, loved Jesus. They explained that the piece of land they had been trying to sell since 1948; however, nobody wanted to buy it as nobody could get planning permission. In fact just 6 months before we came a big estate agent tried to get planning permission but was refused. They said I could have the plot but doubted very much I would get planning permission.

None of this information put me off. I had a word from God and that was good enough for me. We agreed a price which took all our savings. I never considered any problems. I was a welder and knew nothing about building. Looking back with what I know now, I don't think I would have purchased it, but it does show that **too much information can be a hindrance to faith.**

We put our application for planning permission in to Essex County Council and as expected, we got refused. We weren't put off as I have always said, **the wrong expectation leads to**

disillusionment. So the decision didn't phase us. I looked at the Council's reasons for refusal and didn't agree with them. We decided to hire a solicitor to take this to an appeal. The months followed. I had written so many letters trying to chase our application up. I could see our wedding day fast approaching. It felt like the heavens and everyone had gone silent. Frustration became part of our life as the wedding day grew closer. It all got a bit much for Daph. She used to say – "*all you have is a bit of dirt, and we have very little money and no-where to live*". Even the Pastor was having his doubts. Other young couples in the church were getting married. Even my workmates thought I was foolish being so young with no experience of building.

I finally succumbed to pressure and said to Daph that as the wedding was only 3 months away, it looked that we would have to live in the front upstairs room at her mum's house. A little council house is not a very good start, I know. But if we hadn't heard by the time we were married we would try again to look at the property market. That would be our deadline.

Quite often I would see in the bible that God would show up at the last minute. To me, at that time, it seemed like the last second, as it was only a few months away and we would be walking down the aisle with no place of our own.

Instead of collapsing on the inside, I now had someone I could trust. Once again in my little bedroom, I would kneel down by the side of my bunk bed with my hands together and pray. I had learned to pray specific prayers as I needed specific answers. I said:

"*Father, I believe this was your word and will for us to build a house. I don't understand why everyone has gone silent on me. Can you sort this out? Thank you*".

Almost immediately, the thought came to me and said – 'write to the MP'. That had never occurred to me before. So I wrote to the MP at Chelmsford which was St John Stevas, a Conservative, explaining my predicament. Within 2 weeks, I had a letter from the Ministry of Housing, Mr Crossman as Labour was in power at the time, to inform me that my application for planning permission had been successful. Wow! What a result. God is faithful to His word. At least we could get married knowing we have the assurance we could build. To think this plot of land in Broomfield got refused by so many authorities since 1948 – it went to the highest authority in the land right to parliament who approved of our application. Thank God. Because we believe we went to the highest authority, the ultimate authority, our Lord Jesus Christ, who is seated by the right hand of God the Father, praying for His people. I just had my 21st birthday. Daph was 19 years of age. We now had hope – something to look forward to – building our own home.

We also knew we would have to pay for our wedding. But Dad did fulfil his responsibility and pay for the taxis, which was the custom of the day that the Bridegroom's father pays for the taxis. Unknown to me at the time, Dad had got the taxis on the cheap. We knew something was wrong when the bride failed to arrive on time, but 40 minutes later. It so happened of all days to happen, the top hose blew on the taxi. Steam was coming out everywhere. After that was quickly fixed, Daph was then dropped off at the slaughterhouse behind the church. Meanwhile I was sweating as the registrar informed me he had another wedding to go to and would soon be leaving. Panic! I could feel it creeping all over me. The organist, Mr Ken Tween, wasn't a well man, and was suffering a blood condition, just kept playing in the background, while the congregation of people were all getting restless, and kept looking at the back of the church wondering if the bride had changed her mind.

Then, at last, I was beckoned to go to the minor hall at the back of the church, and there was Daph, dressed so beautifully, all in white, with such a pretty veil over her face, looking so radiant. We were then told we must say the wedding vows and sign the register, as the registrar wanted to go. It all seemed rather rushed. Not what I had expected, but hey, what's new? My life seemed full of the unexpected. I was thinking, I hope this isn't prophetic of what is to come. Then I made a mistake and trod on Daph's veil almost ripping it off her head. The look she gave me. All can say is I didn't easily forget that.

The wedding ceremony started almost one hour late with Daph walking down the aisle and all the people, I think, smiling with relief. They were so happy but didn't realise we were already married. For the benefit of everyone we had to say the wedding vows again. I was thinking about when we get to the part, does anyone object? I thought, too bad, we're already married.

Our dear Pastor valued every one of his congregation so much that he would always treat every ceremony, whether it be a wedding or dedicating a baby to our Lord, with a very personal touch. I can remember him wearing a crown of evergreen laurels as that was the meaning of Daph's name, and then he tied our centre legs together like we were running a three-legged race, and explained that when we keep in step with each other we will go a lot further in life, and married life would be a lot easier instead of competing against each other.

The reception was held at the County Hotel, and I was to

make a speech to compliment on the bridesmaids. But God had spoken to me about what I should say. I stood up in front of 100 guests and I publically thanked God for my dad who had given me life, and I thanked him for the way he had brought me up. On this day of all days, I wanted to honour my dad despite our differences. He knew what was best for me, although I couldn't see it through all the abuse. I just wanted to take this opportunity to thank him for instilling in me to live a righteous life.

Nobody knew what happened behind closed doors in our little council terrace house. But I know that Jesus, who I invited in my heart as a young teenager, had been changing me on the inside. I never held any grudges or unforgiveness against Dad. If you had taken a bet this attitude of heart would have been against all odds considering the backdrop of our culture of living. This was the right time as I would be leaving home for good to set up my own home. Today I am so grateful to my Heavenly Father that I was able to honour my dad. Little did I know, I would now be eligible for that promise God gave in the 4th Commandment – to honour your father and mother that it may be well with you.

Not one of us knows another person's heart. It is so easy to pass judgement based on external behaviour.

I found out later in life that Dad was illegitimate. His mother worked as a maid in a mansion-type house in Hastings and we believe she was taken advantage of by a French Naval Officer, leaving Dad's mum with a baby boy. Not being married carried a lot of stigma in those days of the 1920's. If you ever watch the film, Gosford Park; this really highlights this type of shame.

His mother tried to look after Dad until he was 2. We don't know the reason why, but Dad entered foster care for most of his early life, until his mum married a metropolitan policeman in London who despised Dad as he wasn't his own kid. Dad suffered so much rejection and abandonment that when World War 2 came along, he lied about his age so he could join the Royal Air Force and become an engineer, just so he could get out of home which was like a war zone. He dreaded leave, unlike his friends, who looked forward to going home. Because he knew he wasn't wanted, he carried those feelings of being unsafe, unprotected, with no bonding, living in an emotional exile. It's no wonder he had so many angry outbursts and fits of rage and frustration.

Today I can honestly say, as I did on my wedding, I honour him, love him and I miss him, and wish I could turn the clock back, as with what I know now, I would have treated him better.

We left the County Hotel in a little 1960 Austin A40 with balloons and foam all over the car. The hubcaps were filled with coins, and nuts and bolts to make as much noise as possible as we drove away. We also had four 6 foot lengths of rope with half a dozen empty baked bean cans on each length. We had cars behind us bibbing their horns as they followed us for about 6 miles. Eventually, I found a quiet country lane and in my lovely new suit, laid under the car untying all the ropes with the cans on.

We arrived at our honeymoon destination, a small hotel on the seafront in Southsea, which is opposite the Isle of Wight, dead on 10 pm, bang on time. I opened the boot of the car only to find the 2 suitcases had been chained together and locked by a padlock. Fortunately, I had some of my tools with me. I had a tiny file, so with much perspiration managed half an hour later to remove one of the links so that we could remove the chain.

We then checked in, trying not to look too conspicuous. Our room, although it had a sea view, was like a box room. The bed was ¾ size and my feet hung over the edge of the bed when I laid down. By now I didn't want to complain as I didn't want anything else to go wrong or spoil what seemed like a day filled with obstacles.

We opened the cases, and loads of confetti fell out all over the carpet. It was everywhere. On our knees, we picked up every bit of confetti so no-one would know we were newlyweds.

The morning arrived. We sat in the dining room and ordered our breakfast. While waiting for it to arrive the manager of the hotel came over to us at our table and said, "*You must be the newlyweds*". Well, so much for trying to disguise that fact. He then went on to explain that he had had a phone call from the Registry Office in Chelmsford and that we must go to the Council Office in Portsmouth as there seemed to be a problem registering the wedding!

My first thought was, Oh no! Perhaps we are not married after all, legally. I could feel the temperature in my body rising as my face became red with embarrassment. I didn't know what to believe. Nothing had gone smoothly. It seemed whatever could go wrong, had done. Even cutting the cake the knife bent. I thought it was going to break off as the cake was so hard. Unbelievable, I kept saying.

Straight after breakfast, we arrived at a very large, cold looking building. We stepped into the entrance. Confronting us was a very wide oak staircase with people everywhere.

We started asking questions as to where the Registry office was. We had it pointed out to us that we were to go up the staircase. We eventually found the office and I started to explain to the lady behind the counter about what had happened in Chelmsford and that we had been married twice. She looked astonished and perplexed.

Daph decided to step in too and started to explain again. While she was talking in the air of confusion, I was praying, and then the thought popped into my head. It was a hoax! My friends back in Chelmsford had all got together and cooked up the scheme. Then Daph's head turned in the middle of the conversation with the lady behind the counter and she knew. The penny had dropped. We had been had! We couldn't get out of there quick enough. What a start to married life! Certainly not what you would call normal, but looking back the whole experience created memories we shall never forget. Once again, the attitude I was used to was, get on with it, you can't change anything now. It's like we were robbed in so many ways, yet that was all we knew in those days. Carry on regardless. No questions asked. Just bury your heads in the sand and push through. That was the only way we knew at the time.

Chapter 5

CHANGE IS BREWING

Starting married life living with mother in law and Daph's two brothers, Alan and Barry, was not an ideal situation. All we had to ourselves was the front bedroom with a lamppost outside our window, right by a bus stop, but we now had infused in us the hope that soon we would have our own home.

The detailed planning application wasn't accepted, so we decided to just agree with the local council so we could start building as soon as possible.

We agreed with the builder we would do as much as we were able to. Digging a 100-foot trench with a depth of 3 foot isn't what I think Daph had in mind when we agreed to help, especially as this work was done each evening after working nine and a half hours during the day. I would use the pickaxe and shovel as the ground was full of stones. Daph would be on wheelbarrow duty as well as holding a torch. It was very tiring, but also it was fun as we were part of seeing a word from God being fulfilled before our eyes. After a rough winter with snow falling on and off, we moved into the new home in 1970. We had two deck chairs, no cupboards, no fridge (we just kept our milk in buckets of water). And a bed. That was the sum total of our belongings. We had the structure of the house; that was the important thing. 'We have the rest of our lives to add to it', I used to say.

Anybody who knows anything about building houses knows there are usually unforeseen problems which inevitably means it's going to cost more money.

Looking back, I can see God's wisdom in providing a room at Daph's mum's house. We couldn't borrow any more money from anywhere, but as we were both working and Daph's mum, Bett, never charged us any rent for that bedroom, that really helped.

I just thank God I didn't know all the problems in building a property in advance, but even at 21 I had a foundation in my faith that God would honour His word. If I had known all the problems beforehand I don't think I would have started the project. Looking back, we just took a step at a time, and whatever obstacle we faced, we would overcome by committing everything to God in prayer.

We were so pleased to discover that the number allocated to us was 7. I believe names and numbers in the bible are very significant and can carry hidden meanings. To us, at the time the number 7 meant completion and rest – the perfect number. I would often say with much delight that life was going well. I was now no longer singing soprano and was now in the tenor section of the church choir. Daph had joined the choir and was singing in the soprano section. We were full of enthusiasm and faith. We had seen God work in practical ways for us. We went to prayer meetings, and bible studies as well as the youth meetings. It was quite normal for different young people to speak publically at those meetings, so it was no surprise that eventually I would be asked to speak. I felt a bit nervous as I had never spoken to more than 2 or 3 people at a time, let alone a group of 30 young people.

I stood by a short table and began speaking what I believe God had given me. I got off to a good start till I reached a point of trying to explain something. It was as if the blackboard in my mind had a blank canvas. I searched everywhere in my head to continue my talk, but there was a block. I felt so embarrassed as I looked at all the young people who I felt at this stage, were staring at me. Minutes passed by which felt like eternity. I couldn't understand why my train of thought had been interrupted by this memory block. It was like I had changed tracks and was at a dead end.

The silence was even waiting for me to continue. I did eventually manage to get the talk over with. I now knew I had a problem in communicating. I remember now there had been other times when I would think of a word, and when I spoke the opposite would come out of me, and other times I could experience odd words that I would miss out of a conversation which, too, was embarrassing.

In those days, it was almost unheard of people being diagnosed with these type of issues. Yet now we seem to have so many names like autism describing people; mental health. With the attitude I was used to: you can't change it, get on with life, I just shrugged this issue off. Public speaking became the instrument that really highlighted I had a problem. This experience certainly got my attention so much so, that I would avoid positioning myself in that situation again. I found it difficult to accept that I had a disability, and wouldn't admit that to anyone. Now I know that was pride; not admitting my weakness.

I then found it difficult to accept another word God had given me years previously.

> *"The Spirit of the Lord God is upon Me, Because the Lord has anointed Me To preach good tidings to the poor; He has sent Me to heal the brokenhearted, To proclaim liberty to the captives, And the opening of the prison to those who are bound; To proclaim the acceptable year of the Lord, And the day of vengeance of our God; To comfort all who mourn, To console those who mourn in Zion, To give them beauty for ashes, The oil of joy for mourning, The garment of praise for the spirit of heaviness; That they may be called trees of righteousness, The planting of the Lord, that He may be glorified"*.
>
> (Isaiah 61: 1-3 NKJV)

I didn't understand what all these verses meant, but somehow they made such a deep impression on me that I have always kept with me. Often on our journey in life, God speaks to us through the bible; His written word, and His words stay with us. I have since learnt that **God's word abides with us no matter what our circumstances are and how they change.** But there are thoughts that come from Satan, the enemy of our soul. We often call him the devil, or Lucifer, which was his name in heaven before he lost his position of authority to come to earth. His thoughts come and go, and are usually of a negative nature.

Within the church structure I started getting areas of responsibility such as making sure all the chairs used in Sunday school were put away, and that the chairs were put out for the main church service. I enjoyed working, and being a practical person, this suited me, until all the other volunteers became unreliable. I also became part of the youth committee, what church calls today, youth leadership. It wasn't long before Pastor Anthony approached me and asked me to stand for election by the church members to become a Deacon. This is an office held within the local Pentecostal church where you officially become part of the authority structure to serve the people. I immediately thought, who am I? As I was only 21 and there were so many men of stature with so much more experience of life and God than me.

It felt very humbling to be asked. It was something I had never thought about and didn't particularly really want. It was with much prayer and fear I accepted, and would consider it God's will if the members of the church voted for me.

There was an annual meeting once a year where the voting would take place, along with other church activities being discussed. In quite a surprise to me; I officially became a deacon of the church with a congregation of about 150-200 people. Apparently the youngest deacon ever elected at the age of 21 in this local Pentecostal church.

I didn't know whether to laugh or cry. All I knew was that God must know what He's doing. I would have to attend deacons' meetings and pray and seek God for the spiritual welfare of the church. In those days, we didn't have elders. We were considered to fulfil both roles as elders and deacons, being practical as it states in scripture, serving the people but also being involved in the oversight of the church. By this time, I was growing in confidence within myself and all that I had achieved. Life didn't seem to have enough hours in the day; there was always something to do. I was becoming more passionate about my faith in Jesus day by day and the life He had given me that I truly felt so alive and happy. I had a secure job which I loved and that suited me travelling to different parts of Essex, repairing broken machinery like JCB, Dumpers and Mixers. I had a gorgeous wife, and our own house that was designed by me. After living with poverty and emotional pain this now seemed like a small taste of heaven, and to cap it all now I was one of the leaders in the church despite my limited educational abilities. I knew this was impossible for me to have achieved in my own strength, it must have been God, for which I am eternally grateful to my Heavenly Father for all His provision in my life. It is no wonder I was so passionate talking about Jesus Christ and how He can change lives, and accepts you as you are with all the emotional and spiritual baggage we carry!

We both wanted to start a family. I said to Daph, being practical, that as we were both working, let's build the home first which I estimated would take about 3 years. It was in the year 1973 Daph conceived and we were ecstatic with joy when we found out. Life couldn't get any better. Everything, I thought, was on schedule and there was an order about life, no confusion. Everything was just so brilliant. Daph would now be under the supervision and care of St John's Hospital in Chelmsford.

During a routine blood test that pregnancy brings, it was discovered that Daph was O negative with antibodies in her blood. I was found to be O positive. Apparently, the combination of the two blood groups are incompatible, hence the formation of antibodies. What normally happens on this discovery is the mother will have an anti-globulin injection which prevents any problems when the baby is born, but you must have the injection before the child is born, otherwise it doesn't work. Unfortunately for us, Daph already had the antibodies in her blood, and the only way Daph could have got them was by a blood transfusion or a miscarriage. To her knowledge, she hadn't had either. This became a mystery to us.

This meant complications for us. Daph would now be under strict supervision from the doctors at the hospital. It entailed Daph having a large injection to drain fluid out from the womb, an amniocentesis. Fluid was then sent away for testing. This blood condition can cause severe complications to the unborn child.

We were informed that is was too dangerous for Daph to go full term in carrying the baby; it would be safer if the child was induced early.

While we were coming to terms with the diagnosis we heard of a Church of England church in Hainault, Essex, called St Pauls, where people were coming from all over the country to attend a Tuesday meeting. We heard that people were getting healed and people were so full of joy they were dancing in the church. I was concerned as a number of our church members were going. I was quite inquisitive about it but felt I didn't need to go as I had everything I needed from God. I had been baptized by full immersion and was baptized in the Holy Spirit. I was on fire for God. Full of passion. I spoke in another tongue and I prophesied. Why should I need to go elsewhere? I was very satisfied with my present experience, but as we know, **experience is only a gateway, not an end.** These meetings at St

Pauls in Hainault had gone on for about three years and were still going strong. It had got quite a reputation. It became quite concerning as more of our congregation were going. It reached a point that two of my fellow deacons were so concerned that we needed to go for ourselves to see what on earth was going on. Still reluctant, I was persuaded to go with them. Daph was heavily pregnant with our first child, so we decided to go and check it out once and for all, and then that would be the end of the matter.

We arrived at 7 pm and had to queue for an 8 pm start at this boring red brick church in the middle of a housing estate in the middle of winter with Daph, it seemed, expanding by the hour with a baby that couldn't keep still. I felt sorry for Daph. Her back was really aching. At last the doors opened. We walked in and immediately I just knew God was in this place. Nobody said anything. People were struggling to find a seat. But it was the atmosphere that struck me. It was like being bathed in liquid love. People were now sitting on the windowsills. I think there must have been well over 400 people, although it looked like the church only seated 200.

I felt I was at home among people that appeared quite ordinary; no dress code. There were people off the streets. There was such a diversity of people, yet the atmosphere was so filled with expectancy. I loved it. Yet nobody had said or done anything. Then a young couple led us in worship. They looked as if they were caught up in heaven. So ordinary. So natural. Just beautiful. The song they sang I will always remember as I associate it with that meeting – Alleluia, Alleluia. This repeats itself about eight times, and with the same tone we progress with the words *"Lord we love you and thou art worthy"*. We had gone past praise and it felt we were in the presence of a Holy God. Now our spirit was connecting with His Spirit, and we were in union, having fellowship with the Almighty God.

We were all still very conscious of who God is – the Almighty who calls each star by name, with us being mere human beings. Being loved by someone who knew everything about us – even our thoughts can't be hidden from His eyes. Yet, we were accepted and here we were, worshipping in spirit and truth. I knew the verse in John 4:23 (NKJV) when Jesus spoke to the Samaritan woman:

> *"But the hour is coming, and now is, when the true worshipers will worship the Father in spirit and truth; for the Father is seeking such to worship Him".*

We were not just related to God as His children, but through a fellowship so natural it just felt like a river of life was flowing. There came a time when the whole congregation started singing in a heavenly tongue, which felt like being part of a heavenly orchestra, each person as an instrument. All so different but in total harmony. Our conductor was the Lord and the Holy Spirit was flowing through each of us. It was like angels were joining with us. I didn't want it to stop.

The power of His presence and the fellowship in the Spirit impacted me. I knew I would never be the same again. The memory would stay with me forever. There was no sense of the spirit of excellence or performance, or being entertained. We were caught up in pure, unadulterated worship. This lasted for about an hour. The couple were so unassuming. They didn't keep stopping to talk in between. There was no need. There was just a flow about the whole worship experience. We were more conscious of God than the songs or the couple. Our whole inner focus was the Lord himself, who is alive and who gave His life for us sinners who really need him.

After the worship, we sat down. The vicar of St Pauls, Reverend Trevor Deering, spoke. He looked like he had been through a hedge backwards. His hair was longer than mine and went past his shoulders. He looked like a wreck of a man; not an ounce of self-confidence, even though he wore his white ring of confidence around his neck. There was a total absence of pride, yet when he spoke there was so much love and life in his voice. He did have his C of E robes on, but that was to be expected. Despite no natural attraction, I couldn't take my eyes off him. He seemed to radiate such a presence, a glory, that I couldn't explain. We were more conscious of Jesus than him. My heart was warmed to him talking about God choosing the weak things of the world. This really takes the biscuit (1 Corinthians 1:27-29 NIV):

> *"But God chose the foolish things of the world to shame the wise; God chose the weak things of the world to shame the strong. God chose the lowly things of this world and the despised things—and the things that are not—to nullify the things that are, so that no one may boast before him".*

We then had a time where people of such diversity stood up all over the place testifying of what God had done, so spontaneously. Without introduction, people were also reading letters from all over the UK, and many parts of the world, about how God had intervened in lives by the power of His presence in answer to the prayers regularly prayed in the prayer hour in the service. Many cancers had disappeared, the deaf were healed and marriages were also healed. So many testimonies. And this was just the one night I had attended.

What I found out years later reading the first book written about the visitation of God at St Pauls, Hainault (the book was called Evict the Devil – not a brilliant title I thought) was that doctors were also present to verify the claims of healing of this wonderful Jesus and His power.

Trevor Deering spoke a very simple gospel message. He mentioned that he himself had had a nervous breakdown and had so much wrong with him physically, and suffered so much fear he was paranoid and had time out of school in his younger days, but was now transformed by Jesus Christ, the Son of the Living God. After preaching the word, people just flocked to the front giving their lives to Jesus. It was almost like a stampede. I hadn't seen anything like this up until this time. I was used to a few people just putting their hands up at the end of the gospel service on a Sunday evening.

Now there came a time to minister to those with deeper needs. There were so many people who had fallen from a standing position to be laying all over the place on the floor. It looked like a bomb had exploded. The political correctness brigade would have had kittens – not to mention the fire brigade.

For the first time in my life, I heard a loud, piercing shriek, that caused my hair to stand on end as demonic spirits started manifesting and were leaving people. Some were waving their arms and shouting out. No one was constraining them or rushing to get them out of the building. I think you would normally see this type of behaviour in a mental hospital. Amazing! The people there didn't seem to mind so much noise going on. Sometimes when one started, another person started. What looked like confusion wasn't. I was very conscious of authority being present as Jesus just delivered and met these people at their point of need.

Coming from a Pentecostal background I would often hear the quote from the bible in 1 Corinthians 14:40 (NKJV):

"Let all things be done decently and in order".

I often used to think it was ok to constrain people rather than bring freedom. When you think about it you first must do it, then the rest follows. **I would rather experience the life of the nursery, than the life of the cemetery.**

That day I was witnessing here in a Church of England what I always believed would happen if God showed up in a meeting.

As I looked on and watched, the Lord Jesus just touched so many lives. I kept thinking the thought – *"IS THERE ANOTHER JESUS?"* as all we seemed to do was to pray for the doctor and that the Lord would guide their hands. Once again, I had this experience and later on the Lord showed me a verse in 2 Corinthians 11:4:

"For if he who comes preaches another Jesus whom we have not preached, or if you receive a different spirit which you have not received, or a different gospel which you have not accepted—you may well put up with it!"

Paul was saying there is another Jesus, another gospel, another spirit at work in the earth. When you think about it, where would Satan concentrate his attack? In the earth, as he is the master of disguise and he knows what proud people we are, that we don't like to admit we could be wrong in some of our belief systems. It's no wonder that he would target the church to make us ineffective.

The experience at Hainault certainly gave me so much to think about. The impact on me personally changed me forever. **Sometimes in life, the things of God are caught before they are taught,** and for me this certainly was the case.

Daph and I came away from the meeting never to be the same. We had got separated from my two fellow deacons. I wondered how they had got on. I was soon to find out when we had our next deacons meeting.

With great excitement, I was waiting to share as we all gathered together. We got through all the business side of running the church, then the other two deacons shared their experiences of attending the Tuesday evening meeting at Hainault. Well, I couldn't believe what I was hearing. Only negativity came from their lips. I began to wonder, what planet are you on? Didn't you see and experience the presence of God? My report appeared contradictory to theirs. There was so much freedom and life there. Why? Because Jesus Christ was Lord, and in 2 Corinthians 3:17 (NIV):

"where the Spirit of the Lord is, there is freedom".

I know freedom isn't about waving your arms about and just dancing down the aisle. We know you can see that at a pop concert, or singing as loud as you can. The difference there was **JESUS CHRIST WAS LORD.** We know in life you go through many seasons (Ecclesiastes 3). There are 28 seasons mentioned and 14 are opposites e.g. there is a time to be born and a time to die. There is a time of war and a time of peace. In a person's life we, at some point, will go through the seasons of the spirit. For example, when someone is grieving and someone is celebrating the birth of their newborn baby. Opposite seasons. But when we yield to the Lordship of Jesus in that season then, and only then, do we have true liberty. It would be sad if we didn't, and just carried on regardless just as we are, as we would be missing the beautiful wonder of the Lordship of His presence ministering to us and through us. It is sad when you watch people with a fake smile just carrying on the treadmill of trying to please God. We cannot please God like this.

What happened at Hainault began about 1970 and lasted approximately 5 years. God, in His sovereign will, was already beginning a new season in the church called the Charismatic Renewal. Thousands of people gave their lives to Jesus Christ and were transformed in this insignificant and unlikely church who enjoyed, just once a week, the power and presence of Almighty God.

Personally, I only needed to go once. The fire in my heart was ignited once again.

I remember watching a documentary by the network that was then, Thames Television, called This Week, about what was happening in the church. It became the focal point of misunderstanding and misrepresentation which is no surprise as wherever God is moving with life, not far away there will be those that will ignore it or oppose it, but it goes to show how accurate the scriptures are, as Jesus was opposed by those who should have known better.

What transpired in me that day was to fuel not just a memory, but a desire to see this happen in my own life and the life of the church. I knew then, that in the 21st century, the Jesus of the bible was the same today and is able to heal the sick and cast out demons and meet us at our point of need. The experience infused a new hope. Something that I always believed possible, as I believe all the word of God, that it is totally inspired, written by 40 writers, 66 books over a period of a couple of thousand years, yet one author, God Himself:

> *"All Scripture is God-breathed and is useful for teaching, rebuking, correcting and training in righteousness".*
> (2 Timothy 3:16 NIV)

We heard of another person God was visiting about the same time with a different emphasis, also a Church of England vicar called Colin Urquart, who was a vicar in Luton. He seemed to be having a different emphasis, particularly on faith which seemed to be the main thrust of his message. He wrote a number of books; one that blessed me was "My Father is the Gardener" which was such a blessing at the time.

Chapter 6

NOT WHAT I EXPECTED

It never ceases to amaze me that when God wants to impart some truth to you it quite often comes when you are not trying so hard to hear God, but in the normal flow of life. God's word stands out irrespective of all that is happening around us.

On this occasion I was flicking through the pages of my bible on a Sunday morning, just waiting for the service to start and my eye was drawn to the book of Matthew, chapter 24, verse 13 (NKJV) *"But he who endures to the end shall be saved"*, and then still flicking through the bible another verse of scripture just stood out from all the other passages of scripture, and this was in Timothy 3:12 (NKJV), *"and all who desire to live godly in Christ Jesus will suffer persecution"*.

I just knew God was speaking to me about my life being a Christian.

My first reactions to these verses was as I looked at my present experience and modern Christianity in the Western World. I thought, surely this doesn't apply now to me, personally, as I am very happy at the moment. Our baby would be coming soon and I just felt so content. I could never envisage any situation when this scenario would be remotely possible. Anyway, I thought, what happens if I don't endure? Will I never make it into heaven? Do I no longer have a Saviour? And why would living in a godly Christian life cause one to suffer in the Western World? I could understand it if the verse applied to the Eastern bloc, but not here in the UK. Also, it didn't say persecution might happen, but will happen. If this was so, what form would this take?

The service then commenced but these 2 verses of scripture remained with me, even to this day. Was God planting a seed of truth to forewarn of what would happen sometime in the future?

Anyway, I had so much to look forward to; a baby on the way and no more antenatal classes. Brilliant!

We had a date that Daph would be admitted to St John's hospital in Chelmsford to be put on a drip that would induce the baby as the baby wasn't allowed to go to the full term of 39 weeks because of the Rhesus problem that existed.

Now with so much excitement and feeling a little nervous, Daph had this drip connected to her arm on March 11th.

Ten long hours later feeling exasperated as nothing visible had happened, thank the Lord I was a bit prepared with lots of books to read, contractions then started and lasted another 10 hours. You definitely couldn't fall asleep due to the noise level on the ward. It felt a bit like Hell. So many screams and noises were filling the air. I felt so sorry for Daph. I kept covering her ears to limit the trauma that was going on. I lost count of breathing with her in stages at 1.23am. I was worn out so goodness knows how Daph was feeling.

Then, at last, out popped this gorgeous little boy. With tears streaming down our faces, our whole beings so full of emotion, joy and relief. The baby was certainly here. Daph then spoke out without premeditation "We have a little Patrick". I immediately thought, Daph, you have just declared the name for our baby (we hadn't really decided on a name because we didn't know the sex of the baby). So, now there were three Patrick's in the family – my father, myself and baby Patrick. I wasn't going to argue. We were so loved up. And to be honest – some marathons weren't that long!

After some cuddles, Patrick was taken to the Special Care Baby Unit to be monitored. He gained the nickname "Jumbo", as he was 8lbs 4oz, and most of the other babies were really small. If he had gone full term he would have been over 10lbs.

It wasn't long before Patrick was having a battle on his hands. The antibodies weren't the only problems, we were told. He also had yellow jaundice which kept increasing despite being under a lot of blue lights for over 3 days. In those days, the babies were only allowed treatment for 24 hours at a time. The jaundice had now reached a critical point. We had a discussion with the doctors who explained that Patrick's level of jaundice had reached point 16, and apparently if it continued rising above 18 his brain would be damaged.

The medical answer would be to change all his blood, which was available from the blood bank at Brentwood. This was now arranged. I really felt uncomfortable about this, so I contacted

Pastor Anthony, and that evening Pastor Anthony and myself prayed for Patrick, that God would heal him. I can't say I was full of faith, but I now knew Jesus is alive today and is healing people and changing lives.

The doctors came the following day to prescribe the blood transfusion for Patrick, and it came to their notice that Patrick was improving. To be honest, Patrick looked as yellow as a banana, even his eyes were yellow. Slowly but surely Patrick made a total recovery. Doctors being doctors still edged on the side of caution by warning us that Patrick wouldn't have a lot of life in him, and might be rather slow and backward in the first year of life, and for us not to raise our expectations too high regarding his behaviour. Well, I can honestly say that wasn't the case. I didn't receive those words that could have acted as a pronouncement over our son. Patrick was the very opposite, so full of life and energy. He was a living miracle. Within 10 months he was walking.

At that period of time we had no concept that the enemy of our souls that we call Satan, would try to rob him of life. God had a plan before time began that Patrick would be raised up to minister to the young people of our nation, and also to many parts of the world, to share the good news that Jesus Christ is the only saviour that would open up heaven to humanity. What better time to take Patrick out but at birth?

Everything was going to plan. I thought to myself – what a wonderful age we live in. Changes were taking place, not only in our home, but they were also to take place in the church.

The Student Union in Chelmsford approached the church to see if they could use the church building as they wanted to invite Trevor Deering from St Paul's Hainault. It appeared at that time there wasn't a church in Chelmsford that would open doors to him.

Pastor Anthony was a very godly man. He didn't quite understand all that had happened at Hainault as he had never been and the press really wasn't helpful. There seemed too many divided opinions about what had happened in Hainault. I knew Pastor Anthony was a man that understood the ways of the Spirit of God as well as being a bible teacher.

I went to him on one occasion as I had an experience of an evil presence in my bedroom that caused my hair to stand on end. He shared with me he, too, had many experiences when he felt evil in his house that had even tried to strangle him. He never spoke publically about the experiences.

I felt he really wanted Trevor Deering to come but was conscious of the Pentecostal movement he was accountable to. Although a little hesitant, he did agree for the church to be used.

The evening arrived and I really couldn't wait. I so wanted the church to move into this new wave of the Spirit of God that had started to sweep across our nation. People just came from all walks of life, every chair was occupied by people. Even at the back of the church people were standing and had overspilled into the porch area and outside. Just like they did in the New Testament, people flocked to see this Jesus, the Son of God. It goes to show that when Jesus is raised higher than any group, denomination or personality, He just draws the crowds because He comes with authority and power and people's lives are changed.

Trevor Deering spoke on the foolishness of God and how the foolishness of God is greater than all the wisdom of the world, and how what appears in the natural understanding of things and viewed with our natural eyes is just our perspective. We miss out on the divine realities.

Who would ever think that 2 million Israelites marching around the walls of Jericho for 6 days in silence, on the seventh day would blow some trumpets and 30-foot walls with houses on them would fall down. How foolish from our perspective is that? How does it work? The God of Heaven has the power to do anything He wants. He loves a people who don't believe in Him, who want to live life their way independent of Him. He sent His only Son to come and be born of a virgin, to be beaten to pulp, so much so He was hardly recognisable as a human being, let alone the Son of God, and die on a cross. He suffered to take the penalty of our wrongdoings (sins) and it pleased Him to see His Son suffer so much to bring a way for humanity to have eternal life, as it would be impossible for humanity to spend eternity in the presence of a Holy God knowing what we are like. How foolish is that? What appeared defeat with our natural eyes and understanding was the greatest victory this world has ever seen, as Jesus Christ opened up a way for us to have a personal relationship with the Father God, who brought this world of ours into existence (John 14:6). God's ways appear foolish to the way we think in this tiny little world of ours.

And what an example we see in front of our eyes that God chose this weak Reverend, with a history of mental issues, to be an instrument that His divine power and life could flow out from unhindered to reach this generation.

The invitation was given out by Trevor Deering for those who wanted to turn from living life their way and to surrender their life to Jesus Christ. I was astounded at the sheer numbers of people almost running to the front of the church crying. I could see tears running down so many faces with such conviction. Some were shouting Jesus, Jesus, Jesus. I was deeply moved to witness the work of the Holy Spirit bringing the presence of Jesus into our midst. I was used to just a few people raising their hands at the appeal of the gospel service. Once again this must have been what it was like in the New Testament. I felt humbled and privileged to be part of this. One couldn't help thinking what love the Heavenly Father has for us, and what is so dreadful that God would go to such lengths to save us? We often hear the words Hell used in relationship to peoples' experiences, when things are tough and there is no escape, but really do we have any concept of what Hell is? Judging from what God was doing on our midst, it seemed as if salvation wasn't about only going to heaven, but allowing heaven to come into our experience. I have often thought **so many people want to go to heaven but nobody wants to die...**

I now realised as the people flocked to the front of the church in response to the invitation, that the student union hadn't planned for such a response, and hadn't organised a team of counsellors to pray with these people.

I quickly managed to get the attention of people I knew would be willing to pray for these dear people. I led them to an upper room at the back of the church while the worship continued.

I spoke to a guy, and the first thing he did was grasp both of my hands. Strange, I thought. He wanted to see if I was a manual worker. After discovering my hands weren't soft and smooth, but very rough, he allowed me to continue. He just needed someone he could relate to. He then gave his heart and life to Jesus. It wasn't long before he became an active member of the church.

I was very much aware of Pastor Anthony's predicament and

the risk he took in allowing somebody quite controversial both in the eyes of the world and the church to minister here, but now my Pastor had seen and heard demons coming out of people, and seen the sick being healed, but most of all to experience the Glory of God's presence with a greater intensity than he was used to.

Looking back on that meeting, it was in so many ways disorganised, yet everything just seemed to flow naturally. People weren't trying so hard to get everything right or perfect. Their political correct spirit was not at work, yet there was authority and love and order.

Change was here now, and one of the changes that would be taking place in the life of the church was Pastor Anthony's retirement, due sometime within the year. He had no choice as it was a requirement of that time for all its ministers to retire by reaching the age of 65.

To prepare the church for change the leadership at the church would interview people that H.Q. thought would be suitable to take over from the existing Pastor.

We interviewed a Pastor who had a different outlook on church. He was a man of vision. He would like to build a bigger church to allow for church growth. He also had a history of starting a full-time day nursery and was very much interested in young people. The new pastor would work alongside Pastor Anthony in a transition period so the life of the church would continue without too much disruption. After much prayer and seeking the mind of God, it was agreed he would start.

Pastor Anthony had been in the church 25 years and we were very much a family. He wasn't trained by the Pentecostal movement. His previous employment was working as a Foreman at the Ford Motor Company at Dagenham in Essex. During this period of transition I watched the changes going on and the effect it was having on him. He would never verbalise them publically. I could see how hard it was for him to let the reins go, but with so much dignity he went along with it with honour.

He was very much a Spiritual Father to me and in so many ways. He recommended for me to read the daily readings by Oswald Chambers, the book entitled 'My Utmost for His Highest'. This is the only daily reading book I have come across that isn't about us, but about our relationship with our Lord Jesus, who is the foundation of our Christian life.

"For no other foundation can anyone lay than that which is laid, which is Jesus Christ".

(1 Corinthians 3:11 NKJV)

This book still speaks volumes to me today after walking with Jesus for over 50 years.

One of my major values in life would be to determine to live my utmost for His Highest. This emphasis was at the very heart of Pastor Anthony's ministry. This message would be the vein that connects all his messages. He told me he had never preached the same message twice in the local church. Today we would call him prophetic. When asked what he would like to be known for he said very sheepishly 'A Man of God'.

What an example to me. He feared God more than living in the fear of other people's opinions.

Halfway through this transitional stage of church life, God spoke to me in a dream. It felt like it was almost audible. He said, "Moses must go now. Joshua has come". I didn't have a clue what that meant but it was very real and made an impact in my spirit. I had a notebook beside my bed and for the next weeks following that experience, I had other thoughts come to me relating to the dream. Still not knowing what all this meant, I just kept thinking God must have a purpose for speaking in this way.

Two weeks had passed after this dream. I heard on the Tuesday that Pastor Anthony was taken to Broomfield Hospital after a heart attack. The new pastor contacted me and told me what had happened, and that he had gone to hospital. Pastor Anthony, in his last hours alive on the earth, wanted me, of all people, to speak at the church at the following Sunday's Communion Service. After being informed of this, the shock hit me as to what had taken place. Immediately I thought, 'I didn't have a chance to say goodbye'. I felt I had not only lost my spiritual father but a really close friend whom I could trust with my life. He knew all about me and my family and all the abuse we had lived through, yet he was never judgemental to any members of the family. He was strict with me and taught me about having my own boundaries. His life was a demonstration of the life of God flowing through his words and actions. He was always accessible to all members of the church.

I am so glad God is Sovereign and is never taken by surprise. That He sees all and understands all things, even our very frail humanity. If it wasn't for God's foresight preparing me before this major event in church life, I would just be in pieces. Being asked to speak at such a time would have been impossible for me, as I struggle at the best of times with the hidden disability of getting my words back to front and memory block when words disappear from my mind leaving me a blank screen. This was the first and last time the new pastor ever asked me to speak. The church family was now hurting and now entered into a change that no one expected. They really needed to hear a prophetic word from God.

As I stood on the platform on the Sunday morning and explained that God had forewarned by this dream that Moses would die, the anointing of God began to flow through me in such power and life. I didn't need to look at my notes. It felt as if I could stand outside my body and just watch God do all the talking. The clarity of my thinking, the way the words came out without thinking, and watching the people's sorrow and grief lift off them before my eyes as the glory of God came and people were beginning to shine just like Moses in the Old Testament. When he came down the mountain to give the 10 Commandments to Israel, God's people, his face was shining so much the people wanted him to cover his face. One cannot but bow to the awesome God we have. To have a transition that was now sudden. It made one realise that God is the Head of His Church, and will fulfil His plans and purposes. The people were now ready to accept the new pastor. Although still grieving in our hearts we had this assurance still: "God is with us".

What was amazing to me was that nobody knew that Pastor Anthony was going to die and nobody knew God had given me a word 2 weeks before. What was also amazing was that Pastor Anthony knew the mind of Christ before he died. It was impossible for him to know that God had spoken to me. No wonder the early church moved in the fear of the Lord and the comfort of His Holy Spirit.

At times like this we realise that God is the Almighty. He is not remote. He comes for His people. It was a privilege to be one of the bearers to carry the coffin into the church. There were so many dignitaries there. The church was packed. While standing and watching the service take place, trying to be brave, holding back some tears which became an impossible task, the reality of what had just happened began sinking in. That a generation has now come to an end. Pastor Anthony was indeed a man that served the purposes of God in his generation, and it would be wrong to follow a dead man's vision. We must now look to the Lord and support the new pastor. I left that service wondering how things would pan out.

Chapter 7

EMBRACING THE CHANGE

Change, indeed, was here to stay, but when you know it's God it is so much easier to accept, rather than change for the sake of change.

Trevor Deering was once again invited to Chelmsford by the Students Union, and we were approached to see if our church would be willing to let them use our church building again. The new Pastor hadn't been to any of his meetings before. I wondered how he would react to this wave of the Spirit of God.

Once again, the church was packed to overflowing. There was such joy in the place. People wanted to express their worship in dance as well as singing. This was almost unheard of in the seventies. I loved it and was really at home in the atmosphere of anticipation and the unpredictability of what God was going to do. Once again there was a great outpouring of love and freedom, and a great conviction that the Almighty God was in our midst. After everybody had left and we as a leadership met, I sensed a lot of caution and 'it's not really our thing' to embrace it. But they didn't totally dismiss it in the leadership.

The reality was, church would carry on as usual with everybody fulfilling their various functions. This left me a bit empty. It's like you've tasted cream, and nothing else can match up to it. But I knew now there was more to Christianity than fulfilling the status quo. I had birthed in me a desire to seek more of God, even if it meant going outside my denomination parameters.

I had recommended to me a book called "Disciple" written by an Argentinian Pastor, Juan Carlos Ortiz, that was challenging many traditions and habits of church world. I spoke to my pastor about it and he wasn't very keen on it. In fact, he felt it was dangerous to read. This book was bringing a biblical view of discipleship and exposing the merry go round of religion. I could see to those who were locked in tradition it would be quite a threat to this belief system. I loved it, because he saw the church as one, not broken down with walls keeping everybody separate. My appetite was now wet. I needed to find out more of what the Spirit of God was doing in the world.

I heard the Spirit of God was moving in Chad in Somerset, with people like Harry Greenwood, a guy called Uncle Sid, and Ian Andrews. I found out the person they called Uncle Sid was coming to Chelmsford and was invited by the Chelmsford Christian Fellowship. He was holding a meeting in a room in St John's Hospital. I felt quite strange as I sat there at the back, hoping nobody would recognise me; a bit how Nicodemus felt when visiting Jesus by night. He didn't really want his fellow Pharisees to recognise him (John 3).

This man, Uncle Sid, had another message I hadn't heard of before. He was talking about Jesus the deliverer, and how Jesus can set you free from fear, rejection, lust, etc. This puzzled me as I didn't believe a Christian could be affected by Satan and his minions, as we were always taught that you really ignore Satan as he can't hurt you, because you are protected by the shed blood of Jesus. I then heard people testifying of a newfound freedom in their lives. I really couldn't get my head round that, and came away puzzled, with a lot of questions going on inside of me. That wasn't the only occasion my belief system would be challenged.

I decided to investigate further. I saw advertised about a Bible School in Hampstead, London, called Hampstead Bible School of Faith. They were putting a meeting on, so I decided to go on the train, all by myself, to see what this group taught. Their main emphasis was a teaching on Faith and Sonship. This stirred my heart, as I have often thought – what is God's main purpose for creating us? What would be his real objective? In Romans 8:29 and Ephesians 1:5 we learn that God's heart is that we would be conformed to the image of His son, Jesus. These truths resonated in me. I just knew this was the truth. When I looked into John 1:12:

> *"Yet to all who did receive him, to those who believed in his name, he gave the right to become children of God".*

But then in Romans 8:14 (NKJV):

> *"For as many as are led by the Spirit of God, these are sons of God".*

To me this was amazing revelation. When we received Jesus as our Saviour we became a child of God, but when we grow and mature in God we become a son, who is led by the Spirit of God. It's like in the natural order of the world. A child who is just born cannot be led by anything, but when it grows up through the toddler and teenager stages, they can then come into a place of maturity and inherit the Father's business. I loved this teaching. This is my desire, to be a son of God, just like Jesus, led by the Holy Spirit. Another thought occurred to me – what happens in life if we are not led by the Spirit of God? Do we remain at baby/toddler stage? Knowing this helps one to prepare for the journey with the Lord, and not just be parked somewhere. **Nothing will ever follow a parked car.** Jesus spoke to his disciples and said to go in His name and signs would follow (Mark 16:15-18). Was the season changing for the church to be mobilised? This gave me food for thought.

I started to think – why are we so resistant to change? Why does the leadership try to confine us to their denominational way of thinking and doing things? Why are reading and going to places that are outside of our particular church fellowship frowned upon? I really felt our choice was being taken away. Even God gave Adam and Eve choice in a perfect environment. I don't believe anyone has the right to touch our free will. Even God doesn't do that. What was really sad for me to hear was that a well-known bible teacher heard some rumours that were spreading, and said that this was all cultish. It goes to show what I have always believed. **What people don't understand, they fear, and what they fear, they fight.**

Isn't this true in the world? Great men of God like Dr Martin Luther King, William Wilberforce, William Booth of the Salvation Army, and so many others paved the way as a minority in order to bring lasting change – years later now we have faith camps and ministries in the UK.

My own observation is that we can be afraid to acknowledge the truth of a circumstance and instead try to twist God's arm through our intellectual knowledge. I saw this years later when a lady in the church had cancer and was confessing her healing. I spoke with her and she was adamant she was healed. The problem was that I could see death all over her. However, I felt it wasn't my place to undermine her faith in case I was wrong. She died within the year. The problem, I felt, was that her confession was on a mental level. God's revelations had not reached her heart in faith, because within faith there is a rest. You can't work it up, it's what God releases. Confession through faith brings transformation due to the working of the Holy Spirit. Confession of words, on the other hand, can tap into magic. It will work to a point, as the Law of Faith will work to a certain level here, but the release of the power of God is absent. Acknowledging that cancer was present in her body did not mean that she was in agreement with the disease or death, but would have allowed the reality and vulnerability of the situation to be realised and dealt with at a deeper level, allowing God to work. We must always remember that **acknowledgement is not the same as agreement, and to follow the Lord of Life, not just a doctrine.** John Wimber used to say "Follow the horse not the cart as life goes before the doctrine".

> *"For it is with your heart that you believe and are justified, and it is with your mouth that you profess your faith and are saved".* (Romans 10:10 NIV)

I am so glad I went to the Hampstead School of Faith. More seeds of truth were being sown in me that were to help me continue my journey in life. How exciting and encouraging for me to hear truth communicated in accordance to what I believed in my heart, but not having the ability to communicate myself.

The Spirit of God is the Spirit of Truth and when you hear truth being proclaimed something in you just resonates that this is God. Your natural mind might not understand it, particularly if it's the first time you have heard it, and it will often argue with your spirit, but all of us, no matter what country, class or ethnic group we belong are made in the image of God with a spirit. That is the only way we communicate, spirit to Spirit. We miss out so much by being closed to the Spirit of God through prejudice and belief systems that have been ingrained in us. I thank God for all His love and patience and grace to continually want the best for us. He doesn't want us to miss out on enjoying this love relationship with Him as our Father, and also our birth-right and our inheritance as sons of God (Romans 8: 15-17). The bible tells us we are God's children, but it is only the Spirit of God that reinforces that truth to us personally; to each of us in our hearts as God's children.

If we don't have this assurance within our hearts and only have a 'hope so' attitude, I doubt very much we are yet part of God's family.

That condition can be changed by responding to the love of God that is wooing you as a lover for the deep, personal intimacy with Father God. **Jesus Christ is the way but the destination is the Father** (John 14:6). A way is meaningless unless it takes us somewhere.

On a later date, I was seated at the back of a Ukrainian

Airlines plane heading off to the Ukraine to see some friends of mine. I did ask not to be seated at the rear of the plane as I didn't want to sit near the toilets, and would rather be seated in the middle of the aircraft. With a big smile, the gentleman behind the departure desk said that unfortunately, the only seats available were at the back – the worst seat possible for me. But God had another plan, different from my own. I sat next to the window with a space next to me. Then occupying the next seat was a businessman who owned a number of high street shops in the UK. We got talking before the plane landed and he told me about his last divorce costing £2.4 million and he was now on the way to meet his new wife. We talked about football, and also about God. He mentioned that his father went to church and considered himself a Christian. I shared a simple illustration that **you can live in a garage but it doesn't make you a car.** Going to church doesn't make you a Christian. This man had a lot of wealth but I asked him, "What does all that mean compared to spending eternity outside of God's presence?"

He replied, "But I must want God to want that".

I had the privilege of praying for him at the back of the aircraft while people were standing in the aisle right by the side of him. He responded to the love of the Father who had planned this meeting.

I was aware now that I was changing and wanted to pioneer more of what God was doing, and what he was revealing in my generation. As a very practical person who hated reading and studying anything academic, I had this inner thirst and desire to explore God's Word more. I never even read the paper, yet somehow this desire became all-consuming.

I had no desire in learning doctrine for doctrine's sake. There are many views, for example, on how the second coming of Jesus is going to happen. I had no interest at that time to enter what I felt were needless arguments. I was interested in what affects my life now. I really wanted to understand the laws and principles of life. I didn't want to become aimless:

> *"Therefore I do not run like someone running aimlessly; I do not fight like a boxer beating the air".*
> (1 Corinthians 9:26 NIV)

That made sense to me. To have a purpose and not be woolly. I needed to hit the target in prayer. I really need to understand as I am very simple and can't cope with things being far too complicated, which is why I sought revelation knowledge that would feed my spirit and bring change, not just information. I knew that **the Devil knows the bible better than I do and he is not going to heaven.** I had had a hard life and was fed up of being beaten up despite how hard I tried to do the right thing.

God started to show me a basic problem I had and I believe is affecting people in life today. It goes back to the story of Adam and Eve in the Garden of Eden. God planted a garden and in that garden were 2 trees, one was called the Tree of Life, and the other was called the Tree of Knowledge of Good and Evil. God said to Adam:

> *"but you must not eat from the tree of the knowledge of good and evil, for when you eat from it you will certainly die".*
> (Genesis 2:17 NIV)

It seemed the source of Satan's power was rooted in the tree of knowledge. He knew it was poison to Adam and Eve. As you probably know, in this well-known story, Satan disguised himself as a serpent and tempted Eve. Eve had not heard the command from God, only through Adam, which is probably why Satan tempted Eve and not Adam. Adam, who was standing next to Eve, knew the command of God, yet did nothing to protect Eve. Eve may have thought – Adam got it wrong – the fruit looks so good. They both took the fruit and death entered them. It wasn't just the sin of disobedience that brought death, but the fruit itself was poison to them; the fruit of the tree of the knowledge of good and evil.

This tree of knowledge just conveys information, but does not bring life. In this day and age, we need to embrace the Tree of Life, which is Jesus Christ. I needed to feed from the Tree of Life. Revelation knowledge brings life, not death. I realised now why at times I was so bored with some sermons, despite the accuracy and true facts. They were only carrying death with them, not the life of the Son of God which has such an effect on me, which is the Bread of Life. I just couldn't get enough of it.

My belief system was being challenged slowly but surely. The hardness of my soul, that was impenetrable to change, was being chipped away along with my security in my belief system. This would begin to expose my real identity. An identity I had been out of touch with all these years, as I had learned to live behind a mask of acceptability where I was appreciated and my true self was hidden somewhere deep within the cavern of my soul. I had lost touch with who I really was. This work of the Spirit of God was so full of love and grace and not like a bulldozer with no respect for who I am. Yet God knows who 'I AM' and with His grace and knowledge of all my sins, weakness and failure,

He still loved me and wanted to bring change. The wonderful truth is that **the God of the Universe has all the knowledge of us before time began, yet still calls us, knowing us.**

> *"In him we were also chosen, having been predestined according to the plan of him who works out everything in conformity with the purpose of his will".*
>
> (Ephesians 1:11 NIV)

Knowing me, left to myself, I wouldn't have done that.

Chapter 8

FACING A CRISIS

The difficulty that I didn't embrace at the time was that Daph was having enough changes happening in her life too; finding she was pregnant with our second child and our honeymoon period was well and truly over. We both found married life quite difficult. I was finding it hard to cope with Daph's view of seeing the glass half empty, when I would see it as half full.

Daph came from a dysfunctional family too. Her mother had eventually divorced her husband after so much abuse when Daph was only 12 years of age. She had to grow up fast as she had 2 younger brothers who missed having a father figure and Daph had to assume a parental role. This all affected Daph mentally and emotionally. Both of us coming from dysfunctional families that had so much abuse wasn't a good combination.

It was a recipe for disaster really, but God has His ways which later on in life we would both be able to see.

In the meantime, my attitude to life was still in place: you can't change things, make the best of it. That's how I dealt with not only marriage, but the change of leadership in the church. I got more involved in church world.

The new Pastor's vision was to reach children in their schools, so clubs were set up in many schools around Chelmsford. These clubs would then feed into the Sunday School. We had well over 100 children coming from outside the locality of the church. I became responsible to provide recreation every month for the youth for over 150 children as well as Sunday School outings. It was great fun.

As the due date was approaching for the birth of our second child, the visits to the hospital became very regular due to the rhesus blood problem we have. I felt so, so sorry for Daph, to keep on having the amniocentesis test where the doctors would drain fluid from the baby sack where the baby was within Daph.

The day arrived when I would take Daph to St John's hospital. We were so excited and couldn't wait for the arrival of a little baby brother for Patrick. I had done all the necessary preparations. I had decorated the little room at the back of the house. The cot was brought down from the attic and it fitted perfectly in the beautiful room full of colour. Lots of blues. Once again, I had brought a load of books to read remembering the last time Daph gave birth to Patrick. No way was I going to be unprepared. Everything just seemed so perfect.

This time the baby would be induced even earlier than Patrick as after each pregnancy, more antibodies build up in the blood.

The day seemed to drag on, waiting for the baby to arrive.

I lost count of how many drips Daph had to help the baby on its way.

Now it was evening. Secondary contractions were still happening with great intensity. Midnight came and went. Waters had to be broken to speed things up. I started to feel very uneasy, thinking this baby is never going to come. It was as if nature was saying, he isn't ready yet, but I knew he wasn't allowed to go full term of 39 weeks. We had no choice but to wait.

Then, at last, a bright pink little boy emerged and soon slid out. He was laying in front of me as they cut the cord. We were both crying with such love and joy and relief. Totally exhausted.... Our son, Matthew, had eventually arrived.

After all the tests and waiting, nothing else can really explain that moment of a new life. But I did happen to notice the nurses weren't so full of joy. They had a worried look.

My feelings changed as I noticed his little chest was breathing irregularly, as if he had swallowed some chewing gum and it had got stuck somewhere. The next thing I knew he was taken away and put in the special care baby unit. I felt this was all a bit sudden. No cuddles, no touching, no nothing. To me he looked perfectly formed apart from the breathing – you could see he was struggling to get his next breath.

We were both now mentally and physically exhausted; we hadn't slept for 48 hours. I went back home. Daph looked quite distraught not being able to hold baby Matthew.

I went straight to sleep for the rest of the day, what was left of it. There was nothing I could do so I went back to work. They didn't have open visiting in those days.

The following day it wasn't long before the foreman called me into the office to answer a call from the hospital. They wanted me to come to the hospital immediately. It felt for a moment like my blood had drained from my body, and the life within me had gone. I felt almost like a corpse. I knew this was serious.

I arrived at St John's Hospital first of all, to see how Daph was coping. I was being led to a private little room outside of the ward. On the way, I looked to my right. Behind some glass windows were a number of white coats all around baby Matthew, who was laying on a little mattress with no tubes in him. I suddenly felt a shudder of fear and panic which almost made me breathless. I just knew something was wrong. I began shaking on the inside as I arrived in the little room. Daph was sitting on a white, wooden chair, still all gowned up with her dressing gown on to keep her warm. She looked so tired and worn out and worried. She was crying, asking; "where's my baby?" "what's happening?" "What's going on?"

I sat down next to her to try to console her. I really didn't know what to say. All that came to me was – God knows everything, everything will be okay.

I said, "God is in charge, everything is in His hands. We just have to trust Him. We can't do anything". Actually, my emotions were all over the place. We were too distraught to pray.

The nurse came in and said that an ambulance had been called to take baby Matthew to London University Hospital as he needed special treatment.

The next thing I knew the nurse returned and asked me to step out of the room, as she didn't want Daph to hear what she had to say. She explained that Matthew had stopped breathing. By this stage I was numb. It was like I had entered an extreme nightmare I couldn't get out of... there just wasn't a way. Trying to keep it all together and appear strong, I now had to tell Daph. I wanted to do so before a stranger did.

I asked the nurse if we could see him. We hadn't been able to have a good look at him before as he had been taken away so fast to the incubator. The nurse brought our little boy, Matthew Paul. He only weighed 4lb 6oz. He was wrapped in a white woolly blanket. He was held so close to her chest that we only saw his little pink face, which now was lifeless. With that Daph let out an almighty scream, which the whole hospital must have heard. They took him away. They wouldn't let us touch or hold him, as the thinking in the seventies was that it would help us if we didn't form any bond. We never saw him again.

We were both totally distraught, with tears pouring out all over the place. Daph was almost inconsolable.

I insisted that it was in our best interest to go home. It would serve no purpose being in a maternity ward with babies every-where. It would only accentuate the pain. I don't even remember how we got home. The precious gift we felt God had given us was taken away.

As we were leaving the hospital, I was asked if they could have my permission to do an autopsy. They were apologising, saying it wasn't an appropriate time but a decision had to be taken. I agreed but, to be honest, we were both all over the place. We didn't really have time to process that and what it all meant. I found out they didn't do one in the end which I was pleased about.

It's not right. It's just not right. It doesn't make any sense at all. Something is wrong, I kept thinking. This is not how a loving Heavenly Father treats His children. I wouldn't put my children through this! Why? At that point in time, I had no answers.

I do remember coming home and staring at an empty cot and a decorated room feeling numb and very empty.

We were asked if we wanted Matthew buried in a community grave in Writtle Road Cemetery. I felt I owed him something as his dad. The least I could do was buy a plot and have a proper burial.

About 50 people turned up to support us as we stood by this massive hole in the ground. It must have been over 8 feet in depth. We watched this little white shoebox being lowered into the darkness of this massive hole in the ground. I watched with tears rolling down both cheeks as they lowered the ladder and placed the tiny box in the bottom of this hole.

Then the Spirit of God rose up in within me and I started to sing an old chorus:

> 'Because He lives, I can face tomorrow
> Because He lives, all fear is gone.
> Because I know He holds the future
> I can face tomorrow just because He lives'.

Everybody joined in. The presence of our Heavenly Father was almost tangible.

I knew deep in my heart that because Jesus died and rose again from the grave in resurrection life, I can face the future and one day I have this hope within me that I will see my son, Matthew Paul Regan, again.

The new Pastor spoke on 2 Samuel 12; how King David's son died because of judgement. I really couldn't take it in at the time. It was beyond my present understanding.

After the funeral, I would spend my evenings just sitting in the lounge with the lights dimmed, just speechless. Daph would be upstairs in bed, still in shock and grieving. I felt so confused. I just couldn't understand it. I was so full of unanswered questions. The verse from John 10:10 (NKJV) came to mind:

"I have come that they may have life, and that they may have it more abundantly".

"This surely isn't abundant life? This is so wrong," I kept thinking. I had never really thought about the first part of the verse:

"The thief does not come except to steal, and to kill, and to destroy".

Who was this thief, who has a job description of stealing and murdering and wants to obliterate you? I knew Jesus was talking about Satan. I had read the book of Job in the Old Testament where Job was the most righteous man in all the earth, how Satan walked the earth looking for trouble, how he appeared with the other angels in the Court of Heaven, and how God removed the hedge of protection around Job's life. Job lost his 7 sons, daughter, servants and all his livestock. I noticed from this passage that Satan was able to use different groups of people like Chaldeans and Sabeans to accomplish his will. He was also able to use fire and destroy the home, as well as use a tornado. He affected Job's health and to crown it all his wife spoke the same words Satan said in Heaven:

"Curse God and die!"   (Job 2:9 NKJV)

This made me think that Satan has all this power at his disposal. But how did he do it? As he had to walk he couldn't be omnipresent. I knew this story as a story, just theology, that God was trying to teach us to rise from the ashes as Job did at the end of the story. Is there a reality to this that affects our world today? How did Satan rob my son of his life? I didn't have any experience regarding this enemy of our lives, only the devastation we feel as we try to rebuild our lives after his destruction. I noticed too that Satan could only operate in the parameters that God allowed.

In the months that followed Daph had to go back to the hospital for check-ups. The waiting room she was put in was with people who wanted to terminate their babies. I felt the cruelty of that. It felt like there was someone who wanted to afflict even more pain, as if we hadn't had enough.

We both saw the consultant who explained there had been a mistake over the dates and Matthew was born too early and should have been left, as his lungs were not properly developed. They are apparently the last part of the body to develop.

We were now advised that because of the high level of anti-bodies we shouldn't consider having any more children. Despite all the questions going on on the inside of me, as to why this happened, I felt it's no use telling Daph that as we both had an inner desire which wouldn't go away to have more children.

It wasn't long before that desire became a reality. Daph became pregnant again. Due to the mistakes made with the birth of Matthew, all the testing and checks regarding Daph and the baby were to be double-checked by London University Hospital. I really couldn't go through the experience of losing a child again.

The paediatrician in charge of Daph was a Christian that

went to the same church as us, a Dr Andrew Gibson. We felt this was God's provision for us.

During the pregnancy, we had a Pastor come to our church called John Barr. He shared how he watched his little boy cross the road in the East End of London. He watched as a car hit him and killed him. At his son's funeral, he walked across to the guy who killed his son and said, "I forgive you". He said it was the longest and hardest walk he had ever made. We spoke to his wife Hazel after the service. We all felt that God had brought us together for this specific time in our lives. He had sent us each someone who understood how it felt, and knew what it was like to walk through the valley of the shadow of death. Daph and I were really comforted. I didn't know at that time that John would be an instrument in the hand of God - one of the mentors I would need in the future.

Daph was now 8 months pregnant. It was 13 months since Matthew had died.

I heard Trevor Deering, the Pastor God used in Hainault all those years ago, was holding a healing service in the C of E, High Street, Ongar. We both decided we needed to go where we knew God's presence would be manifest among us. We just worshipped God and just knew God was in the place. Although still feeling quite fragile, we felt it was right to respond to the invitation for prayer. Daph went forward as one of the team had what is known as a Word of Knowledge, one of the gifts of the Holy Spirit. (1 Corinthians 12:8). The guy just said, "Your baby will be fine". Nothing externally appeared to happen but Daph received that as a word from the Lord Jesus by faith; a simple agreement.

The time came for Daph to be induced again, with all these

drips put in her arm to bring the baby on early. I had a call while at work to go to the hospital. I decided to go home from work, get washed and changed, select several books, as I thought I needed to prepare for another marathon. I arrived at the hospital ward I had left Daph in the night before. I opened the door only to discover I had interrupted another dear lady giving birth. With great embarrassment, I went to the nurse's station and found the correct room. Within half an hour, our dearest daughter Rebecca was born, which was such a surprise. I just assumed we would have another boy as in my family, I have 3 brothers. We were so grateful to God – everything had gone like clockwork.

But, as expected, Rebecca had to go to the special care unit for the normal testings. They had blood prepared if Rebecca needed a transfusion. Everything was cross-matched so no more mistakes. When the final test results came through the doctors came round to Daph's bedside and with sheer amazement they said they could find no antibodies in the blood!!! They explained they had never seen this before and that it could not be explained. The only explanation they could find to satisfy their technical minds was, they suggested, there must have been a different father! With that, I thought that Daph would get out of bed and give them one!!!

So, Rebecca became another miracle in our family. It looks like the Lord Jesus changed the blood in Daph's womb. There was no way the hospital could wriggle out of this being a miracle as everything had been checked by London University Hospital and St Johns.

We weren't used to seeing the world at war, with invisible forces out to destroy and rob us of life. This just wasn't our vocabulary at the time, for as far as we were concerned we both recognised we had had a hard life. We felt like ordinary people trying to make the best of life. Little did we know the greatest victory we were celebrating would make us vulnerable once again to be hit emotionally and spiritually.

This became a reality and a lesson we were learning – we are more vulnerable of being 'hit' again after a victory. After the birth of Rebecca we noticed her stomach had started to swell. It looked as if she had swallowed a balloon and every now and again someone would just pump it up a bit.

A few nights later, while Patrick and I were staying at friend's house, I had a call from the hospital just past midnight to say I was urgently needed as the nurses couldn't calm my wife down. I thought, now what? Everything appeared fine when I left. One of the nurses had told Daph that Rebecca was seriously ill and might have to go to the London Hospital. Daph's emotions had immediately kicked in and thought the nightmare had started again: that we could lose Rebecca. I got down to the hospital, calmed Daph down and prayed for Rebecca. The mucus she had swallowed during birth had become stuck and was the cause of her stomach enlarging. The Peace of God just came. God just released faith. The very next day the mucus dissolved and Rebecca's stomach shape returned to normal. Another crisis over with. Phew!

Still, throughout these crises, more and more questions started to arise in me. I remember asking the leadership, "Why did our son die?" All the answers I received never satisfied me. Some had said God wanted him. I replied, "Tough, I wanted him". I don't believe God created him then decided to have him killed. It didn't make sense to me.

I found that I was dealing with my pain by becoming very busy. I just buried the pain along with all the pain of my early years growing up with so much abuse. This was my culture. I hadn't yet seen or found any other way. I am not the sort of person to go to medication. I was the sort that would continue to push through as that was what I was used to. That was what worked for me. Denying my pain and not facing it was my way – a bit like the old Frank Sinatra song, "I'll do it my way".

Chapter 9

ENOUGH IS ENOUGH

It wasn't long before the vision the new pastor had was implemented. A new church was built that would be multi-functional that would be used every day of the week. The full-time day nursery was up and running and was a great help in paying for the mortgage for the new church. Every department seemed to grow.

I was asked to take charge of the mission department which involved monthly prayer meetings. Also, I would be responsible for ministering in a local care home called Spains Lodge in Broomfield which is now Madalayne Court. With much enthusiasm and passion, I fulfilled all these responsibilities along with existing commitments. I love being busy and working hard.

Our marriage, however, was put under more strain, as we didn't seem to have quality time together. Daph has an amazing teaching gift and taught the teenagers every Sunday. We loved what we were doing as we knew we were doing it for the Lord Jesus.

The new Pastor didn't seem to connect with me. Somehow I felt there was quite a distance. The church just grew and the Pastor had his friend from Wales join him as a co-Pastor. On the outside, everything seemed to be going well, but on the inside of me I knew brokenness was changing me.

There was one particular Sunday morning communion service that was going to make an impact on me. It was after the new church had been running for a few years. I was sitting on the platform, which was the tradition of the deacons in those days. I had such a heart full of praise and couldn't wait for the open time when the congregation could participate in the service. I just stood up and was about to worship God when the wind of the Spirit of God flowed right through me. It literally took the wind out of my sails and left me empty. God had another agenda. A lady whom I hadn't heard prophesy before gave a strong prophetic word. I shall never forget what she said as it resonated in my heart. The Lord was directing our attention back to Him and was saying that we had lost our focus and we had become like children in the playground, and we needed to repent and turn back to Him.

The Fear of God and the Majesty of God swept through the building. I fell to my knees, then the Spirit of God spoke to me and said that He had put desires within me. These were not natural desires at that time. After this, it came within me, this desire to seek His face with all my heart by reading and going to conferences, and to seek God with such a thirst that my whole heart was involved. Once again, I realised this explained what was happening to me. I couldn't stop reading and going to places to discover more about Jesus. It just amazed me. God Himself created this desire. He has a programme for our lives and just wants us to respond to Him and make right choices, despite possible consequences, as He is calling us to follow Him.

Finally, the time came in my life when I could no longer keep the lid on all the turmoil that was going on in the inside of me. My belief system had been challenged, not only by reading books, listening to others and His word, but through my own life experience.

I didn't believe my life matched up to what I thought a Christian life should be. I was in my thirties. I had 2 wonderful children, my own house, a secure job and a lovely wife, all given by God as I followed the leading of His Spirit within me. Yet what did it all mean? I had, in some people's life view, reached the top, apart from being the Pastor, yet I hadn't a clue how to help people at their point of need. I would pray for people with little expectation that things would change. I was really dissatisfied with my Christian life. I had lost the most precious thing to me, my precious son, Matthew. To me, nothing is as important as life. You can't buy it. I knew if I put my hand to something and I really wanted it I would be able to get it. Now, here I was. Not a clue of what was happening to me. I thought, if the disciples were here they would at least understand what was going on.

I was feeling more helpless by the day, and was losing faith as a Christian. What was I doing? I had been a leader for over 15 years. How long does it take to be able to do the works of Jesus? Let alone the greater works. The disciples took three and a half years. It just was not right. I couldn't invest the rest of my life in something I didn't believe was working, because everything God does works.

So what was missing?

Yes. We had a bigger church. Yes, we had more people. Yes, we had more departments, forming what we would call ministries today, but what does it all mean? If God is the focus surely He would be manifesting Himself among us instead of us spending our time saying God's presence is here. If that was so, why do the sick and broken come in among us, and then go out the same? Why do we pray for the doctors instead of healing the sick and casting out demons? Church growth, to me, isn't an indication that God is among us; for example, a political party can grow and sing their anthems, but their growth does not mean God is with them. It is not about numbers. I personally felt, enough is enough. What's the point wasting my life having the talk, but yet being powerless in so many ways? **I cannot be an echo to somebody else's experience. I need to be a voice.** I needed my own experience.

When I looked at Paul the apostle in the New Testament and his visit to the church at Corinth, he didn't have great communication skills, which related to me. He said he didn't come just to talk, but to demonstrate the power of God (1 Corinthians 2:5). Yet I am a good Pentecostal leader, baptised and filled with the Holy Spirit. I speak in tongues and prophesy. So, what's gone wrong? I know God isn't interested in status as there is no status in His Kingdom. But I felt I could not live on this merry-go-round of predictability. I believe that God is bigger than our traditions, our formulas and our wisdom. I believe the truth stands out by being distinctive through its message and by the presence of God in this world of ours. God's word is absolute.

I looked at the book of Acts and saw two believers called Annanias and Sapphira. What seemed to me was that all they did was lie to the Holy Spirit! And they were both struck down and died instantly. No wonder the Fear of God and Comfort of the Holy Spirit would be the hallmark of the early Christians, yet people feared to join them. "Wow!"

I believe God hasn't changed: that He is the same yesterday and the same today. Somehow have we lost our way. Are we no longer salt that is distinctive and affects everything we touch, and light which exposes all darkness and compromise? Have we lost our cutting edge in that we compensate for His presence by our own abilities and gifts? By now, I was crying from my heart: we want You to be God among us, so we can do the things we can't do unless you come. To be raised up higher than any celebrity, preacher or group; until we are more conscious of You than the person ministering to us. We desperately want your Kingdom to come on earth as it is in heaven, the alignment of the Lord's will in the prayer He taught the disciples.

For well over a year, I would cry and seek God every day. **I no longer wanted to treat God like my butler** and keep asking Him to bless me. I wanted to follow Him, as He is so much bigger than I am. I believe we all should follow God, not expect God to follow us. As Job found out in the Old Testament, despite all his own righteousness and pride and arrogance, he was faced with the Almighty God in his trials, and had to bow the knee in brokenness when the Almighty God spoke to him:

> *"Where were you when I laid the earth's foundation? Tell me, if you understand. Who marked off its dimensions?"*
>
> (Job 38:4 NIV)

And the dialogue of the Lord goes on, asking Job – Do you know all the laws of Heaven? Can you raise your voice to the clouds and cover yourself with a flood of water?

No wonder Job said:

> *"I know that you can do all things; no purpose of yours can be thwarted"*.   (Job 42:2 NIV)

God is the Almighty. I don't want a God that I can control and make do everything I want. Within me is the life of the Son of God and I will never be satisfied unless there is complete union with Him. I am fed up with religion and dead works. I have seen the Lord Almighty moving within the glory of His presence, which has impregnated the atmosphere without anyone speaking. I have seen love that was penetrated to heal the sick and cast out demons and fill us up so much so we couldn't contain the joy of His presence. I don't want just signs and wonders. I know there are those that practise such things, but haven't come through the real Jesus, but have come another way. (John 10:1) I also don't want just the benefits of God's Kingdom without Him committing Himself to me, as in John 2:24-25 (NKJV). Jesus healed the sick but would not commit because he knew what was in our hearts. I desperately wanted God for himself and not what He could do. I didn't want success to make me feel good.

I was still pouring out my heart every day for well over a year. It was so hard as the heavens felt like brass. It seemed I just wasn't getting through. I was feeling lost and broken, getting more disillusioned as time went by. I questioned my faith. I knew I was born again. I felt the power of the Life of the Son of God coming into me when I was a teenager. I had such a revelation of the Father's heart and His love, and that He accepted me because of the shed blood of Jesus which made me righteous and Holy in His sight. I wasn't conscious at that time of any sin in my life. I knew the hand of God in finding me a job as a welder, knew His guidance in finding me a wife, and also giving me the desire and faith to build my own house at 21.

I know I am imperfect with various weaknesses in my communication because my words get muddled. I felt like Jacob of old in the Old Testament when he wouldn't let God go at a place called Peniel (Genesis 32:26). There was such a determination in my spirit. The brokenness of all that I had gone through was having a work in me. I couldn't make God speak to me in the same way I couldn't make my wife Daph speak just because I picked the 'phone up. There was nothing I could control. I had nowhere to go and I didn't want to go anywhere. I was desperate to hear God.

Then one evening I was on my knees before my Heavenly Father. This day seemed the same as any other day, when it appeared this voice of God was crystal clear:

"I WANT YOUR LIFE".

I didn't understand. I responded by saying "I have given you my life, my time, my talents, my money. We hardly have a marriage as we are so busy".

"Son – you have given your life to the church. I want it".

To be honest, this had never occurred to me before and wasn't what I was expecting to hear after so long seeking His face.

I just didn't quite understand as everything I ever did I thought I did it for the Lord, now I realised it was indeed for Him but not with Him.

I was meant to follow Him and not expect Him, the Almighty God, to follow me.

Some church people might misunderstand that. Church isn't wrong, as Jesus is building His church, the people of God, as the church in the New Testament is never referred to as a building. For me, church had come in place of God and was taking over my heart. I had been gradually seduced away from listening to and relying on God for everything, but I honestly didn't know that I was doing this, which is why I was puzzled by God's response. He reminded me of 2 biblical principles that I needed to apply in following the Lord: "*Jesus replied, "No one who puts a hand to the plough and looks back is fit for service in the kingdom of God"* (Luke 9:62 NIV) and Luke (6:46-49 NIV) that it is a wise man who counts the cost.

I was now getting in touch with my true identity, which was one of fear and anxiety that had been buried from all the abuse I had in my earlier years. The hardness of my emotions and my need to control was melting in His presence as I realised I couldn't say yes to God at that moment of time. The fear was becoming overwhelming as the reality of what God was asking just caused me to weep. I was being paralysed, it felt, in every part of me. I knew I wasn't ready to commit to God in this way and not be able to look back. I knew this wasn't an emotional decision. It was once and for all. I knew what the prophets and those disciples in the New Testament faced. They got stoned, rejected and misunderstood. I really needed time to count the cost of what this would mean for my life. At the present time I was in charge of a number of departments in the church and had various teams that were working for me. Also, it came to me that I might be sent to places I didn't want to go and told to say things I didn't really want to say.

I thought of Jonah who had a message for a place called Ninevah, but went in the opposite direction and was swallowed by a big fish. Jonah learnt his lesson the hard way. I thought, it's better to play deaf. Unfortunately, you can't hide from God. He has a perfect plan for our lives and treats us all as individuals.

I knew God knew my heart and the sort of person I am. I knew I just couldn't say religious prayers. I could only pray from my heart as I did when I first asked Jesus into my heart in my teenage years, otherwise it would be a waste of time.

Months went past as I continued to meditate and seek His face, but I knew something of the Love of God, and that love just grew and grew and was poured into my soul until it became like Niagra. It was overwhelming. It was so strong and beautiful that my fears seemed to retreat into insignificance. I finally said, as the Lord became my soul focus "Yes Lord. I yield to you. I come fully into your Kingdom. Have full reign in me". I had become strong and successful and independent, and now I looked back and was sorry. I allowed myself to fall away from listening and obeying God's voice. I know in my spirit that **blessing comes from obedience** (Deuteronomy 28:1-2). I had only known about the gospel of salvation, but now I realised as I read the bible that Jesus only preached the gospel of the Kingdom (Mark 1:15) and there was only one way in.

> *"We must through many tribulations enter the kingdom of God".*   (Acts 14:22 NKJV)

It certainly hasn't been an easy route, but I couldn't go back and carry on a treadmill that to me would be death. I now needed to follow the continuous leading of the Spirit of God (Romans 8:14). This would be my lifestyle. I was scared as I didn't really know the areas of my life where God didn't reign. I was only too aware of my weakness and failings, but I had trusted God in the past. The hardest thing for me would be my relationships, particularly with my wife, as Daph wasn't where I was on the journey with the Lord. The grief of losing Matthew, I knew, was so deep within her, and those I love so dearly. In fact, when you consider the word "life" it is total: all my plans, my future, my emotions and all my feelings, and work and finances, my church family, everything. I know the bible talks about the heart because it is deceitful above all things, who can know it? (Jeremiah 17:9). What would the searchlight of the Holy Spirit, which is the Finger of God, find in me that I didn't even know I had? Do I have so much shame and fear that it is covering things up? At this stage, the Lord had my life, and my permission to show me. I would humble myself to put things right because I trusted the Lord God. This was the only way I could approach the Lord. Decision made for me.

I knew I couldn't stay in the boat of security, but like Peter of old, I was stepping out into the insecurity of not knowing what was going to happen next. All I did know was that I couldn't go back into my own way of life. It had to be His way of life.

No longer would I be a Christian rebel, but now I would be submitted to the King of all Kings. My life would now be merged with the life of the Lord Jesus. Now I have met the condition of being a true overcomer:

"They triumphed over him (Satan) by the blood of the Lamb

and by the word of their testimony; they did not love their lives so much as to shrink from death."

(Revelation 12:11 NIV)

Also, I was now entering a covenant with God by the laying down of my own life, just as in a marriage union when both promise to lay their lives down – a sacrifice which is a type of death. What we are saying is: I have left all others to be one with you. I will put you before all others. You will be first. I entered the covenant of marriage through death to my own rights and Daph did the same. Only then did we come into the union of intimacy as we shared our lives together. The essence of the marriage covenant is that we no longer desire living for ourselves (Hebrews 9:16-17), we become one.

I now knew I wasn't going to trust any man, or any denomination or group, nor was I going to follow signs and wonders, power and anointing. But I would follow only Jesus, the love of my life, who rescued me out of darkness and gave me a purpose in living. His life would be my life.

Little did I know at the time what lay ahead of me. One thing I did know however, is that when you enter into a covenant relationship with God, He is committed to you. He is totally trustworthy. But this journey would be on a narrow road that would get narrower and narrower as I walked on it with the Lord. **This is the only road that leads to life.** I hadn't noticed before in these verses: it doesn't say the path leads to heaven, but life, and only a few find it.

"Enter through the narrow gate. For wide is the gate and broad is the road that leads to destruction, and many enter

through it. But small is the gate and narrow the road that leads to life, and only a few find it".

(Matthew 7:13-14 NIV)

Prayer

Dear Lord,

I have nowhere else to go now. Although I have opened up my heart to you as my Lord and saviour, I realise you are calling me into a total surrender. All I can say from the depth of my being is that I ask you to be Lord of my life, Lord of my family and all of my relationships, Lord of my finances, Lord of my emotions and all of my feelings, Lord of my sexuality and all of its expression, Lord of my mind and all of my attitudes and thinking, Lord of my will and decisions, Lord of my body and physical health, Lord of my work, Lord of my material goods, Lord of my spirit and worship. Dear Lord I give you permission to show me what you're not Lord of.

In Jesus name,

Amen

Chapter 10

THE KINGDOM OF GOD IS HERE

It never ceases to surprise me that when you have an experience with God that the Holy Spirit has been leading you into, you begin to notice principles of truth in His word. When Jesus was speaking to the disciples about His second coming back to the earth, he describes the sort of activities that would be taking place in Luke 17:20-37; eating, drinking, getting married, buying and selling and building, yet none of these activities are sin. I really thought when Jesus mentioned the day of Noah and Lot he would highlight sexual perversion and the occult, yet these 'normal' activities can distract us from seeing the day when the full manifestation of His Kingdom comes to the earth. Now we only experience a taste of what is to come in part. WOW! How important it is to be alert and aware of our lifestyles, and assess how much, in these days, we are submitting to the reign of Jesus in our lives. It certainly enhances the fear of God in my life.

I noticed, after taking that decision of yielding my life to God, that revelation, authority and power became much more evident in my life. I was seeing things in the invisible realm that I had never seen before. It was as if a veil had come off my eyes. One example is that on one occasion as I was walking up the stairs in the church, my friend's daughter turned round and her face became contorted. It seemed as if a demon spirit had come to the surface. That was so weird, I thought. I had never seen her look like that before. I just knew this wasn't her, but a demonic spirit manifesting.

While seeking God at home about the prayer meeting I was to lead that night, the Lord spoke to me and said, tell Mum 'I AM' going to baptise her in the Holy Spirit tonight. I couldn't wait to tell Mum and encourage her, as Mum had been seeking God for over 13 years to receive this gift. I knocked on the front door at her house and explained what I felt God had told me. Her excitement level was zero. I was hit by this attitude. So what had changed?

Reluctantly Mum said she would come to the meeting. It turned out that Mum had started to believe she had committed the unforgivable sin (Mark 3:29) and she wasn't worthy to receive the gifts of the Spirit. When I arrived at the church, I positioned the chairs in a semi-circle so I could see all their faces. There must have been about 40 people present.

It appeared everyone was very subdued. The meeting would have appeared on the outside, quite dead. People prayed and worshipped with little enthusiasm. On the inside of me was such amazing peace and confidence that I didn't care what was going on externally. Mum was going to receive that night.

The time came. I stood up and made an announcement – who wants to receive the Holy Spirit tonight? The silence seemed to have a volume of its own. I said, please raise your hand as the Lord is going to fill you tonight. Dear Mum... after a few minutes Mum's hand was raised... the only one. She looked at me, as though to say, well, you told me, here I am. It was like I was operating in a gift of Faith. I walked over to her. She looked like concrete. No emotion. I just prayed, "Receive the Holy Spirit" and Mum went flying backwards. It was like a stick of dynamite was under her seat. The 5th person along from Mum who sat at the end of the row also at the same time, flew off her chair. It was like an electric bolt went through the row of chairs. It felt as if our Lord Jesus was standing in our midst with such compassion and grace, just ministering to Mum. I was surprised as much as Mum was. I heard from Mum later that when she got home she couldn't stop speaking in tongues (another language), trying to understand what happened. But what had happened was that after 13 years of so many waiting meetings I felt that Mum had such a wall of disappointment that it led to more disappointments, which led to unbelief. She had just switched off and got harder.

But God knew and gave her a mighty baptism of the Holy Spirit that would empower her to live this Christian life, rather than at times just working in the soul realm using her own will power.

That night, as the Power of the Kingdom of God came among us, I saw business people growling and somebody's face also contorting, yet nobody else seemed to notice. Once again, I thought, what's happening to me? Everything seemed to be changing since I made the commitment to enter the Kingdom of His Rule.

As leaders of the church, we would be the ones that prayed for the people during the morning services. People began to fall over backwards, occasionally forwards, and some would just collapse as the power of God was manifest. I was amazed but so grateful to God that the Loving Christ who had been raised from the dead was here among us by the power of the Holy Spirit and was ministering to His people.

I still was concerned about how they were after the experience of falling to the floor, rather than just looking at this phenomenon at face value. This started happening more regularly now, but I did notice there seemed some resistance to this, even to the extent that the other leaders formed a circle around the remaining people left for prayer. Strange, I thought. It reminded me of the resistance to those meetings in Hainault and when Trevor Deering came to Chelmsford. It started to trouble me. What's happening? Don't we want the people to change? Who cares who is praying for who? Let's judge by the fruit. People are receiving more joy, being set free and getting healed. When we keep saying God's presence is here and God shows up in ways we are not used to, who are we to complain? Or have we made God in our image in that He is subject to us and our rules and traditions? Crazy, I thought. I can't believe all these reactions. It didn't make sense. Once again, more questions were building up inside of me. I started to evaluate what in reality was going on. Have we become so organised that we are serving the spirit of excellence and political correctness? Have we become so perfectionist in our meetings that we have to be able to predict and control everything? Are we just operating on our gifts and abilities meaning that we have just tapped into the law of faith, which anyone can do, rather than the power of God? What is the source of the power? What is the difference between us and a business corporation? What would stand out to the man on the street, except from our church language? Whose church is it? Does it belong to us or is it God's church? If it's God's church, where is He? What's He doing? Have we today fallen into the trap like the religious people of the days of Jesus, who were good people who fasted and prayed and read the bible, yet by all their doctrine and traditions, nullified the power of God? (Mark 7:13)

Has the DNA of our church now become a spiritual template confining how we do things? Are we are governed by that instead of the living Christ, living and moving through every member of the body of believers who lives under His banner and operates only through His name, the name of Jesus?

Being a welding engineer, I like to know how things work. If I am going to make something I need to look at the plans so I have an overall picture and then I know what I am building or repairing. I can then follow the instructions, to ensure it is going to withstand external pressure like a house or a large excavator bucket.

It is no surprise God treats us as individuals and knows what we need before we do. I was convicted by a verse of scripture:

> *"Love not the world, neither the things that are in the world. If any man love the world, the love of the Father is not in him."* (1 John 2:15 KJV)

This certainly is not one of those scriptures that you associate with your promise box of scripture verses. It is not normally used in conversation. I have never heard anyone preach or explain this verse, but it certainly gripped my attention. I am one that believes all the bible to be the written word of God (Hebrews 4:12). It would be wrong for me to pick and choose what is truth and what isn't and become selective; otherwise I would be in danger of creating a god in my own image – and who am I anyway? What a statement!

What do we mean by the word 'world'? I started to reflect on my limited knowledge of the bible and discovered there are two Greek words for world, one is the 'kosmos'. The other is 'aion'. The one in our text is kosmos and has a number of aspects to it:

- The material world.

  "The God who made the world and everything in it".
  (Acts 17:24 NIV)

  "Go into all the world…" (Mark 16:15 NIV)

The 'world' here is referring to the earth.

- Then we have the world of people.

  "For God so loved the world…" (John 3:16 NIV)

  "He was in the world, and though the world was made through him, the world did not recognize him".
  (John 1:10 NIV)

- The things of the world: a social world order which operates behind the things of the world. Something that is invisible – a planned system or order of thinking.

- The ruler of this world which is Satan, the prince of this world, and this world order has shown itself hostile to God.

"I will not say much more to you, for the prince of this world is coming. He has no hold over me..."

(John 14:30 NIV)

"For since in the wisdom of God the world through its wisdom did not know him..."

(1 Corinthians 1:21 NIV)

"We know that we are children of God, and that the whole world is under the control of the evil one".

(1 John 5:19 NIV)

- The wisdom of this world which is foolishness to God.

"For since in the wisdom of God the world through its wisdom did not know him".

(1 Corinthians 3:19 NIV)

- The spirit of the world

"What we have received is not the spirit of the world, but the Spirit who is from God".   (1 Corinthians 2:12)

These are only a few scriptures that mention the world, but when I think of what is in the world you see a world of politics, a world of religions and education, literature and science and technology. A world that is independent and unaccountable to God. The focus is on man. The kosmos is a social world order with a mastermind who planned it. One must ask oneself, what is the ultimate goal of its development? Where is it all leading?

We are living on this earth. We are people living in a world, educated by a world system, with its values and perspectives and goals which scripture attributes to Satan, the god of this world. The values of this world are so temporal. When Jesus spoke to his disciples *"What good will it be for someone to gain the whole world, yet forfeit their soul? Or what can anyone give in exchange for their soul?"* (Matthew 16:26). All that achievement and success and money and position and philosophy one can have, yet Jesus has passed sentence on the wisdom and spirit of this world order. *"Now is the time for judgment on this world; now the prince of this world will be driven out"* (John 12:31). The world of external value – success, pride, outward appearances and outward strength – is not the value of the Kingdom. God chose the weak things of the world, the despised, the rejected. He calls the poor in spirit blessed. God chooses anointing over abilities. He chose people who need to rely on Him for everything so that He receives the glory.

Let's think. Before Adam and Eve disobeyed God by eating the forbidden fruit from the Tree of the Knowledge of Good and Evil, there was the earth, which has now been opened up through the sin of rebellion – a 'world'. And the prince of this world has control of their minds and will keep the human race feeding from the knowledge of good and evil. In this one event, death was injected into the blood stream of Adam – the law of decay – and all that was under Adam's authority in the natural world also became subject to the law of death. Before, they had experienced a beautiful intimacy and communion with Almighty God.

The world after Adam's fall was now subject to having this knowledge as part of the human's DNA. A way to think, to behave, and all the values that come from a temporary system that ultimately will have final judgement from God. We could say before Adam fell we had the earth, after the fall we now have a world, a new social order, a mind behind, a system of thinking.

In James 4:4 we read that friendship of this world is an enemy of God. The spirit of this world will hate those who are not of it.

I love the dialogue between the Roman Governor Pilate and Jesus as Jesus stood trial. In John 18:36 (NIV) he said, *"My Kingdom is not of this world"*. Jesus was laying down His life in full authority. It wasn't taken from him. He had already overcome because His Kingdom has different values and purposes and ways of doing things:

> *"Who is he who overcomes the world, but he who believes that Jesus is the Son of God?"*　　(1 John 5:5 NKJV)

There is this conflict in the earth. A world system whose mastermind is Satan versus the Kingdom of God. Even whilst I was writing this I could sense the power of the world trying to touch me. I am always checking my motivation for why I do what I do. Is what I do going to be beneficial or is it going to lead me away from Christ? We are in this world but like Christ, we can say we are not of it (John 17:14).

In James 1:27 (NIV), "*keep oneself from being polluted by the world*". For example – music, the arts and money – you can see it's nature when it isn't submitted to a consecrated life. I know Watchman Nee said once; you can't walk down a dusty road without picking up some dust. It's so true. Receiving revelation from God's word in prayer cleans our spirit.

Salvation is our exit out of the world's system and its values. The church in Greek is called the "Ecclesia", "the called out ones"; called out from the destruction of the prince of the world order.

No wonder water baptism is a picture of a world under judgement, as in Noah's day when God brought judgement on a world order that was full of corruption. Noah left that life behind and went 40 days through the water of death and came through into life.

As we are buried in the waters of baptism we rise up into a new order – the Kingdom of God – where Jesus Christ reigns in our hearts. No wonder we have to undo so much of the world's way of doing things:

> "*And do not be conformed to this world, but be transformed by the renewing of your mind, that you may prove what is that good and acceptable and perfect will of God.*"
> (Romans 12:2 NKJV)

We, as true believers, are like those Israelites (God's people), all leaving Egypt and its values and ways to go through the wilderness to meet with God as He is the one who transforms.

There is a common illustration that paints the picture of a ship on the water which looks all right, but the water in the ship is all wrong. At a fundamental level, the 'world' being in the church is wrong.

Now that I am more aware of this revelation I must do something about it in my life. If I am to walk in the light as Jesus is the Light, I must obey His word in my heart and not walk in darkness otherwise what's the point of asking God for more revelation if I am not walking in the revelation He has already given me?

As I check my own heart, could it be the world values and ways and mind of the world system are preventing the blessing of His manifest presence among us in church world?

At this point of my life, I had no idea of how much the power of the world was touching me.

This world can never be our home. As true believers know we have been born from above. Through the life of the Son that came into us when we were born again by receiving Jesus in our hearts, we become citizens of heaven and are only passing through in this journey of life.

We can live knowing on the inside of us we are being detached from the world's social order and the mind behind this system.

I have had the privilege of witnessing to a lovely elderly couple who minister in the power of the Holy Spirit in such weakness physically, yet with so much authority. On another occasion, I saw an ex DJ talk what appeared to me a load of waffle yet 50 people responded by giving their lives to Jesus. I remember thinking it appears no matter what the DJ says, the anointing of God just breaks all the yokes and all darkness. I was amazed.

Also, at the beginning of establishing the full gospel businessmen in Chelmsford, the four leaders chosen were given an office that wasn't natural to any of them. Once again, I could see their weakness provided God with the opportunity to receive all the glory. They were all very competent people. God's kingdom is so opposite to this world system masterminded by Satan. Every leader was out of his comfort zone and we saw through their weakness how God used them.

If you can see this operating in or around you, never judge the people, as we are dealing with an invisible structure and an invisible mind that has been operating a long time since the fall of Adam in the Garden of Eden.

The word 'world' can be translated as 'AGE'. The disciples asked Jesus in Matthew (24:3 NIV):

> *"and what will be the sign of your coming and of the end of the age? (world)?"*

In Romans 12:2 it talks about not being conformed to the pattern of this world, so how can we be changed? The answer is in Romans 12:2 (NIV):

> *"but be transformed by the renewing of your mind".*

We have to change our thinking from the mind behind the world's system (Satan) who is ruling this age (world). Paul talks about this in Galatians 1:4 (NIV), as to Jesus,

> *"who gave himself for our sins to rescue us from the present evil age, according to the will of our God and Father".*

There must be within us a detachment from the world's thinking as this age (world) is coming to an end. I know the line of separation began when I made that covenant commitment to the Lord – a detachment from the present age and it's thinking, which is masterminded by Satan, was the beginning of revelation to my spirit, which causes me to see and enables me to repent and change my thinking. I realise this is on-going, as I have been trained as most of us have, by the world and its standards and values. Thank God for the work of the cross at Calvary, which has rescued us from this massive deception and enabled us to begin to see the many disguises Satan has through his philosophies in this world.

When we look into the word of God we can see God's choices and values are so much higher than ours. In today's world, I can't imagine many John the Baptists sitting in our churches, clothes made of camel hair, whose diet is locusts and honey. Quite a wild man who was a voice, a voice in the wilderness. Yet today God is still speaking through us in the middle of this world. We who have ears to hear and eyes to see what is going on will respond to the voice of God.

Chapter 11

CHANGING PERSPECTIVES

The revelation that the Kingdom of God is in opposition to the world's social order under the mastermind, Satan, who can influence us by his way of thinking, had such a profound effect on me. I could now see the overall picture of the invisible war we are in. I felt I was slowly being drawn into a change of perspective from looking at things on face value only, and now becoming aware of the invisible world with all its hidden meanings. This spiritual sensing is called discernment and it comes from within a man, particularly those filled with the Holy Spirit. Being a very practical person, this hasn't come easily to me.

> *"So we fix our eyes not on what is seen, but on what is unseen, since what is seen is temporary, but what is unseen is eternal".*   (2 Corinthians 4:17 NIV)

The natural man will view things from what is visible and operate and take decisions based on that, but the spiritual man will look at things differently and take decisions based not on what's on the surface, but by listening and sensing what the Spirit of God is saying to him.

By now, I have already felt the power of the world around me, as well as seeing the demonic spirits operating. I have also known the power and purity of God's love, welling up in my spirit, overflowing in my emotions and body with such acceptance. It was as if I was as good as dead, but came alive with the Heavenly Father's acceptance of me, because He sent His Son to die on a cross instead of me.

Now I could see that God's intention is that we live and move and are led by the Spirit of God in life, and not by our natural minds that have been trained by the world's mastermind, Satan. No wonder that there can be conflict within as the natural mind is an enemy. *"The mind governed by the flesh is hostile to God"* (Romans 8:7 NIV) and cannot understand the things of God, which does explain why there is conflict among Christians. One can look at a situation one way on a practical level. The other will be sensitive to His Spirit and come to a different conclusion. It is just so important to love each other as we are on this journey together and need each other.

Jesus lived His life listening and hearing and obeying His Heavenly Father by using His Spirit (John 5:19, John 12:49) which is the life intended for us all to live as sons of God. Romans 8:14 (NKJV) says,

> *"For as many as are led by the Spirit of God, these are sons of God"*.

It's as if I have been trained in Egypt (a type of 'world'), like Moses in the Old Testament, yet I belong to another kingdom, the Kingdom of God.

To illustrate the invisible world we only have to look at the story of Cain and Abel in Genesis 4. Both gave an offering to God. Cain gave a fruit offering to the Lord and Abel gave a meat offering, from the first born in his flock. Abel's offering was accepted by God but Cain's was rejected. Abel understood the universal principle which was the way to approach God was through the shedding of blood as a sacrifice. Cain brought an offering from his own labour by working the land, which was under a curse, yet to the natural man's understanding, he did his best. Hence Cain got judged and was then marked for the rest of his life. The mark was visible, yet carried a message from God in the invisible realm, that nobody was allowed to kill him. It makes you wonder what is going on in the spiritual realm when people obtain a permanent tattoo. I wonder what they represent and what are the consequences of being marked for the rest of your life?

Another illustration was when Jesus was in the wilderness and being tempted by Satan to worship him, and in Matthew 4:4 (NIV) Jesus replied by using the word of God as a weapon, saying *"it is written"*. We see in Ephesians 6:17 that the Word of God is a sword. You can't see it, but when it is spoken it has the power to defeat the enemy of our souls. We see this principle again in those that love not their life unto death – those are the ones that overcome the enemy by confessing God's word as Jesus did (Revelation 12:11). It is amazing that proclaiming the Word of God in faith, which is invisible, can have so much power.

One more illustration just to bring the point home is found

in Mark 12:42. This is the story of when Jesus watched the rich people put money in the offering and along came a poor widow who put in 2 copper coins. She gave all that she had. There was nothing left: no stockpile, it was everything. We know that money has such a power in the world's system, but she transferred more than money in the invisible realm. She gave her life. This was more than an offering. This was such an expression of what was going on on the inside of her. No wonder we can't see so much today as we only look at the surface. It is so important to look beyond what we can see with our natural eyes.

The Word of God has to be approached, not just from a doctrinal view, but the view that the Word of God has the Breath of God in it. If you look beyond the black and white print, you will discover this written Word also contains the Living Word that can speak to us today. The natural man who is still under the world's system of logic and reasoning cannot understand it (1 Corinthians 2:14), but the man whose spirit is alive will connect with the Spirit of God that is inbreathed in the written word (2 Timothy 3:16).

Somehow the understanding comes like a light to us, beyond any visible revelation. It's as if within a few seconds you could write a book on the revelation the Spirit of God is giving to you. Faith, which is also invisible, connects us like a light switch to this revelation, which can lead us into action.

Jesus spoke to the religious people of the day and told them that their traditions had nullified the word of God and its power (Mark 7:13). It is possible to follow our traditions as we meet as believers and as we live our lives, without listening and living with Jesus 24 hours a day as a person. We can get so caught up with the ways of the world: no matter how good they are, they are still on a temporal level. Jesus Christ is the Living Word. In 2 Corinthians 3:18 (NKJV) as we behold the Lord, not as we hear about Him, we *"are being transformed into the same image from glory to glory"*. The moment we see using our spirit to connect us to Jesus we are being changed. Even the disciples who had walked with Jesus on the Emmaus Road after Jesus had been crucified didn't recognise Jesus, and He was speaking to them for miles. In Mark 16:12, Jesus appeared to them in a different form. They weren't expecting Jesus to come the way He did. In Psalm 29, the voice of God comes to us in many different ways, a majestic voice, a still, calming voice. We can get so caught up with our doctrine when we come as a corporate body of believers and not hear! Jesus is alive!

Prophetically, I was becoming more spiritually aware. The word of God used to quicken my spirit. I would have no peace until I released it. Daph found it difficult to cope with as quite often there was a reaction from other people, which was not always positive.

I started to realise I could no longer hold the various offices I had in the church. I started to release them one by one. I had such a hunger to discover the truth and felt I was compromising what the Lord was showing me by continuing. It was tough. But I knew I was too busy working full time and having two children. I needed time out to seek the face of God. I was losing faith in what I was doing. I knew the principle: Whatever isn't faith is sin, and I always endeavour to maintain the position of living in faith.

The reaction that came my way after my resignation shocked me! I was given what was called the "evil eye". Rejection seemed to be the order of the day. People would go silent on me. I started to think, where is the love of God? Aren't we supposed to love each other, and are we not known for our love? That's a joke, I thought. So what we are implying is that I am only loved by performing, by working and there is no respect. I wanted space in order to seek God.

I wouldn't let this get to me so I made another inner vow. I will love everyone no matter what they do or say about me. I was determined I didn't want to be a hypocrite. All I know is I am far from perfect but I do know Christ accepts me as I am, warts as well, and I want to be an ambassador of His life and love.

What is the point of having a message about the love of God if we cannot love each other? What sort of Christianity is that? It didn't make sense to me. I was never thought of this way while I was Mr Popular, while I was giving my life to the life of the church. I had known what rejection was like from the abuse I had growing up. I know too, that I had coped with it by becoming harder in my emotions, but since my encounter with the Lord, the effect it was having on me was that I felt so sad. What was going on? I used to come home from leadership meetings and just weep. Daph used to say, why don't you just give up and not bother? It was the love of God and the love of God's people that kept me in my last remaining office in the church. I just sensed in my spirit I wasn't released to go fully, and needed to keep faithful to the message God was birthing in me.

This invisible dimension of being led by the Spirit of God was to be the way God would train me. Before the fall, Adam walked with God as His Spirit was in charge of his life on earth, and

Adam communed with God's Spirit. Since eating of the Tree of the Knowledge of Good and Evil, Adam was now opened up to a world of knowledge. Sin had brought separation.

This union with God was re-established after Jesus paid our penalty for sin and we became born again. We became a temple of God. His dwelling place, and our spirit that was dead to God has now become alive. We can now have direct contact, spirit to Spirit. But unfortunately, we have been trained by the world system and often in our walk with God we have our soul directing the terms as to how we are to live and behave, rather than our spirit being placed in subordination to the Spirit of God.

Now I was on a journey to undo that, so my spirit could grow from being just a child of God, to a place of maturity and become a son of God, led by the Spirit of God, as in Romans 8:14. I am just grateful, looking back, that the Lord is my Shepherd, as my goal is to conform to His image:

> *"For whom He foreknew, He also predestined to be conformed to the image of His Son".*
>
> (Romans 8:29 NKJV)

I thank God He chose us, and that we, in freedom, can choose Him, remembering that God never controls us in any way. He just presents us with choices.

Chapter 12

THE CIRCLE OF LOVE

A couple called Pete and Shirley invited Daph and myself to a conference in a C of E convent run by a couple called Bill and Molly Worboys on wholeness.

They were C of E people and had been missionaries in Uganda while the revival at the time was on. Also, they had worked alongside Trevor Deering at Hainault in Essex.

I sensed in my spirit I needed to go, but was not quite sure of being in a convent, but well, I thought, it's only a week. I'm sure I won't turn into a nun. There were about 20 people there. They didn't advertise it but prayed God would send the people He wanted.

It was so quiet. I didn't realise silence would be so noisy. Very different from my Pentecostal background. That week I learnt a far greater depth of the love of God, not just by what they taught, but by their demonstration, particularly the love and honour and respect with which they treated the older generation. There were Church of England vicars there, whose identity was wearing what is known as the "dog collar", or in some circles, the "ring of confidence". I felt strange as I was the youngest there, and I wasn't used to being in such close quarters with older people. I realised I had a limitation on my love. I needed the love to go deeper into me and not be so selective between young and old.

They taught what they called "The Circle of God's Love". The complete salvation which Jesus purchased by becoming a sacrifice for humanity on the Cross of Calvary.

> *"...but to us who are being saved it is the power of God".*
> (1 Corinthians 1:18 NKJV)

They divided the circle into many segments, each segment contained an aspect of salvation:

- Emotional healing from abuse, rejection, dealing with shame, being abandoned and not feeling wanted or accepted.

- Mental health problems, anxiety and fears and worries and depression

- Healing from sickness, disease and infirmities

- Bondage and defilements

It seemed that all needs are part of salvation; emotional, physical, mental and spiritual. Salvation means to become whole and complete, living in total freedom without the effects of sin and trauma affecting the way we live our lives.

The Greek word in the New Testament for salvation is "sozo" which means healing, rescuing, deliverance and salvation, and is only found in the name of Jesus.

> *"Nor is there salvation in any other, for there is no other name under heaven given among men by which we must be saved."* (Acts 4:12 NKJV)

I thought I was saved, past tense. I had got my ticket to heaven and that was it – end of story. I hadn't realised Jesus accomplished so much at the Cross of Calvary in that there was total provision for all humanity's needs.

This incredible salvation, which is perfect and complete, really made me think.

There was a depth that can only be described as extravagant, which expresses God's love that was demonstrated at the Cross at Calvary. I realised I had only just entered in to a fraction of what had been purchased for me. No wonder the apostle Paul wrote in Ephesians 3:18, there is a love beyond knowledge that has a height and depth and width to it.

It is a reality that this salvation, the expression of love and forgiveness, would bring us to a place of becoming whole (1 Thessalonians 5:23). We can have freedom from all our weaknesses and our failures and various bondages, even those we inherited in our DNA (John 10:10). This abundant life the enemy of our souls can't take away and it is present and on-going, not just in the past, nor just in the future, but it is for the present. It's our birthright, our inheritance as the sons of God.

The God of Heaven sent Jesus, who became the door that opens us up to a complete salvation. Amazing yet very humbling. I really didn't know I could get free. I was so used to coping my way and making inner vows. I thought salvation was automatic. I didn't realise it was **a process of being saved.**

It seemed I came to the door, which is Jesus, and just stood in the hallway of a big mansion and never explored or entered into any other room in this magnificent mansion of love extravagant.

The revelation of what salvation really is brings so much hope today when so many people are turning to philosophies and putting their hope in these working for them. Others are turning to the occult, whether it be astrology or horoscopes (not happy-scopes) for some sort of answer. Also, people want to relieve stress by turning to all types of meditations like yoga and eastern meditations from Buddhism and TM (Transcendental meditation). There are those who suffer grief and sickness and go to the spiritualist. Also, there are those who experience reflexology and acupuncture, and have even been to a hypnotist to get rid of all sorts of sickness and addictions and fears.

When Peter and John in the New Testament visited the temple they saw a crippled beggar and the beggar shouted 'give me some money', and they said 'silver and gold we haven't got but LOOK AT US. What we do have we give to you' (Acts 3:3-4), and the beggar was made well. The Greek is sozo (salvation).

The healing which is part of salvation came to him. I am so glad that there are those who know they have something more than words to give to people who are in need.

This man was healed and it was only in the name of Jesus (Acts 3:16).

Jesus Christ has provided the eternal salvation. By His grace we are saved through faith (Ephesians 2:8). It is God's gift to us. If we agree with His word in our hearts as He speaks to us and then speak it out, we can enjoy a little more in this salvation (Romans 10:9-10 NKJV):

> *"That if you confess with your mouth the Lord Jesus and believe in your heart that God has raised Him from the dead, you will be saved. For with the heart one believes unto righteousness, and with the mouth confession is made unto salvation".*

The love that was present in the convent that day enabled me to open my heart and allow the Holy Spirit to start to bring healing to those emotions that had been damaged in my earlier years, they had become an open door to so much fear and anxiety.

I had felt people were controlling, judging or talking about me, so I found it hard to trust them. It just wasn't safe. I have always felt **your heart is like a safe. You don't give the key to many people.**

For me, this was just the beginning of my healing and would allow the Holy Spirit to flow through my spirit unhindered.

I came away from what I initially thought was a dead place, more alive within me. One thing that particularly stood out was I felt so clean on the inside of me, it was as if somebody had given me a bath on the inside. The peace of God was so amazing: an inner stillness that was so calm. This was the real thing, and the other activities the Devil affects are but a counterfeit of the real thing. The Devil is not creative and can only counterfeit what is already in circulation. Today you wouldn't counterfeit what was then the 10 bob note as it isn't in circulation now. Jesus Christ is the real deal.

This sense of cleanness and peace was amazing. I felt I didn't even want to read the newspaper, and I love keeping up with the news, as I wanted the "cleanness" to stay.

The presence of God was changing me on the inside. It did make me think again, about what I had been missing all these years. Why do we have to try so hard to bring the presence of God to be manifest in church meetings and our lives? Was it because God was no longer our focus and our focus has been on the vehicle we are using to bring the presence of God, such as the worship or the preaching?

I was to visit this conference for a number of years. I just wanted more of the living water of life and to come away from the pollution of this world's system.

Looking back at the conference I can see I was a bit of a nightmare to them. Having been a Christian for some time, I thought I had my doctrine in place as to what I believe, yet it seemed I was the one with all the questions.

One thing I disagreed with a lot and couldn't accept at the time was the power of generational sin and the generational cycle. I just couldn't get my head around it. I got so defensive and argued my case that this wasn't true. I felt the cut-off point of this affecting me was the cross: when I gave my life to the Lord Jesus and became a new person. This teaching just didn't fit my theology. This led me to search the scriptures for myself. I suppose I was like a lot of people – just accepting what I was told and just echoing the denominational view.

When I allowed my wall of prejudice to come down and looked into the Word of God I could see right from the first person God created, Adam, that through his rebellion the seed of rebellion, which is the nature of Satan, changed the DNA of the human race. Now all the human race have that rebellious nature, which is why you don't have to teach a 6-month-old baby to be disobedient. The baby wants to be independent which is why the parents spend their lives guiding the child to do the right thing, yet the rebellious nature is still there.

I understand Christ, when He came, was called the last Adam, and started a new human race as the Spirit of God joined Himself to our spirit and we became alive to God. The barrier of sin was taken away for us as we chose to believe in Jesus for our salvation. This new nature was given to us by the Holy Spirit which makes us a new person.

I found that when I became a Christian I never got a new soul or a new body, the soul being the psychological side of me – my mind and will and emotions.

I can see from many passages of scripture like Exodus 20:5-6, that there was a punishment of the sin of idolatry that the third and fourth generation became affected. Also, I discovered that sexual sin would affect up to 10 generations (Deuteronomy 23:2). I looked at different patterns of behaviour following Abraham's DNA and what his genes carried. In Genesis 20:2 we read that Abraham told a lie about Sarah being his wife – he told the king that she was his sister. 40 years later, Isaac, Abraham's son, in Genesis 26:7 told the same king his wife was his sister. The same lie. Then we find Isaac's son Jacob telling lies in Genesis 27:19. Not only are the behaviour and traits coming through our genes, but the word that explains it all is "**consequences**" (Romans 6:23). We cannot bear the guilt of our father's sin, but the consequences of ancestral sin affect the descendants. No wonder the expression, "just like your dad, a chip off the old block". Also, it makes sense as to why the doctor wants to know if you have an illness in your family. For us, as Christians, it points to a potential judgement of certain sins in our ancestral lines which are affecting our lives today.

Thank God that Jesus purchased a full and complete salvation where we don't have to live with these consequences and they can be renounced (which means to speak off) as we confess our ancestral sin.

No wonder the Devil hates God's word. In John 8:32 (NKJV):

> *"And you shall know the truth, and the truth shall make you free".*

No wonder Satan doesn't like us to search the word of God, as his tactic that still works today as he tempted Eve in the Garden of Eden. *"Did God really say?"* (Genesis 3:1 NIV), casts doubt on God's word.

Satan is the father of lies (John 8:44) and always will be.

Years later, when I was in London, a lady came to me and said she couldn't conceive and was barren. I asked her had she committed an abortion. She said no: my mother had an abortion. I said, will you confess the ancestral sin of your mother. She said she would. We broke the power of ancestral sin in the name of Jesus and within a year, she had a baby.

On another occasion, one of my mother's neighbours who is an unbeliever, suffered from hay fever. Apparently, his father also had hay fever and was really bad when the pollen count went up. With his wife standing by the side of me I said, I realise you are not a Christian, but I believe if you can agree with me for a short while and you renounce the hay fever that has almost stopped you working, our Lord Jesus will come to you by the power of His Holy Spirit and will bring freedom to you. He did that out of desperation as nothing he had tried worked before, and now he is completely free.

We discovered many addictions have a root in our family lines, as well as divorce and certain fears. When I looked back, I remember the message preached at my son Matthew's grave, about how King David sinned and his son died in 2 Samuel 12:1-24. Was this answer I had been looking for as to why? I knew God never created him to die, but once again I was reminded of the spiritual law of sowing and reaping. It didn't seem fair, but thank God He established His justice through the cross of Christ, and we can appropriate by faith, the salvation which Jesus purchased for us (Philippians 2:12).

Prayer:

Father God,

I come to you now in the name of Jesus Christ and I confess that I and my ancestors have sinned. I now confess (specifically, any curses, pronouncements, weaknesses, infirmities and any dedication that the Lord shows you). I now renounce the consequences of these sins in my life and family. I unreservedly forgive my ancestors. I now cancel every assignment, curse/s, and patterns that Satan is using to bring me into bondage. I declare I am a child of God, saved by the Blood of Jesus. I cancel all Satan's rights now, in Jesus name,

Amen

Chapter 13

THE WILDERNESS BEGINS

My situation at work had started to change. My company had been taken over by an ex-gypsy who seemed to be rolling in money. He would appear in the work yard with a bright silver shining Rolls Royce. I knew something was wrong. He didn't seem interested in the company or the employees. I saw him sack a dozen people before Christmas when work was slack with no conscience. My friend the foreman, Arnold left. He was a lovely Christian, yet within 6 months, he had a heart attack and died. He was only 34. I felt it was the stress he was under. I watched my friends, people who had been in the company for over 30 years being signed off work, yet each took him to the tribunal and won their case.

I used to enjoy my work. I knew God had given me this job when I left school. I would travel all round Essex looking after over 300 plant machines. Now the atmosphere had changed from one of peace and serenity to living in fear and tension, as you never knew what was going to happen next.

This seemed to be going hand in hand with the other major part of my life, being involved in church. Tension seemed to be part of this world of church. I was asked on a number of occasions to explain my actions and theology, as so many people had been coming to receive prayer ministry and were getting healed and coming into a new freedom and being filled with the Spirit of God.

I can remember coming away from such a meeting feeling I had been interrogated as if I had done something wrong.

The conflict within me grew as did the distance with the new Pastor. I was beginning to feel we weren't speaking from the same page. I had at this point now resigned the last position I held in the church as part of the authority structure: being a Deacon/Elder.

The prophetic word seemed to increase in me. I had only stayed on the leadership as I felt I was a voice for so many people who weren't being heard. I loved my church family and I owed it so much. However, now I was changing and the conflict within me grew.

One Sunday morning, I sat in the congregation weeping on the inside because of what God was showing me, to the degree I just couldn't keep in my seat any longer. I walked to the front of the church at an appropriate time in the communion service and read Philippians 3:17-21 (NKJV) and shared have we become *"enemies of the cross"* (v18): that our appetite, particularly for food, has become too important to us rather than denying ourselves? Have we allowed the spirit of the age (world) to affect our thinking, and do we really need to change our thinking (repent) because we are citizens of heaven and our lifestyle should reflect this?

I was shaking. I knew there would be consequences. But I had the fear of God within me and would not allow the fear of man to intimidate me. My heart so longed for the church to be filled with God's glory. I wanted the best for His people. I grew up having communion (intimacy with God) within the act of the communion service. Unfortunately, like so many prophetic words given over the years, they don't seem to register to the hearers apart from being written in a book. Often nothing appears to change outwardly. It's like we are on a merry-go-round and can't get off, yet it's killing us on the inside.

Despite encouragement from other pastors outside the local church, I felt very much alone and was in grief as to how we were moving as a church. My wife, Daph, felt I was rocking the boat and I needed to try and keep the peace, and keep quiet. I said, "We are not listening to the living God anymore". It seemed that we were locked in our ways and doctrine, yet Jesus was speaking and we were just carrying on as usual. What was happening to us as people of God? This was causing so much grief within me, particularly since having the experience of entering the Kingdom of God, and seeing the demonstration of His presence changing lives. I heard people share their testimony of coming into a new freedom which they had never known before, despite being Christians for years.

I shall never forget a young couple. They lived in one of the poorest places in Chelmsford. The area had a bad reputation for trouble. She had diabetes. She injected herself with insulin every day. They were in their 20's. They came to see us. They had no church background. They were dressed very scruffily, being so poor. They touched my heart. I knew what poverty was. This was my background. As we prayed, the Lord came and just brought such freedom from very deep rejection and abandonment and grief. Her mother had died when she was so young. He was into the New Age philosophy and had lots of tattoos, but he really needed a dad, someone to father him. They experienced so much inner pain. In those days in the seventies and eighties we could only minister with the measure of light we had. After quite a few sessions, she was asked to sing a solo to a packed church of over 350 people. One Sunday evening she sang from her heart. I can't remember the words, but the anointing of the presence of a Holy God flowing through this healed broken vessel was amazing. It was like listening to the voice of an angel. It was beautiful. The atmosphere seemed so clean and there was a sense of the awe of God and being pure, not defiled by the music or beat of the world. You could have heard a pin drop, as the beautiful, sweet presence of God just flowed across the people. Just amazing. I am so grateful to God that He had given us the privilege to minister to this broken couple – filled with such pain with little hope of anything changing. Witnessing this so blessed me. They would now be releasing the presence of God to their people group, a group that the church would be foreign to, with no shame, only glory. For me, it was worth it all, remaining true to myself and what God had shown me despite the resistance from some quarters to try to keep me quiet.

Looking back, I wish I had known more at the time as there was still so much that needed to be done, but I am grateful for the little, and the lives I saw God change, in that season.

Now came a new season I was about to enter into. God had been speaking to me about the wilderness. The verses He gave me were Hebrews 11:24-27. This talked about how Moses would have to leave the comforts of Egypt by faith and obey God and go into the wilderness.

It wasn't long before this would become my experience. But I didn't know how to go about it and really, what did it mean? There were no books in the seventies as far as I knew. I know John Bevere brought one out in the early nineties called 'Victory in the Wilderness', but wilderness was only a word to me at that time. I had no idea what that meant. It was very rare for anyone to leave their church family without a specific call in those days, but God was moving His church, His people, into a new season. The Charismatic Renewal had already started and I was to get a divine boot.

One Sunday afternoon, the two ministers of the church asked to come round to have a chat with my wife and me in our home. The message they bought was that I was no longer welcome any more in the church and that I should leave. My wife and children didn't have to leave, but I did. Voices were raised and it wasn't very pleasant, but with much conviction, I said I am sorry – it is God's church and you don't have that authority. I will be coming back next week.

We were left shocked and traumatised. We were both crying and feeling distraught. We had grown up there and we were part of the family. These new pastors hadn't been there half as long as we had. We were broken. It was a sword that was put into our marriage to destroy us. Daph was now giving me such a hard time by saying it was all my fault. If only I had just kept quiet and carried on. I was becoming numb like when I was growing up with so much rejection and pain. There was a baptismal service that evening. We were so distraught. What were we going to do? We were now outcasts. Not wanted. What was our crime? So many thoughts were hitting me. I didn't help matters as my rebellion kicked in and I said, unless I hear from God, we will be back in church next week, and you will have to physically remove us.

I had no idea what God was up to. All I knew was that I had to be living in a place of faith, otherwise I would be in sin (Romans 14:23). I hadn't got a word from God, so I knew it wasn't wise to move.

I felt for my two children, Patrick and Becky, having to leave their friends too. What was going to happen to them? What about all the friends we had grown up with? The air seemed filled with confusion and fear and anxiety. What were we going to do? What was going on?

The Monday following 'Bombshell Sunday' we had already booked and paid to go to the Full Gospel Business meeting in Woodford. It's where Christians invite their friends to a Christian Fellowship to have a meal and listen to somebody's testimony. Our friends Robin and Julie were doing the worship and they had a visiting speaker sharing his experience of life. We sat at these lovely round tables in what seemed a really posh hotel with everything 'just so'. Everybody was really dressed up.

The guy spoke about leaving a church when it was the call of God. At that moment, my spirit rejoiced as the word confirmed to me that God was in this and had called us out. With tears of relief, we left that place with the assurance that God was with us and now we were to enter the wilderness – not really knowing what that meant, or knowing where we were going, or why we had to go through the experience. All I knew at that stage was that I trusted God, because I knew He was with us and with the Living Word no matter what came our way, we would be okay, because our God is our Heavenly Dad.

I had a secure job with a regular income but we didn't have a spiritual home or family around us, or anywhere to go now on Sundays as a family.

At this stage of my journey in life, I had a measure of peace, as I knew I was not in rebellion to God.

I have had to say many times in my life to my wife Daph, "please forgive me. I can only follow what I believe God is saying to me, but I know I can't go back and be an echo any more of somebody else's teaching or doctrine, or the latest fad or book that's going around. I have to be a voice as it is my life. I trust God that He knows what He is doing but in the natural, life is looking like a mess exploding with internal pressure. But God is God. And we are His children. I believe that".

After that Monday we left the church. A letter was read publically about me to the congregation which wasn't the complete truth.

I heard within 6-7 months over 70 people had also left the church.

The season of the wilderness began, but it appeared a lot of that change was to become a reason to blame me. None of our friends contacted us. We were called the 'Family of Rebellion'.

After we had left, I put on a Christmas party for 100 people who I knew now were in the wilderness. God had scattered His people across the UK, as He was already doing all over the place.

We needed to have fellowship with a few friends, Alan, Sarah and Jan. We met with them in Alan and Sarah's house, as a small group, united by the call and love of God. At first, it felt a bit strange with us meeting just round the corner from our old church. Although it was a hard and tough time, when we worshipped it became like an open heaven.

One of the last things I can remember was a dear old lady called Mrs Forsyth prophesying for over 6 months about entering God's rest. In Hebrews 4: 9-10 (NKJV):

> *"There remains therefore a rest for the people of God. For he who has entered His rest has himself also ceased from his works as God did from His".*

I was very conscious that this was what God was saying to me, but being such an active person who just loves to work, it seemed I couldn't get into His rest. With my past experiences and the amount of uncertainty I was living in, this call to enter His rest just seemed impossible. Then I heard some time after leaving the church that this dear lady, Mrs Forsyth, was in the later stages of life in our local hospital.

Daph and I went to visit her before she died. With little strength and a feeble voice she laid in the hospital bed and started to prophesy again and was now saying we would touch the nations of the earth with God's message. I thought at that point in time the furthest I had ever been was Jersey on holiday, let alone the nations of the earth. But those words never left me, as I was learning still. **It is God's word that abides and doesn't return to Him void, but it's Satan's words that come and go.** They can change with the weather, but God's Word remains deep within us.

Daph and I had an invitation to a short conference in a

Church of England convent in Bedfordshire. My friends Bill and Molly Worboys would be there with a young American called Ken. He had only been a Christian for a few years. The other speaker was the Reverend John Barr, who was well-known in the UK as a Pentecostal Pastor, but one who was used very much in operating in the Word of Knowledge (one of the gifts of the Spirit). He also had a strong prophetic edge to his ministry.

The meeting was very quiet and Pentecostal with no hype whatsoever. There were about 26 people present. We sat around the walls of the room. In one of the sessions I found myself in the middle of the room waiting for prayer ministry with a few others. I started to feel embarrassed. I didn't know what I was out of my seat for. I couldn't even remember getting up. I really wanted to get back to my seat, but I felt I had passed the point of no return. Molly approached me with Ken, the young American, and just said, "Pat, the Lord is taking the stress and tension you are carrying and He is just lifting it all off you". I started to well up. Tears started to flow down my cheeks as each of the muscles and the pressure within my body and head started to relax. This was amazing. I was so used to living as someone who was numb on the inside, and this was the Lord's presence and His love. He cared enough about me in my lost state of not knowing what is happening to just touch me with the power of His Love. It was so strange, as all I was used to was rejection after rejection, standing up for injustice and as a voice for the Lord. The loneliness at times was hard to bear.

I believe we have to be people of our word. I made a decision I wouldn't look back. I knew I couldn't hide anything from God. Yet today it felt as if He had come to me in person.

The next moment Ken the American just said this "Pat, when

will you enter God's rest?" This was the experience I sought so long and hard for yet it seemed to evade me. I took the decision in faith to enter, as a veil in the Spirit just opened up to me. I just stepped into the rest of God. I had come to the end of all I had tried to achieve for the Lord. I was a broken man. Peace and security just filled my soul, my whole being. It felt like something of heaven had touched me. Nothing on earth had ever come close to this. It was a place of power, no striving, no performance, nothing about meeting my own needs. But it was about a deeper walk with Father God within the Holy of Holies. It was so personal. "Who am I that He should care?" A son. This was what mattered to me. Looking back I can see I have left that rest at times, and have come and gone out from it. But this is more than information or another doctrine. It is a reality: our birth-right and part of our inheritance as God's children. The Word has now become flesh. I would never be the same again.

> *"In repentance and rest is your salvation,*
> *in quietness and trust is your strength"*
>
> (Isaiah 30:13 NIV)

The Prince of Peace, our Lord Jesus, died and gave His life that we may be partakers of the inheritance due to us as sons of God.

It's amazing how many people would like to go to Heaven yet don't want to die. **God isn't trying to get us to Heaven. He is trying to get Heaven into us.** If only we would cease from our works and follow the Lord instead of asking God to follow us and just bless our plans. **God isn't our butler.**

I had been a Christian over 20 years yet hadn't had this wonderful experience. I always seemed to learn the hard way; when I had come to the end of my own resources. The rest I found isn't doing nothing, but a base on which to work with the Lord.

Daph, on the other hand, had had enough and wanted to walk out of this conference. She didn't want to know and was giving me a hard time.

I saw one of the leaders. They shared a principle and said, you can only help to bring Daph to a place of faith. Would I release Daph in faith to the Invisible God? I went back to my room and knelt by my bed on my knees. I felt like Abraham of old when he offered Isaac, the son of promise on the altar of death, and trusted God with him.

I did that in the Spirit and put Daph on the altar and left her there without rescuing her, and trusted God that He would deal with Daph in His time.

That was one of the hardest decisions – to take my own hands off, to have no control and willingly take Daph, whom I love very much, and leave her with the Living God. It is something I knew I had to do. I knew Daph's fears, and the abuse she had suffered, let alone all the shame she carried, which would be insurmountable at the present time. But I don't set the time and season. God was on the move and I had to follow Him. I can't just sit in church listening to sermons week in and out. I had set my heart to discover the reality, the truth of living with the person, Jesus, in my life, day by day.

I hadn't a clue where this journey was going to take me, but I was reminded in the Hall of Faithful men and women in Hebrews 11 who lived and died without seeing what they believed, but they still lived and died by faith.

God had given me some verses of scripture I didn't understand right at the beginning of this journey into the wilderness:

"My son, do not despise the chastening of the Lord,
Nor be discouraged when you are rebuked by Him;
For whom the Lord loves He chastens,
And scourges every son whom He receives".

(Hebrews: 12:5-6 NKJV)

At the time I felt I was a good guy. I hadn't done anything really bad. However, this became one of those verses that would become clearer along the journey, but I can say at that stage the new pastor did what was right by throwing me out as at that point in time I wasn't conscious of what was wrong with me. I hadn't asked to be brought up in abuse and this affected my behaviour. I'm so glad our Lord Jesus came to save sinners like me, not saints. I was to discover that God never gives up on us although at times it feels we give up on ourselves. It was His grace that would open me up to the truth. Jesus is *"full of grace and truth"* (John 1:14 NKJV). Grace always comes before truth. This was the lesson I had to learn in relationships as God gave so much grace to me first, before He showed me the truth.

Part Two

Chapter 14

AN UNEXPECTED
VISITATION

For the last 2 years God had been speaking to me about working for him full time by going self-employed. I knew my fears were greater than my faith at the time especially after all we had gone through leaving the church. I knew I couldn't go there and dwell on those thoughts. It's as if I had put a brick wall up with the voice of God calling me from the other side.

Now I was sitting at home by my dining room table just a few days after the conference in a totally new place in my faith after entering God's rest. I said to the Lord "when would you like me to start this welding business and go self-employed?"

Almost immediately the Lord said "June 1st". It was so clear, with no time for me to form a barrier. I couldn't mistake it being from God. I thought I'd better check the date as June 1st must be on a Monday and not any day during the week. Lo and behold, it was a Monday. Shivers ran down my spine. This is really happening to me. God is serious about this. Now I know what Peter, the disciple of the Lord, felt like stepping out of the boat into the impossible, walking on water with no props and all alone. I was different now. My fears were still there but the Lord had prepared me for this season. The Lord gave me just 2 weeks' notice. I had been in the company for 18 years. There was a recession on. I had a wife and 2 children and a mortgage. Daph was giving me a hard time saying, "How stupid and ridiculous is this? Giving up a secure job with a regular income and going into a totally unknown lifestyle."

I bought a really cheap and rusty short wheelbase transit van with so many rusty panels it was an embarrassment to look at, let alone turn up to a welding job for people's cars or heavy plant machinery. After paying for the first advertisement in the local paper, I had about £10 left. My mother's friend felt so sorry for me he gave me a job that would take about 2 days to do.

Looking back it was perfect timing as I heard that the remaining people who I had worked with for 18 years were leaving the company the same week, yet nobody had told me. The voices I had to contend with: "nobody in their right mind would do such a thing", "it is irresponsible", "you have a wife and family, financial commitments". The last week was the most difficult, working through my notice period at work. One day I would be in a place of faith, just like Peter the Disciple, on the water with my spirit focussing on the Lord. He is the Lord, and I am His child. The next day it was like a cloud of blackness descended on me and I couldn't see the way ahead. My fears and worries combined with all the negative voices around me telling me it's not going to work, too many other people were losing their jobs. I can see now why the Lord said to give short notice. I don't think mentally and emotionally I would have been able to cope much longer which is why I found strength, having the word of God within me which gave me the endurance to be able to stand and resist all that was thrown against me.

In one way, it was a relief leaving L.A. Carty. Since the company had been taken over, I had worked in fear and abuse, but in the middle of that God also taught me to love my new governor, but it didn't mean I had to like him.

This new adventure was scary, yet exciting, as I was committing myself to live day by day by faith. I said to my wife Daph, "I have had enough of listening to talks on faith, reading about other people's faith. I have to outwork my faith beyond theory as otherwise it is still dead", as James 2:14-26 describes.

Once again, I would say to Daph, "Please forgive me if I am wrong, but I can only trust what I believe our Lord Jesus is saying to me today". I have chosen that I don't want to live by the system of religion, but as I have proved in the past through the faithfulness of trusting God against all odds, I can trust the indwelling living presence of God. This is my inbuilt guidance. He has never let me down. Following Jesus is my way of life. This is more normal to me. There is a peace and security when you are not in charge of your life, especially when you have got out the boat of comfortability and onto the water of insecurity. You are never alone. Living by faith does bring one to be disciplined – to keep your inner focus on the one who is calling you, our Lord Jesus. So the responsibility is His, not mine. I am trusting Him, I know I am a very practical person and like things in order. I also want to understand things but I know my own limitations in the natural realm. **I couldn't take this decision to live by faith and then not do it, as** I understand that if I look to myself I would be putting myself under a curse.

> *"Cursed is the man who trusts in man".*
>
> (Jeremiah 17:5 NKJV)

My own feelings were all over the place. I hadn't a clue what the next step was, but I did know we have a Heavenly Father who is working all things out in my life.

> *"for it is God who works in you both to will and to do for His good pleasure".*
>
> (Philippians 2:13 NKJV)

His life is my life.

I loved going round people's houses welding up their cars, preparing them for the M.O.T. or getting them through when their vehicle had failed. I found though, that I wasn't relating to people. I think it took me about 4 years to get deprogrammed from the Christian bubble I had lived in in church world with all the Christian jargon. I hadn't realised how religious I had become. God's church and His people are great. It's the system I have a problem with. All the political correctness which seems more important than the people. In that season God was shaking everyone up and moving so many of us around.

I heard of an American preacher called John Wimber, who

was coming to a conference in Wembley, London. He was the founder of the Vineyard group of churches. A number of friends had booked as a small group so I decided to join them.

The freedom and the beauty of the intimacy of worship really touched my heart. I have always felt worship is a journey to meet with the God of Heaven. I love praise. It's good to activate our souls to worship but praise is only a gateway with thanksgiving on the way to the Holy Place, to meet face to face in intimacy. Often staying in praise has become a goal and not part of the journey.

But here they definitely had a revelation on worship, which means to kiss. That's how intimate it is. Within us as believers our spirit needs this union to go beyond our songs, to bow in His presence and come to the place where He is the Lord Almighty. God is in charge. With 3,000 people there the presence of God was very tangible. We were no longer worshipping the worship, the means to approach our God. The plushness of the really big soft seat was just beautiful, instead of being squashed up, sitting on hard chairs.

We had worshipped and reached a special place of intimacy, then one by one, various prophetic words from the heart of Father God just flowed. There must have been about half a dozen people who were moved to speak. There was a vein running through each prophetic voice. Each gave a part that added to another part. It felt indeed like, one word from Father God. It was strong. We had allowed sin to enter through our hurts and inner pain causing judgements and bitterness. There was a call to repent. To turn in another direction, to change our minds and confess our sins.

There was a spontaneous response all over the auditorium

that came from our hearts, in complete unity and agreement. Such a deep sense we were in the presence of the One who created the Universe and holds each star in place. It felt like all our self-importance and position and ego and status were nothing in His eyes. We were all in this together, rich or poor, high profile church leaders I knew. There were no celebrities, no raising up of anyone. Indeed, we truly felt insignificant and aware that the garment of our souls was stained, unclean, by the presence of sin.

People all over the place were crying, wailing, some even screaming as if they were in Hell. Others were laying in the aisle, face down on the floor. It was like a hurricane had come into the place and was swirling round and round but not going anywhere.

I looked up after 15 minutes to the top of the building and sensed within me that the Spirit of Repentance that had been released wasn't going anywhere. I asked the question, why? Isn't God receiving our repentance as we confess our sins to Him? I felt the Lord say, "I know how fickle you are. I want to see the work of repentance that goes beyond your words and changes you from the inside."

So another 15 minutes. The wailing got louder along with the screams. I remember thinking to myself, this sounds like Hell, with just desperation and no escape. We can't get out. The eyes of the Lord are everywhere. No excuses. No projections of our sins on others. Each of us accountable only to the Magnificent, Majestic God who sits on the throne with angels all around who was visiting us that day.

I haven't ever felt such intensity as I did in that meeting with the depths of pain and tears that poured out of me. We have so many meetings today about us, but this day was where Almighty God was in charge. We were meeting Him, heart to heart, spirit to Spirit, as a united body of Christ – his people called the church.

For half an hour, which was a long time to be under the Spirit of Repentance, with our stomachs aching and tear-stained faces and with much relief, Father God accepted our repentance. This really is His gift to us, as we continually repent. **Without Him giving us this gift we can keep saying sorry but as we know there is little change.** Obeying the Law as a duty isn't enough. God came in and changed our hearts and accepted and healed us. What love our Heavenly Father, the Almighty God, has for us. None of us deserved the gift that day. It was His grace. He knew He had called us into the wilderness as His people, and just like Israel of old on their journey, dealt with our sins, our rejection and realigned us once again. We weren't conscious of John Wimber. He too was with us on our knees. We had met with God. The type of meeting reminded me a little of when I went to church and we came out knowing we had met with God. Where the Spirit of the Lord is, there is Liberty (2 Corinthians 2:17).

After God had received our repentance, John Wimber then approached the lectern, opened his bible to read from 1 Corinthians 13 – the love chapter – and down on the right-hand side of the centre aisle a lady started laughing her head off. It was infectious. I looked at John Wimber. He had only announced the reading. He allowed this individual to carry on laughing for about 5 minutes. She was almost falling off her chair. It felt a bit strange at first because we had been at the other end of the scale about 30 minutes ago when we were in grief and sorrow.

Then John Wimber started pointing to various people. I was sitting quite high up in the stalls and I felt he was pointing at me. The next minute I knew I couldn't stop laughing. It was so deep, this joy, that was flowing so deep I was now aching on the inside of me. The people around me started laughing. I suppose looking back, it was as if I had become a catalyst for those around me. Well, for another 15 minutes, the whole place erupted like a volcano of pure, clean joy. Once again, all this was so spontaneous as the body of Christ, His people just responded with so much joy. I think part of this was that we were so grateful. At last, God had received us. We then moved into spontaneous worship, dancing before the Lord. It wasn't the charismatic up and down on the spot, but every fibre of our being just had to worship. I even saw a number of nuns with all their regalia on worshipping with no inhibitions. I saw people doing cartwheels between the stalls. The joy and expression of freedom had come to His people in the wilderness. This was a season where God was bringing transformation.

That visitation of God took place on the Thursday of that week. The next and last meeting was on the Friday. John Wimber spoke and said, "What a great party God threw for us". Boy, did we need it. I have never been in a meeting of that size when God granted us the gift of repentance.

I thank God that in our wilderness we are never out of God's sight, just like Israel of old, but there are times and seasons that God initiates.

I thank God for leadership that has so much authority and is so secure in God, yet not exercising control. This was a model that to me was so beautiful, that God's people met with God and went away more conscious of God than any personality.

I came away thinking about how much fear and control props up a system, particularly when the Spirit of God moves in ways we are unaccustomed to. In that season everywhere we went the theme was: "**God wants the church back**".

***

I can see now, when we look at the scriptures, we see true repentance begins with God releasing a gift to us, not with man. It is the free sovereign grace of God. John the Baptist preached a baptism of repentance to prepare the way of the Lord (Mark 1:3-4, Luke 24:46-47). Repentance was preached before the remission of sins, even on the day of Pentecost when Peter stood up in response to a question from the crowd of over 3,000 people after hearing about Jesus Christ. The people cried out in Acts 2:37 (NIV) "*What shall we do?*" Peter replied "*repent and be baptised*" (Acts 2:38 NIV). We also see in Hebrews 6 one of the six basic doctrines is repentance from dead works.

The repentance we experienced wasn't remorse, when we were just sorry but a "*godly sorrow produces repentance leading to salvation*" (2 Corinthians 7:10 NKJV). **The sin and pain we experienced would be producing the formation of the Son of God within us.** When we received the Lord we were as a child (John 1:12). Now we were in the process of growth where we were on the way to come into sonship (Galatians 4:19), where our Heavenly Father can trust us with a lot more. We recognise that what is happening in the natural realm is also happening in the spiritual realm.

I just love the reality that **repentance leads not only to faith, but to joy,** to be free from guilt and the weight of the power of sin. What I am continuously learning is that the experience isn't a one off experience. My life would become a life of repentance as God continued to bring me into more of his salvation. I used to think everything was automatic. How wrong I was. No wonder Paul encourages us to work out our salvation in fear and trembling (Philippians 2:12-13).

Confession is part of this experience. As we confess our sins we are bringing to the light what was hidden in darkness.

When I attended the meeting I wasn't conscious of any sin. It goes to show – we really don't know our own hearts. But when the Holy Spirit came it brought conviction, and the vehicle of repentance was given to bring freedom.

Once again, I didn't realise this wasn't automatic. How could it be if I didn't know my sin?

> *"Whoever conceals their sins does not prosper,*
> *but the one who confesses and renounces them finds mercy".*
> (Proverbs 28:13 NIV)

> *"Then I acknowledged my sin to you*
> *and did not cover up my iniquity.*
> *I said, "I will confess*
> *my transgressions to the Lord."*
> *And you forgave*
> *the guilt of my sin".*
> (Psalm 32:5 NIV)

We also know that in James 5:16, James talks about confessing our sins that we might be healed.

My friend John Barr used to say – don't expect God to cover

what we won't uncover.

The Devil loses his grip on us when we bring those unrighteous acts and attitudes into the light. Then the darkness has to flee. We are called to walk always in the light, with no secrets of the darkness.

Being aware of the magnitude of the Almighty God moving among us at the conference certainly highlighted what an awesome God we have, as well as someone who is a Father to His children, not just in name.

The Fear of the Lord was so present. It wasn't a demonic fear that has torment in it, or a religious fear, but the Fear of the Lord is one of the aspects of the Spirit of God found in Revelation 1:4 and Isaiah 11:1-2. The Fear of the Lord not only gives us wisdom and knowledge, but gives us boundaries. It is healthy for us to be accountable to the Almighty God. We can't do as we please. It is a positive attitude that the people of God need to cultivate as freedom exists in the Fear of the Lord. We, as the people of God, are incomplete without it as *"The fear of the Lord leads to life"* (Proverbs 19:23 NKJV). It is our protection on our walk with the Lord on this journey of life. Jesus said we can't just do as we please in John 14:23 (NIV): *"Anyone who loves me will obey my teaching"*. We can't say we love God and live in disobedience to His Word. But the Fear of God will keep us walking in the love of God with its boundaries.

In Acts 9:31 (NKJV) it says: *"And walking in the fear of the Lord and in the comfort of the Holy Spirit, they were multiplied"*. What a wonderful balance from the early church: walking in the Fear of the Lord and the comfort of the Holy Spirit.

Our Father God loves us enough not only to heal us, but

not to leave us as orphans. He sends the Holy Spirit to convict us and bring us into alignment with His plans and purposes. He desires for us to be conformed to the image of His son (Romans 8:29) and no other image or likeness, **that we become the message of His Son, not in words only but by who we are.**

If I said to you I have measles, but you catch chickenpox, what do you think I am carrying? You only catch what I have, not what I say I have. I noticed in working with unbelievers, they soon pick up if you are genuine and carry the truth. Although their minds might not understand it, in their hearts they can perceive the truth.

The world awaits for the Son of God to be revealed (Romans 8:19). Jesus lived in subjection to Father God, and out of that subjection he had dominion. Jesus Christ was the prototype. He led the way to show us how to live as a son of God in this journey of life. It's possible too – we can follow Him.

We can exercise our faith by obeying His word, for we are called to walk by faith, not by sight. One cancels the other out. It is not walking by our physical senses but by faith (2 Corinthians 5:7).

The world says seeing is believing, but it is actually the other way around. We believe first, then we see. It is once again the contrast between the visible and invisible. While we do not look at the things which are seen, but at the things which are not seen.

> *"For the things which are seen are temporary, but the things which are not seen are eternal".*
>
> (2 Corinthians 4:18 NKJV)

Faith connects us to two unseen realities, God Himself and

His Word. We can endure hardships if we turn to God and His Word by faith, and as we do, we will enjoy His life and His goodness.

Chapter 15

SUPERNATURAL INTERVENTIONS

I was to find living through a wilderness experience with no church family, feeling ostracised overnight and now with no regular income, that I was in a position of vulnerability, subject to all the pressures of life, and having to rely on God alone. This was quite nerve-racking. Yet, I had chosen to follow the call of God and live by faith.

The loneliness, I think, was the hardest to cope with, especially as my wife Daph, wasn't in agreement with me. I thank God for those relationships we began to develop as we met as a small house group. It is said there is no fellowship like those in the trenches with you.

It felt as if God was stripping me of all independence on

the world's system and its values of money, success, external comforts and people. I knew I had to continue to go forward in the wilderness which appeared barren and empty to discover who I really was and what I really believed in my heart, and to find who God is.

Each week I would have to pray for the next week's work. There was always a hidden pressure. What if the 'phone didn't ring? At that time I didn't even have enough equipment to do certain welding jobs, so I would buy tools whenever I needed them. But I knew I couldn't look back. I had made the decision to enter the Kingdom of God in my lounge at home. In those early days, the tension in our home was tough. I think every fear and anxiety came to the surface in Daph. I spent many nights lying in my bed, crying, thinking "This is so hard. I don't understand what's happening? Am I wrong?" So many negative thoughts would assail my mind and so few people I could go to would understand. "God has spoken. He must know what He's doing" but it's not really helping me, not knowing. Yet this experience was causing my spirit to grow in faith as I was learning to live by the Spirit of God, and not by sight or feelings. It was comforting to know even Jesus had to grow in his Spirit, it doesn't say in his soul (Luke 2:40 NKJV).

I found the hardest test of faith in that season was doing nothing for the Lord. It was amazing how much unbelief was hidden in me, considering I had always been so busy working for God.

I certainly had to keep my attitude right. I knew when Israel murmured and grumbled in the wilderness experience that God was displeased with them in Exodus 16. Being thankful for everything wasn't easy, but we read in 1 Thessalonians 5:16

"This is the will of God". Changing habits and attitudes doesn't happen overnight, but change must take place. The alternative is to get despondent and fall into unbelief.

I was soon put to the test while welding an old Austin 1100 car. Everything was going wrong. I had never done this job before. Pressure was building up and frustration setting in, particularly as I had time restraints too. The customer wanted the car back that evening. Sweat was pouring out of my brow as I laid under the car. I got up and said, "All I need now is this car to catch fire and that will just about finish me off". Still looking at the car with pressure building in my head, about to explode, I could see smoke rising up from behind the dashboard; then the car was filled with smoke. My heart missed a few beats as panic set in. "I don't believe it! I have a customer's car on fire on my driveway, in front of my house up in the air on axel stands. What if the petrol tank catches fire? Goodbye car. Goodbye front of the house!" At this moment I wasn't thankful for everything! I opened the car doors to let the smoke out, looked under the dashboard and saw all the wires being fused together by the flames. I envisaged no lights, no horn, no starter, no nothing. I hadn't time to ring the fire brigade. By instinct, I put my hands in the flames and pulled out the burning wires. The rubber was melting like liquid, like hot tar, which embedded in my arm. My hands got burnt. I didn't have gloves on. I just ignored the pain, my body shaking in fear, but the good news was that I had managed to restrict the damage to the car. The bad news was there were no lights, winkers – nothing electrical was working. You could not drive the car! It just smelled of smoke and all the wires were a black, crisp mess.

I stood up and looked at the mess of the car and wondered

how on earth I was going to repair the car on time. I was sweating and in pain and anxious. I just spoke it out – "If only Steve was here". (Steve is an auto electrician who worked at Chelmsford Autos).

Literally, a minute later, Daph came out of the house not knowing anything had gone on and said, "Some guy called Steve is on the 'phone".

"Steve!" I said, "Really?" I picked up the 'phone and in amazement explained the situation to him. Steve said he had the day off and had his works van with him. He came round and within a few hours had re-wired the front of the car, much to my relief and nervous system.

Reflecting on what had just happened I realised that I had spoken, out of pressure, the words, "All I needed was for the car to catch fire", and it did. Also, in pressure I spoke out, "if only Steve was here", and within a short space of time Steve was there! Steve had never rung my home and has never to this day rung my home again. A supernatural intervention in a desperate situation.

The Lord reminded me to watch what I speak, as words carry invisible power to bring life and death.

> *"Death and life are in the power of the tongue".*
> (Proverbs 18:21 NKJV)

There are so many scriptures on the use of our words: Matthew 12:37, Proverbs 12:13, Proverbs 13:3, Proverbs 6:2 (NKJV):

> *"You are snared by the words of your mouth; You are taken by the words of your mouth".*

I know people who have said, "This will be the death of me" or "over my dead body". They are no longer with us. One person in Romania said, "over my dead body", in a council meeting opposing Christian orphanage planning permission. He died within a month. Needless to say no one else opposed the building of the orphanage.

This experience certainly impacted me – learning how to speak. How lightly we treat God's word and principles in life. It's so easy to blame God and the Devil, yet we ignore His Word that brings freedom to us. I have the scars on my arm to this day from the burning wires.

Once again, I hadn't any books on watching our confession (that is the things we say), but I am thankful to God for His grace in revealing to me the importance of His word. It is His story, His dealing with humanity giving us principles to live by.

***

Being a mobile welder working outside had many disadvantages. The weather played an important part in my day. If it was pouring with rain it was almost impossible to work especially with all the electrical equipment I carried which was why I really appreciated a lovely sunny day, especially with a clear blue sky and not a cloud to be seen. This is how it was on a day that would open me up to an experience that was completely foreign to me at the time.

I was lying under a Renault car, welding up a floor pan. Really happy, much more conscious that God was still with me, especially after His grace helping me out in my business. I was singing the old chorus, "Majesty, worship His majesty".

While I was singing under the car I noticed these legs standing by the car and I said, "Can I help you?"

He replied, "Are you a Christian?"

I said, "What made you ask?"

"I thought so. I know that song you were singing. Would you like a coffee with me after you have finished your work?"

Strange, I thought. Is this a divine appointment? So I accepted his invitation. He seemed to have such a presence about him.

I had a coffee in the house he was staying in. He introduced himself. He explained he was visiting England from Cyprus and was staying with friends. He was very well-spoken. He knew a lot about the bible, being a Greek Cypriot. He could go into the original language and explain the meaning. His name when translated into English meant Salvation. I was so sure this was a God appointment. He always spoke from his spirit and not with superficial talk. Everything we spoke about seemed to have depth to it. We shared and we both felt it would be good to meet again.

The relationship grew as we met regularly. I introduced him to a number of friends who were interested in developing more bible knowledge. We hired a small hall so we could have regular Sunday services. He invited people he knew. This went on for about a year. My wife's discernment was very different from mine at the time. Daph wasn't very happy about it. I did notice my spirit was coming into some sort of bondage, so I started to seek the Lord about it. I always carried a bible with me at work to meditate. In my lunch break I would read it and the words "Angel of Light" just seemed to stand out on the page. Then I would read about a wolf in sheep's clothing. This happened three times. I couldn't believe it. I kept thinking it was me. I wasn't right. He was such a good person. He would watch every word that came out of his mouth. He was so disciplined. You couldn't point to any sin in his life.

Up to this point in time I had always been in very good health. I never had time off work, but I not only felt my spirit coming into bondage, I knew I wasn't so free on the inside of me. Then the day came when I found myself too weak to work and felt really ill. I didn't even want to get out of bed. My wife, who is a palliative care nurse, kept insisting I go to the doctors. I just wouldn't go. I would try and fight it off, but nothing was working. All my prayers and my confession didn't seem to shift any of this. I could feel I was actually dying. Life was being drained from me. I sat up in bed feeling so much worse. I lifted my arms and it was like my life was flowing out, down my arms, out of my fingers, and I couldn't do anything about it. The pressure increased to go to the doctors as I was becoming pale and looked a lot like death. My wife said, "There are patients in the hospice looking better than you".

"That's not really helping me darling. All I can say is I feel I have been bitten by the serpent".

Then I cried out to God as I became weaker and weaker. I said, "Please Lord, speak to me, and don't make it hard to know if it is you. I don't want to go through an elimination process. Is this the Devil, or is this me, or you God?"

In God's mercy and grace, a blackboard appeared in my mind and I saw writing with a scripture and verse. I asked my wife Daph, "Please pass me my bible". Well, I found the scripture and verse. It said "the serpent has bitten you". I knew then my Heavenly Father heard my cry as I had just spoken the exact words I had just read. God had intervened by His grace. I knew

189

I needed help. I rang Bill and Molly Worboys up in the east of England. They said "Come over" and they would see me.

This dear Anglican Vicar, Bill, who was very short, started singing in tongues over me, then Molly broke a soul tie to the bible teacher. Molly said, "I have never heard Bill sing in the Holy Spirit over anyone before". They both continued to minister to me and life started to increase in me, as the power of the resurrected Christ came.

It must have been about a week before I fully recovered and started to feel normal again. The problem I faced now was getting my friends and family out of this deception.

This was made easy for me when other friends of the bible teacher invited a number of his friends to join us for a Sunday morning service.

I noticed when each of his friends all prayed, they had a particular mannerism. They would all make the sound of a tut in their prayers, the same as his local friends. I knew this was wrong, as God created us to be individuals. We shouldn't be like anyone else. We are part of Christ's body held together by love and peace, not by conformity, only by uniformity (Ephesians 4:3, Colossians 3:14). We are all unique, the eye is very different from the foot etc.

I found the words from another minister who had watched over me, Rev John Barr, came to me, found in 1 John 4:1 – **test the spirit. It doesn't say test the doctrine.** This is so true, we can have the right doctrine but the spirit we operate in can be wrong.

I have been in meetings since when power was manifested in the meeting with so many people laying on the floor in what is often called 'slain in the Spirit', and I and others had to walk out. I was feeling a heavy object like a blacksmith's anvil pushing down on me giving me a headache. POWER WITHOUT PRESENCE IS DANGEROUS.

Other times it is obvious to see when someone is speaking and a spirit of bitterness or resentment is released. You can sense a cutting edge to their voice when a person's spirit is quite hard. There is little softness in these voices. Usually, there would be a deep pain underneath their exterior, or other times which is probably the most common today, when a believer begins to feel a bit crushed or controlled and a false guilt comes upon them mainly because the person doesn't comply with the rest of the congregation. I have friends who have given large sums of money. Quite often this would be the spirit of witchcraft operating. In Galatians 3:1 (NKJV) it says, "Who has bewitched you?" Paul was speaking to believers at the church in Galatia. It translates, who has put you under a spell? It's a form of mind control to bring you to conform, and doesn't respect the individuality and uniqueness of each member of the body of Christ. One of the tests I do to detect this is, do I fear the person? Do I fear giving my view? Of course, you could fear man anyway, but it's strange, isn't it, that some parents can even fear their children because of the control that is being manifested? This is still a spirit of witchcraft.

God will never control us as He has given us free will. Whenever we meet control, we meet Satan's kingdom. Our Lord respects our free will. Unfortunately, what can happen is that the people or person can become spiritually abused. They start to lose their voice as no value is in placed on them or their opinion, and if it goes on, ones identity can actually be spiritually raped. From this there comes a sense of being worthless. Trust becomes a real issue to them.

Reflecting now on my experience, I didn't realise the power of the soul. I was never brought up to distinguish between soul and spirit. Now this experience forced me to examine what the scripture teaches. The most obvious is found in Hebrews 4:12 (NKJV):

"For the word of God is living and powerful, and sharper than any two-edged sword, piercing even to the division of soul and spirit".

Also 1 Thessalonians 5:23 (NKJV):

"Now may the God of peace Himself sanctify you completely; and may your whole spirit, soul, and body be preserved blameless at the coming of our Lord Jesus Christ".

In Luke 1:46-47 (NKJV):

"And Mary said my soul magnifies the Lord, And my spirit has rejoiced in God my Saviour".

Our soul is the vehicle we use to relate to each other which consists of our mind, will and emotions. But our spirit relates to God, who is Spirit, which is why God seeks those to worship Him. The bible states in John 4:23 (NKJV) *"when the true worshipers will worship the Father in spirit and truth"*, not in the soul. It is a spirit to Spirit union. Our soul needs to be stirred up at times, like David used to say in the Psalms (103:1 NIV) *"Praise the Lord, my soul"*, but it's like priming a pump. The union takes place when our spirit is activated to meet with a Holy God which is why when one is suffering from a guilty conscience because of unconfessed sin one finds it's difficult to approach the Throne of Grace. It needs to be in truth as well (Hebrews 10:22).

Looking back I need to understand the spiritual realities taking place:

1. I cannot be led by circumstances just because all seems right on the surface and appears biblical.

2. It's possible for a Christian to have a mixture of spirits within them, enough to affect not only ones mind and body, but one's life.

3. To trust God always, not man, but to listen to the Spirit of God within (Jeremiah 17:5).

4. God will hear us if we are desperate; we are never far from His presence.

5. It is important to be able to test the spirit, rather than the doctrine.

6. Check oneself, that we are walking in the light with a good conscience.

7. Ungodly relationships that join us by agreement on the inside of us can bring bondage and devastation which needs breaking in the name of Jesus. This is often referred to as a soul tie.

8. I examined the power of a soul that is tied to another. I could now understand how the bible said that when people have sex the two become one (1 Corinthians 6:16). There is a joining of their souls. For me this

experience I had was just a friendship, and one that nearly killed me. When you are in a place of vulnerability the enemy takes no prisoners.

Looking into the bible we can see the power of change being illustrated through the life of David. In 1 Samuel 18:1-3 (NKJV) *"the soul of Jonathan was knit to the soul of David, and Jonathan loved him as his own soul"*. David was a young man with a heart after God. He was anointed to be king of Israel. But in the following chapter we read that Jonathan's father Saul wanted to kill David. David now turns to his soul mate for help; before he would have turned to the Lord. His spirit was under the power of Jonathan's soul which was very strong. David's soul was now in conflict and confusion, since the join with Jonathan. He was now a man drawing on the soulish resources of Jonathan. His life was going downhill. He slept in caves and dressed in rags, constantly running for his life. He ended up at Gath impersonating a mad man by pretending to be insane, scribbling crazily on the gates, and letting saliva run down his beard before the King (1 Samuel 21:13).

This was the man after God's own heart – the future King of Israel – who had killed lions and bears and had slain not just thousands, but tens of thousands, reduced to this. He was impersonating being insane. What a sad picture of one anointed by God. But if we look at Jonathan's soul, he was like his father, double-minded, confused and rebellious as we see in 1 Samuel 14:29. He criticized his father, rebelled against his command, and encouraged the men saying they would be better off if they rebelled too.

A relationship can hinder our discernment. I know when we have unmet needs and hurts and unresolved issues we are open to trust man before God. I had felt that I was dying. This really is no game – living in a world that is at war against us, the Kingdom of God and the Life of the Son of God. A life which is in true, born again believers.

It is important for us to have our own identity and be our own voice without the power of any ungodly soul tie influencing in us.

I was in a very large, charismatic church once. It was very obvious to me in that short while that the four leaders were being influenced by a strong leader. It wasn't long before they all started to behave in the same way. They all started growing beards and chewing gum. Often you can look across a congregation and see others that begin to look like a leader or even sound the same. I had my eyes closed once worshipping the Lord. A lady started singing a solo and I thought it was the main worship leader, so strong was this join. However, it is important to remember that **deceived people don't know they are deceived.**

I certainly hadn't known I was, but I could no longer bury my head in the sand and wait for everything to get better. I had to be honest, although at the time didn't fully understand what was happening to me, but I do know God intervened and spoke to me in my desperation, and I needed Bill and Molly from the outside to confirm what God was saying. At times we are so involved in our own world we can't see the wood for the trees. We need another perspective.

I have lost count of the hundreds of people I've met who have had the bondage broken and have come into a glorious freedom. I just love the body of Christ, with all the members being so diverse, so free to express their uniqueness. Each one of us has a unique way to bring the life and love of God to a fallen world. It is no wonder secular counselling doesn't change the spiritual realities that play out in our lives. It's our Lord Jesus who knows better than anyone else. He has the answers.

Prayer

Dear Heavenly Father,

As I come to you in the name of Jesus Christ, I now break every ungodly soul tie affecting my body, soul and spirit, which has existed between myself and .... (name individuals), in the name of Jesus. I specifically speak to every demonic power that has taken advantage of that link and I tell you that you have no right here in the name of Jesus and you must go now. I ask you Lord now to cleanse my body, soul and spirit from any defilement from these ties.

In Jesus name,

Amen

Chapter 16

A MASSIVE EYE OPENER

I didn't think it was possible for a Christian believer to carry within themselves such a deadly power that it could suck the life out of me. I was beginning to realise outside of my Christian bubble, in this wilderness world, there was so much I didn't know.

Who is talking about these spiritual realities? How many people are ill and suffering and just go to the doctor? They just get relief, yet without any intervention from God, when the cause is spiritual? I knew I might not still have been here if God hadn't intervened.

This is something that cannot remain hidden from God's people: that we can be so affected by demonic activity that operates not only in the world's system as explained before, but through ungodly relationships that become a vehicle to destruction and confusion.

I can see why Paul, in 2 Corinthians 7:1, speaks to the Corinthian church to take responsibility and clean themselves up from their defilement. Defilement can come through past relationships and any involvement in the occult, generational sin, and all sexual sin. Some people have had sex, and because of the intensity of the join, they have thought they were in love, but in reality they have just been bonded in lust and realise it's too late once they are married. **We have learnt lust can't wait, but love can.**

Before God we stand forgiven and righteous. Before Him we stand in the righteousness of Christ and have been forgiven as we have accepted Christ as our saviour. We can never improve on the righteousness of God, but as Paul said, the consequences of our past have defiled our spirit and flesh and need to be brought to a conclusion. If we are to walk with God we need to be cleaned up. This isn't an option. **It's as if we catch the fish (people) but nobody cleans them.** It's possible to live in our own bubble, not knowing we need to be cleaned up, but wondering why we have not grown spiritually or have so many issues with our mental and physical health. Jesus died on the cross and rose from the dead so we can experience the fullness of salvation, which is for our body, soul and spirit, and present ourselves before God blameless (1 Thessalonians 5:23). **God is not trying to get us into heaven, he wants to get heaven to live in us.**

I really needed to share this with the fellowship of people we were sharing our lives with. I decided to do this on the way to the Sunday morning meeting we were having round at my mother-in-law's home. I got stuck in a queue of traffic as someone up ahead was turning right and was waiting for the oncoming traffic to stop.

I looked into my rear-view mirror and saw a car approaching me at speed, not knowing that we were in a queue of cars waiting to move. I just felt I was a sitting duck. Half a second later, I heard a loud screeching of brakes, then a massive bang as the car smashed into the back of my car, pushing me into a light coloured Jaguar in front of me.

I just couldn't believe it. There was nothing I could do. Was this coincidence or was the enemy of our souls, Satan, opposing me, trying to take me out another way? I had now begun to expose the world of darkness. I couldn't help thinking at the time – this is more serious than I first thought! So much opposition. It's unbelievable!

This became a deeper reality to me when I was part of a counselling team for the Good News Crusade led by Don Double in Malvern.

After the salvation appeal on the first evening, I would estimate about 100 people came forward to know Jesus Christ. We would then go into a marquee at the back of the main meeting venue and be paired up by the leaders. I was asked to pray with a guy in his 40's. I asked him why he had come forward. He explained he had become a Christian 3 years ago while living in Christchurch in the south of England. He said he had a problem hearing God's voice. I didn't know what to pray. As I was asking the Lord about this within my spirit I felt the Lord say 'it's a spirit of false religion'. I have learnt that God's is usually the first word that comes to you. The next one is the big doubt, so I decided to command the spirit to leave. There was such a corporate anointing present (increase of God's activity). This tall gentleman fell to the ground and was making the noise of a frog. All his neck became very red and was starting to swell up. His neck was expanding. It looked like he was going to explode as the demons were about to leave. I was so focussed and involved in this ministry I had forgotten where I was. All around me were 100 other people, praying and reading the bible and here I was with a 40-year-old lying on the floor making noises and acting like a frog. There was a tap on my shoulder as one of the leaders told me to stop praying. I couldn't believe it! But I knew **one must always submit to the authority one is under as God doesn't bless Christian rebels.** The demonic, I felt, laughed at me and went back down. I had a dressing down. I explained I am only human. I cannot do this, this is the work of the Holy Spirit. Thank God my mate the Rev John Barr, who was also on the site, saw him and the guy came into freedom.

I wondered about him being a young Christian who was honest and wanted freedom. How many church meetings had he sat in and if he continued to for many years, he would have had the same problem. Perhaps in three years' time he would have just adapted his life to live with his problems? I understood now that the word 'occult' means hidden, and it was the Power of the Kingdom of God that exposed the activity of Satan's Kingdom.

When I look at the bible I see Jesus healing the sick and performing miracles, but when Jesus exposed the kingdom of darkness, Satan's rule and authority, the opposition started to rise against him. Looking back, it was no coincidence I had a serious car accident as we were exposing the reality that Christian believers need to be cleaned up from the defilement of the past. Listening to sermons week after week but yet living with the issues from our past wasn't helping. I did this for years, living behind a mask of respectability, hiding my true identity and taking on a false identity only to fit in and not be the odd one out. Also, to be branded a trouble maker. Now I was alone with no-one to fool. I can't fool God. I had no choice but to face the realities of life. I could not hide in the busyness of life. I needed to get in touch with who I really was – my true identity.

I was so naïve in those days, not considering that the enemy of our souls, Satan, could create schemes to try and take us out. I have often read in Ephesians 6 about using armour as a means of protection, but didn't realise in Ephesians 6:11 it says *"Put on the whole armour of God, that you may be able to stand against the wiles of the devil"* (NKJV). The word 'wiles' is translated as schemes. This certainly brought awareness of the necessity to put on and live with the armour on. I can't help thinking of the opposite. "What happens, if like me, we become so complacent?" I hadn't thought it mattered. But what would you think if you were engaged in a national war without wearing any protection? What would happen to you? Would our whole being, our mind, body and soul be exposed to the devil's power and schemes? Personally, I think it's not only ignorance of God's word, but pride. "I didn't believe it was necessary". I was soon to learn as I continued my journey in the wilderness of life that I really needed to get my act together. I had sat in a Christian bubble. For all those years, I had been so busy working for God and trying to save the world. I had little discipline over my inner thoughts and lifestyle. I was now being woken up from a religious lifestyle to face these unseen, invisible realities that affect our daily lives. I can't complain because this is what I wanted, to discover truth whether I liked it or not. God's word is always right.

Without getting into too much detail, I had another four serious car accidents, with cars being written off, each increasing in intensity and damage to our finances as well. I still didn't know what to do about it, as it was never our fault. We never lost a no claims bonus.

This was to change after we had the fourth serious accident.

I was driving back from Southend one Saturday evening. We had had a lovely evening going bowling with all the family and my brothers and their families. I had just bought a brand-new Ford Sierra. It had only done 13,000 miles and was about a year old. Everything seemed really good. We had booked to go to a Christian event called Spring Harvest on the Monday. That was until I saw a brand-new yellow Rover pull into the pub forecourt in front of me and do a u-turn as he was lost. Immediately I applied the brake, yet the car went into a skid, I turned the wheel and got out of the skid in half a second and hit a Volvo head-on who was going the same speed as myself – 55 miles/hour. The impact was about 90 miles an hour. The road was a little damp and the light was just starting to fade.

I then wasn't aware of anything as I had gone unconscious. We didn't have airbags in the in car those days. I woke up to the most excruciating pain in my face and my body I had ever felt. My eye, it seemed, had dropped as my cheek had been crushed in, which is apparently like an egg and supports the eye. I looked to my left. My wife Daph was unconscious and was trapped against the dashboard as the impact caused her seat to flip up out of the floor. My daughter, somehow, had come from the backseat and was thrown between the front seats breaking the femur bone in her leg. I looked to my door and my brother Melvin was trying to open the door, but the door was jammed as the whole of the front of the car was pushed backwards. We had to have fire engines and a number of ambulances to release us. The police arrived at the scene in about ten minutes. My son Patrick had a number of large bruises like eggs around his body. All I could hear lying in the ambulance was Patrick running around shouting, "Is my dad dead?" My mother broke a few ribs and a hand. My niece Amber, who was also in the back of the car suffered some bruising.

I found out later Daph had broken her wrist. She had put it on the dashboard as she saw the oncoming car. She also cracked her ribs on both sides. A bone dislodged in the bottom of her back. Both Daph and Becky, my daughter, had whiplash.

We nearly all died at one moment in time.

Petrol was leaking from the car as another car, a Ford Capri, hit us while we were all unconscious in the middle of the road. People within the pub heard the crash and were coming out smoking. With so much petrol around it was a miracle we weren't burnt alive. My brothers had been following us in the car. One got out to stop any more cars piling into us, and then my other brother chased the guy who caused the accident as he drove away. The police prosecuted the driver of the Rover and said, after speaking to him, we couldn't have had a crash with a more evil person, as he was more concerned about a 35mm scratch on his car which my brother did when he overtook him and almost pushed him into a nearby field.

I knew I couldn't look in a mirror as I was told I wouldn't be recognisable. I didn't want to remember that picture.

What was going on? This was the fourth serious car accident. Why were we being targeted? How could this happen to us as Christian believers? Where was the protection?

This took me over a year to recover. My daughter has a 12 inch scar on her leg as she had to have a metal plate inserted. The right-hand side of my face is numb as the nerves got severed. When your body has that level of impact, the shock and trauma seems to cause every nerve and muscle to move. It felt like life was leaving me. It took about a year to start feeling normal again. When I went through that period of deception, it was about a week before my life came back. This was the same feeling of life being taken out of my body, yet this took a much longer period of time. Daph and Becky went to one hospital, and I went to St John's, another hospital. Thankfully today we have all recovered.

I had lost my first brand new car, months of work and 3 years of my time fighting for compensation. So much had happened since starting this journey of discovering answers, yet I was beating the air again. It goes to show the power of Satan's Kingdom of darkness in doing everything he can to "*steal, and to kill, and to destroy*" (John 10:10 NKJV). He had certainly achieved most of that in my life, except we were not destroyed. **We might be knocked down, but we would never be knocked out.** As greater is the Lord living in us, than anything against us. Yet I was puzzled. This was no joke. The stress and the hassle. It seemed like we lived in shock and trauma. What right had Satan got to do this to us? We had served God faithfully for years. It just wasn't right. I would not accept this... So I continued to seek God and ask yet more questions.

Then one evening the Lord spoke to me. It was such a clear voice "There is a curse from Daph's Dad". This was not the time to argue with God. I didn't know, being a Christian, that a curse could operate against me, but looking back, I felt this about generational sin. But when you have been stripped of all your props and totally committed your life to God He answers and you take note. I just knew that I knew this was the truth. Once again, certain doctrines I lived by had to be put aside. **I was following the Lord, not a doctrine**, that now I know was not necessarily wrong, but incomplete. The doctrines never had any answers. I then said to Daph, "God has shown me now there is a curse from your dad, and we need to break this in faith in the name of Jesus".

Daph was in a bit of a hurry. We now had another Sierra so Daph went to pick our daughter Becky up from a keyboard lesson on the other side of town.

Half an hour later, waiting for them to come home, I had a phone call. Could I come straight away as there has been a serious car accident? Your wife and daughter have been involved. I started to shake as the shock and disbelief hit me again. I kept saying to myself, I would break this curse tonight. This isn't real. It can't be happening.

Daph was driving towards a set of traffic lights approaching our village and someone with too much alcohol in their system decided to overtake her and hit a lamp post on Daph's left which meant Daph had nowhere to go but into his passenger door. The car behind then went into the back of Daph squashing up another Sierra. Fortunately, Daph was approaching the traffic lights and was only going about 25 mph. Five serious car accidents in a matter of a few years. That isn't normal. There is a verse in Proverbs 26:2 which states a **curse cannot land without a cause.**

We broke the power of that particular curse in the name of Jesus. This right is part of our salvation that Jesus accomplished by the finished work of the cross at Calvary, when Jesus not only took our sins and iniquities and shame and rejection, but became a curse. By his completed work we can enjoy our wonderful birth-right, our inheritance, our salvation.

Like most believers at that time, we were brought up thinking everything was automatic, that we did not have to appropriate what Jesus had done. I used to sit back on my laurels in such complacency. I didn't realise there was a battle raging against my life, my health and family, and my finances, and all life problems. I interpreted them as natural and just put up with things; praying, but not really seeing answers. Enough is enough. No wonder Paul says work out your own salvation in fear and trembling (Philippians 2:12) and Paul writes to Timothy in 2 Timothy 4:6-7 (NKJV):

> *"I have fought the good fight, I have finished the race, I have kept the faith"*.

Paul knew there was an invisible war that we live in life. He fought to the end of his life. He said the natural man will not understand the things that happen in the spirit realm because they are spiritually discerned, which I can see now. While I was full of self-confidence, full of my own ability, I didn't need to look beyond what was visible and see what was really going on, which is why I need to constantly keep full of the Holy Spirit.

We have, as Christian believers, been promised a birth-right and an inheritance, our own gold mine purchased because of the sacrificial death and completed work of Jesus Christ, the Son of the Living God. Yet in reality, our gold mine is being diluted by the activity of Satan because of the rights he has in our lives, given to him through disobedience to the voice of God.

Ignorance isn't a blessing as shown in Leviticus 5:17 and in 2 Corinthians 2:11 (NKJV):

> *"lest Satan should take advantage of us; for we are not ignorant of his devices".*

Well, I was not any more. **I will not be an echo of somebody else's interpretation of scripture.**

We know Jesus fulfilled the laws and set us free under the new covenant by His precious blood:

> *"to redeem those who were under the law, that we might receive the adoption as sons".*   (Galatians 4:5 NKJV)

> *"Do not think that I came to destroy the Law or the Prophets. I did not come to destroy but to fulfill. For assuredly, I say to you, till heaven and earth pass away, one jot or one tittle will by no means pass from the law till all is fulfilled".*
> (Matthew 5:17-18 NKJV)

However, the spiritual principle given to us through the written word still holds true in our lives today. If we want to live in blessing we are accountable to the word and voice of God, which is the primary source of blessing.

> *"Now it shall come to pass, if you diligently obey the voice of the Lord your God, to observe carefully all His commandments which I command you today, that the Lord your God will set you high above all nations of the earth.*

*And all these blessings shall come upon you and overtake
you, because you obey the voice of the Lord your God."*
(Deuteronomy 28:1-2 NKJV)

A curse is a sending mechanism and the demonic spirits bring
about the fulfilment of the curse. A curse can bring barrenness
and female problems, various sicknesses, poverty and disease,
mental and emotional breakdown, as well as breakdown of a
marriage and family breakdowns, suicide and unnatural and
untimely death. Sometimes one can be aware of continual struggles and endless frustration.

There are several sources of curses:

1. Bringing cursed objects into our home (Deuteronomy
   7:25-26, Joshua 7):

   This is the story of Achan bringing silver and gold
   garments from the enemies' camp. This caused him and
   his family to die, as well as many good men of Israel.
   This brought defeat. Today some people have jewellery,
   pictures, and ornaments from various places of worship.
   They can carry certain symbols that represent Satan's
   activity: Buddha, totem poles, children's toys that represent magic such as unicorns are very popular today.
   Dragons are also popular. Is it really right as Christian
   ambassadors of Christ in the world to display objects
   that represent Christ's adversaries?

2. Inherited curses:

> We have only to see that there is sickness, divorce, poverty, accidents and mental health issues and all curses that our ancestors have incurred by rebellion and being disobedient to God – concerns and recurring problems that praying alone has not moved.
>
> A lady was brought to us by her leaders, with an abdomen which was swollen. She was in pain no matter how much prayer and help from the doctors she received. Her condition was debilitating. After much prayer the Lord showed me the roots were inherited – roots of an inherited sin of jealousy. We broke that curse as is found in Numbers 5. This young lady made a full recovery.

3. In Genesis 12:2-3 we read a blessing or curse for those who speak for or against God's people, (Jewish people) who are God's natural people on earth. The church is God's spiritual people.

4. In Matthew 27:24-25 (NKJV): The Jewish people answered Pilate when they had Jesus Christ on trial and said "*His blood be on us and on our children*". It's like a hidden veil was placed over the eyes of the Jewish people that tries to stop them from recognising the Messiah.

Curses also operate through oaths, words spoken by those in authority. We had seen that outworking through Daph's Dad, even though Daph hadn't seen him in years.

Anywhere where you are under authority a power is released – a teacher as well as parents for example – if there is ground a curse can land on us.

We read in Genesis 31 the story of Jacob who serves Rachel's father for 7 years. As they left Rachel took some of her father's idols and Jacob didn't know. So when Laban, Rachel's father, caught up with Jacob and accused him, Jacob pronounced a curse. In Genesis 31:32 (NKJV):

"With whomever you find your gods, do not let him live".

Jacob didn't know Rachel, whom he loved, had stolen them. When she gave birth (Genesis 35) Rachel died. How sad is that? Rachel gave the legal right for a curse to land.

There are times when there has been a divorce – the husband has cursed the wife by saying "I hate your guts", hence the lady has stomach problems. Thank God that the curses with roots in our generational line can be pulled out:

"Every plant which My heavenly Father has not planted will be uprooted".   (Matthew 15:13 NKJV)

Words spoken carelessly, without premeditation, and often in anger even though not really meant, will make a mark on the recipient (Matthew 12:36-37). A lady we ministered to told us her father used to say to her as she was growing up, "you are always a misery". No matter what she did in life, she seemed to be fighting an invisible shadow of darkness. It was only when it was broken that the curse lifted off and joy came to her.

"Self-Imposed Curses" are a major block to receiving physical and mental health and healing. Words such as those below which are then received.

"You will always be in pain."
"I will have to work the rest of my life."
"Nothing ever goes right."
"I am tired of living. I am always tired."
"I might as well be dead."
"I never want twins." (Quite often one can die as a result of the curse)
"I don't want a boy." (Quite often they miscarried if they are carrying a boy)
"I hate my own body, my boobs, and everything else about me."
"It runs in the family so I guess I will be next."

The words **always** and **never** are all inclusive words.

When someone leaves an authority structure like church or family and words are pronounced by the leadership of "you will never prosper", "nobody will want you", this will act as a curse and needs to be broken in Jesus name.

Quite often when I attended church I used to say – **God is real, why can't we be real?** – and wonder why we hide our true identities and live with so much going wrong in our lives, rather than dealing with the root issues.

A lovely young couple came to see us. The pastor sent them down. They were sent prophetically from New Zealand to the UK. He was employed by the church fellowship. He lost his job as the church fellowship was going through a hard time. They both had been trying for a baby for a number of years. The pressure in the marriage started rising. They were in their early thirties, and after a number of years of trying to have a baby, went to have IVF.

The results came back which devastated her. They found it was almost impossible for her to have a child as her ovaries had deteriorated to that of a late 40-year-old. She had less that a 5% chance of conceiving. With the pressure in the marriage, living in another culture, no parents to go to, thousands of miles from her support system, she felt she would never be a mum. She went to London Bridge to commit suicide, so great was the pressure. As she was about to jump into the Thames, the Lord spoke to her one thing "WHAT ABOUT THOSE YOU LEAVE BEHIND?" That was enough to release the pressure and bring some sense of rational thinking. She saw the pastor who recommended that we spend some time with her. We spent the best part of a day ministering to her husband and this lovely young lady. It was quite a hard day. The Lord showed us a number of curses operating against them both. I had a lovely letter less than a year later to say she had a lovely baby. They moved to Europe and are really happy. They now have two children and he is working full time.

Their testimony touched so many lives, not only from New Zealand, but also in their local church, that this living Jesus, who was resurrected from the dead by the power of the Holy Spirit, is revealing himself to humanity and bringing revelation and salvation. **It just takes a small key to unlock a big door.**

Once, I was walking through a local town. As I was walking, I passed a lady and then heard this voice speaking out saying, "Hi Pat, have you got a minute? My daughter has a problem. Do you think you could help? She has a lot of pain and has bladder problems and keeps peeing a lot. She has seen the GP who referred her to the hospital, who then referred her to a specialist, yet nobody seems to have any answers. She is losing hope and getting depressed. This is now affecting the whole household as she lives with us."

While she was speaking, the Lord was downloading some biblical principles that I have already shared in this book. First, I said, "Your daughter is suffering from unconscious guilt that needs to be brought to the light and confessed specifically to the Lord. One cannot expect to receive faith and authority if you approach God with a guilty conscience."

"If I regard iniquity in my heart, The Lord will not hear".
(Psalm 66:18 NKJV)

I knew the daughter was an unmarried mum and had slept with someone and now had a baby. The next step would be to break the ungodly soul tie with the guy, as the bible teaches that they have become as one. Her daughter was still joined to the guy, even though he wasn't on the scene anymore. One still has to break this invisible join; **nothing is automatic.** He still had authority over her daughter. After her confession she would now be in a position of faith and authority.

I said to the mum, "Did the guy say anything to your daughter?" "Yes", she replied, "he talked about her having pain". I replied, "He has cursed your daughter and now she must break that curse and tell any demonic spirit to leave".

I never heard anything for about two months. Then the 'phone rang at home. It was the mother again, who explained that her daughter went to her bedroom that night and followed what I believed God was saying. The next day she found she was healed. No more pain. Everything seemed to have returned to normal. Hope had come back and that black cloud of depression had lifted off her and the family. It wasn't long before she was baptised in water and has such a desire now to learn more about the Kingdom of God and follow Jesus. The reason they hadn't let me know earlier was to make sure she was totally healed.

I was particularly blessed as she didn't need me. She just operated in what the bible teaches, that Jesus has purchased a full salvation for us, body, soul and spirit.

Prayer

Lord Jesus,

I confess you are the Son of God, that you died on the cross for my sins and rose again on the third day, you took every curse and became a curse for me. I forgive my mother and father and my ancestors for the curses placed on my life knowingly and unknowingly. I renounce them and I ask you Lord to release me from their consequences. I now break those curses and the power of them on my life in the name of Jesus. I now command every demonic spirit attached to these curses in my life to leave me now. I declare now that I am free because of Jesus death on the cross.

In the name of Jesus, Amen

Chapter 17

CLASH OF TWO KINGDOMS

It's almost impossible to believe so much could happen to us as family. Five serious car accidents in a matter of a few years, yet not losing any no claims bonuses. It's like living in a different world to when everything was safe and secure. To compensate for fellowship and biblical input for my children we would go to Christian camps each bank holiday and also summer camps which provided some sort of light relief amidst all the invisible pressure that existed in our world of experience.

I felt sorry for Daph. This living by faith with no church and no secure income constantly exposed pressures in us both – the fears and insecurities we had, as we both knew what poverty and abuse were. In this time we really abused each other, but this was our culture, this was what we knew. But now we were relying on our Heavenly Father to bring change. I felt sorry for the kids as well as it wasn't easy living in different tensions in the home. I knew this wasn't right and there were more keys to help us come into greater freedom. We had committed to this lifestyle of living in the wilderness, learning to live in the Spirit, and to listen and obey the voice of God.

I was soon to discover the reality of what the Rev John Barr and Bill and Molly were teaching me at that time in my daily world of work, as I was a mobile welding specialist.

One of the welding jobs I was asked to do a long way from our home was for a businessman.

I arrived on site to find I would be working at some riding stables. This is different, I thought. A tall, handsome, man, in his early forties came out and asked me to rebuild the step on his horse box. I always carried enough metal with me, so I knew I could make this step as good as new. During my lunch break the man, called Graham, brought me out a cup of coffee. He started opening up about his life and how he seemed to have lived from one tragedy to another. He had gone through divorce and had had so much loss in his life, and also had had a number of accidents.

Knowing now what I had gone through and what the bible teaches about curses I just said to him, "Graham, I think you are living under a curse, as you haven't had much blessing". He said, "My parents went to church but it's not for me. I don't believe all that rubbish. I am not interested mate, get on with your welding". He left. I finished the job thinking I have gone too far as he looked quite angry and fed up.

About 4 months went by. It was New Year's Eve. The 'phone

rang. It was a call from Graham. "Pat, mate. You must help me. Can you come and see me?" I said, "It's New Year's Eve!" He said, "This is urgent. I nearly died. I was driving my tractor along my driveway and the next minute all I knew was I had slipped into the ditch by the side of my driveway. The tractor turned over and I was laying in the bottom of the ditch. Thankfully, not crushed. I can't stop shaking. I can't take any more! I think there is some truth in what you said, there being a curse. It is just a miracle I didn't die. I can't live like this anymore."

I explained, "I am with the family and I will come after the celebrations in a few days' time". I had learnt I always **do what is important first, not necessarily what is urgent,** and it was more important for me to spend time with my family.

I drove over to see him. It was a very cold, dark evening. The house was beautifully decorated with a lovely York Stone fireplace, and two very large, comfortable settees. I sat and listened to his story and all that had happened. I then explained, "This Jesus who died on the cross isn't just a historical figure, but one who is alive today. His completed work of salvation involves every part of your life, not just a ticket to heaven, but that you may become whole yourself, free from curse and the dominion of sin, and you can live under God's blessing in your life. Will you surrender your life to Jesus and allow him to be at the driving seat of your heart? It will cost you everything and to be honest, what do you have to lose?" He agreed to surrender to Jesus and wave the white flag. He was really desperate. I said, "You speak to Jesus in your own way, then I will pray and break the curse you are under". He wasted no time praying. Then I just prayed as I felt led by the Holy Spirit. The next thing I knew it was like somebody had handed him a live electric cable as he was thrown across the room with his head just missing the York Stone fireplace. He lay on the carpet for a little while as if he was dead. I really wasn't sure what was going on. He eventually got up looking so red in the face with sweat dripping down his face, like he had been in a sauna. Totally surprised and in his very own words he said "I thought you said you were only going to say a little prayer". I said, "Graham, you have met this Jesus who is alive, and today you have come out from a place of darkness that held no hope, no answers, into a living relationship with Jesus Christ, the son of the Living God". I realised that God was in the room. I thought, in for a penny, in for a pound. Let's get him cleaned up a bit. "It's brilliant this new life you have, but I feel it's important now, that you confess any sin the Holy Spirit is showing you that is in your conscious mind. Don't go looking in your past. You will know as the Finger of God, which is the Holy Spirit, will show you, otherwise you will build your own prison again and get weighed down with guilt".

He started to confess his adultery, his addiction to pornography and other ungodly behaviours. We then broke him free from those ungodly soul ties and commanded those invisible forces to leave him. Then, once again he was catapulted across the room, this time just missing the other settee, and lay on the floor as if he was dead. I was thinking, this is crazy. Is this what really happens when there is a clash of two kingdoms and the power of darkness is leaving him? He eventually lifted up his head and stood looking very unsteady. "This is just a little prayer?" he said. I think I was almost in total shock. I had never seen such power demonstrated before. I said, "Jesus is here, and there has been an invasion of his presence in your heart, and as you confessed the darkness that held you prisoner has now been dispelled. The light of the presence of God which we call glory is now within you now. This was a divine appointment. A set up. You gave God permission and He loves you so much".

Just then the front door opened and in walked his wife, a very tall person who looked very confident and very much in charge. She wanted to know what was going on as her husband looked very different. I thought, this is a good time to leg it. I made my excuses and left Graham to explain all that had happened.

I drove home as if I was on cloud nine. I can't remember how I got home. The sheer sense of humility and gratefulness just swept over my soul, as I had just witnessed an invasion of God's Life coming into a human being and removing the darkness and death out of his mortal frame. This reminded me of Hainault all those years ago, at the C of E, where Trevor Deering was ministering. This Jesus is with us in our everyday life. I didn't have to work anything up and we didn't have to go through set prayers or songs. We were just ordinary people sharing life. No arguments of doctrinal difference. Just love and compassion for someone who needed Jesus. I realise that **Jesus didn't die for nice people, but real people.**

Colin Urquhart said once, "We have to be ourselves in order for Christ to set us free from ourselves that we might be like Jesus".

How true it is that Jesus died and gave everything for us sinners. What a wonderful message we have, but it's not only a message, we can carry the presence of God with us wherever we go. This is awesome. **Brokenness is a major key that enables the Lord to flow through us.** As I faced death so many times the Pat Regan opinions and self-interest, everything, had to die so the Son of God could increase His life within me. Now I can understand the scripture in 2 Corinthians 4:11-12 (NIV):

> *"For we who are alive are always being given over to death for Jesus' sake, so that his life may also be revealed in our mortal body. So then, death is at work in us, but life is at work in you".*

A number of weeks went by. Then one Tuesday, Graham rang me. He said, "Pat, something is wrong. My joy and peace seem to have evaporated. What's happened?"

I said, "Graham, where did you lose the sense of God's presence?" Normally, **when you lose something, you will find it where you lost it.**

He thought about that and said, "What comes to me was when I watched the film, 'The Chiller".

I said, "That doesn't sound good. The way forward, Graham, is to repent. To say that you will never watch a horror movie again and just confess that to God, that you opened your heart to darkness again. Then I will pray".

I was thinking, I am not going to travel 60 odd miles return journey, and I was not really expecting a lot to happen. Graham prayed to God. All I did was to break him free from the evil force in the film over the phone. With that, almost immediately, I could hear an almighty roar, as if a lion had been released. My first thought was – where is he? Is there anybody with him? Is he at home or is he at work? I then commanded the evil presence to leave him, then a stillness came. What's happening? I was thinking. A quiet voice came back on the 'phone and now he sounded a bit more normal.

First question – "Where are you, mate?"

His reply – "I am in the office on site lying on the floor in the Porto cabin".

"Is anybody with you, Graham?"

"No mate", was his reply.

I then was wiping my forehead of sweat as I breathed a sigh of relief. I was thinking, people will think we are crazy.

This did, once again, pose more questions to me. I decided to plug him into the local fellowship I knew as I really couldn't pastor him over such a distance. But I thought once again, how many people who receive Jesus Christ are sitting in church with so little glory of God manifest in their lives? That just haven't been cleaned up and are just putting up with loads of issues and are not entering into the freedom Christ died for?

I also thought, he had such a power encounter with Jesus. He knew something was wrong when he defiled his spirit and lost that sense of a Holy God, yet God hadn't left him, but there were invisible consequences to his actions. They were affecting his walk with God. Yet today, I know so many Christians who have watched the Harry Potter films, which is an introduction to witchcraft, yet outwardly look the same, not being aware that we walk with a Holy God and His temple, which is within our bodies, has been defiled by these external influences that have found a gateway into our lives either by ignorance, or false teaching, or basically our flesh as we like watching them. It's still our choice. Those experiences not only changed Graham, but myself as I examined my own walk, and how familiar, at times, I had become with the Almighty God's presence.

Normally I would have viewed these things on a surface level, but I am understanding that the natural mind, or carnal mind, as the bible describes, cannot understand this sort of power and experience as it is an enemy to God. To see the power released in the name of Jesus and then how easily ones spirit can be defiled causing such a loss of peace and joy and the sense of God's presence! I supposed it's easy to say we have a Holy God but live unholy lives.

Certainly living through brokenness gives a greater sensitivity to the voice of God and to what he is saying to us.

Thank God He can give us a gift of repentance, to bring the cleansing within our spirit man and consciousness because Jesus made it possible by shedding His blood, His life for us (Hebrews 13:12) so we can return to walking with God in the spirit. But it does show you even after one becomes a Christian, we are not immune to the activity of Satan.

If you think about it, where are these doorways that create an opening for demonic activity in our lives?

The simplest way as a foundation is to think of the word ROBE, and how each letter stands for a gateway:

R — RELATIONSHIPS

a. We have seen that a soul tie can be formed through wrong relationships or sexual encounters which fuse our souls together to create an invisible bridge in the spirit world for the demonic to cross from one person to another depending on what each person is carrying. E.g. lust, curses and even death, as well as bitterness, etc. For those who have gone through broken relationships like divorce, the pain can be almost unbearable.

In the invisible world quite often each partner cannot get the thoughts from their ex out of their head and emotions, which is why the results can only be dealt with by breaking these ties in Jesus name.

b. Where a person exercises control through manipulation or domination or even flattery they can become so overbearing that freedom is gradually taken away. This leads to abuse as it disrespects others opinions and freedom of choice. Whenever you meet this you meet Satan's Kingdom. It is witchcraft, and it is the greatest hindrance for anyone seeking to fulfil their God-given calling. If the level of control is allowed to go on and one allows this, it's possible to take on their likeness. I have seen a number of congregations where the abuse of authority takes place. Some people begin to look and sound like the other leaders or those who they are joined to in an unhealthy way.

c. When somebody has crossed the line and made an idol of the other relationship, even if it is a dog, they will eventually take on the spirit of the dog, which is why some dog owners look like their dog (Psalm 115:8). Whatever you worship you will become like – anyone or anything. God will not share the throne room of your heart.

The tie is strengthened when there is unrighteous sexual involvement with another person or animal. Not only will their appearance change but their voice will change, which is why some men or women sound like the opposite sex (homosexual). When I was in India years later, I said to my team, look at some of the young girls who worship the elephant god. They are beginning to look like the elephant as their faces had changed with the spirit of the elephant on them.

I was estimating a welding job in the local village. The front door opened and right in front of me was a 4 ft. yellow Buddha statue. A few minutes later another person came in a wheelchair to the door. Apart from the colour they looked like identical twins. I was totally amazed. It just goes to show how accurate God's word is and how practical it is.

We have already seen how generational sin can bring consequences in families with faulty genes which can lead to sickness, certain weaknesses, cancers, addictions and sexual sin, which is an inherited iniquity. Also curses. Thank God Jesus died not only for our sins but iniquities as well.

d. The whole area of unforgiveness is so important as the repercussions are a major block to healing and the freedom Christ promised us. We see in John 20:23 in the parable of the unmerciful servant that "*In anger his master handed him over to the jailers to be tortured, until he should pay back all he owed*" (Matthew 18:34 NIV). The bottom line in this passage is, if we don't forgive all those we hold unforgiveness against, including God and ourselves, God himself sends the tormentors, which might be constant pain, migraine, sleeplessness, sickness. All those things can torment us, and when you think about it, if God sent them, nobody can deliver them. A lady whom we prayed for in Malvern had very bad eyesight and her vision was deteriorating. She had been hurt by her son who was in prison at the time. As she tore up the 'IOU' and forgave him from her heart, her eyesight became clearer. Before, it was very cloudy. Tears just started to fall down her face as that weight of sin lifted and she felt the cleansing power of repentance.

O — OCCULT (which means hidden)

a. This covers so much in our society now as so many practices have been imported from other cultures. It is always so important to find the power source. Just because something works doesn't make it right. Some will work to a degree because it's possible for one to exercise faith, tapping into the invisible law of faith in the universe. In India, when a child is born with weakness or sickness they take the child to the local Hindu temple and the elders then pray to their idol and the child has a measure of recovery. They have tapped into the law of faith but the power source is demonic, and not from God, which locks them into the power of the demonic operating through the idol. God's word is the authority in our lives on how we should live. All committed acts of unrighteousness are against God, as well as ourselves.

b. Look for signs and symbols in homes which represent

the kingdom of darkness. It's a good indication there are spiritual forces at work.

c. The Practise of Yoga (which is a Hindu system of philosophy): with the exercise, mantra and breathing is basically being yoked to a Hindu god. By having an open mind and meditating, this is like an invitation for demonic spirits to affect us mentally, emotionally and physically.

d. Being hypnotised brings us under a spell and a form of mind control.

e. Reflexology: massage of specific parts of the sole of the foot that link to spiritual pathways.

f. Massage: Somebody is laying hands and their intent can be one from the influence of the demonic. There can be an impartation of an ungodly influence.

g. Acupuncture and martial arts, visiting defiled ground like going into a temple where false gods are worshipped, or visiting Stonehenge or witchcraft sites. All these involvements will open you up to demonic influences and these will defile your spirit.

h. Horoscopes, rock music – we know that music can open up a person's soul. Many Christians who haven't had the past cleaned up and brought to a conclusion can release unseen powers as they worship, especially when the emotions take over and one is led more by feelings than the Spirit.

i. Spiritualism: Leviticus 19:31 (NIV) *"Do not turn to mediums or seek out spiritists, for you will be defiled by them. I am the Lord your God"* and Deuteronomy 18:10-12 (NIV) *"Let no one be found among you who sacrifices their son or daughter in the fire, who practices divination or sorcery, interprets omens, engages in witchcraft, or casts spells, or who is a medium or spiritist or who consults the dead. Anyone who does these things is detestable to the Lord; because of these same detestable practices the Lord your God will drive out those nations before you"*. Today this could be levitation, gypsy curses, Ouija board and tarot cards. This also includes astrology, using a pendulum to predict the sex of the baby, hypnosis, superstition, faith healers, drugs and vampires. There is so much in the Word of God warning us of the dangers. It's not my intention to give you list after list, but only to draw your attention to what the bible teaches and the consequences that can be devastating for generations to come (Exodus 20).

We had a young man who came to see us. His friends sent me an email sharing their concerns as he was really depressed and had been on suicide watch. He came from a very large church in London.

As we spoke to him, it turned out that he had visited spiritualist churches for some guidance. He told me that his mother was a pagan worshipper in Siberia and was also involved in shapeshifting. I think our western mind would find that hard to believe! We tend to think of these things happening only in films, like when a human being changes shape into a werewolf. He was desperate. For freedom, he renounced his sins and ancestral sins. The ungodly ties were broken and repented of – he wouldn't participate in spiritualism again. The power of Jesus came, and the kingdom of darkness gave way to the kingdom of light. Depression, hopelessness, despair, suicidal thoughts and death were defeated by the power of the blood of Jesus. He emailed me some months later regarding his newfound freedom.

Another lady we saw once was playing the Ouija board at university. After it had answered her question correctly, the very large coffee table that would take at least 4 very strong men to lift, started to rise and it pinned her against the wall of her dormitory. That freaked her out.

j. False religion and the cults. Coming home from a deliverance meeting in London, I was in my brother's car with 2 of his friends. We all got invited in for coffee. While in conversation, I saw a Mormon spirit on one of the ladies. Before we left I asked if I could pray for her. She agreed. As we prayed the power of God came on her as I commanded this spirit of Mormon to leave in Jesus name. Her face started to contort and was moving all over the place. The spirit left. Speaking to her afterwards she said she had no control over her face moving and how weird it felt. It also came to light that the gateway was in the family as her sister in law belonged to the

Mormon church in Salt Lake City. We didn't know that but her appearance had taken the likeness of a Mormon. No one is meant to be a clone of someone or something. When a likeness comes into a group individuality starts to disappear.

B — BIRTH

Birth is a place of vulnerability. In some cases the womb can turn into a tomb, especially if there has been miscarriage or abortion which will bring the spirit of death. A child can be born with a lust problem if the conception is in lust, not love.

A child's sexual orientation can be altered if an occult practise of swinging a pendulum over the mother while pregnant occurs.

E — EVENTS

a. Laying on of hands: I knew a preacher while in a summer camp. I had a bad vibe about him, even though he had a reputation of seeing people healed. He had a gift of miracles operating. A young girl received prayer from him and couldn't stop screaming. They brought the child out of the meeting. We broke whatever had been imparted by the preacher and she calmed down and came into peace. Since then, years later, I learnt he was in deception and had to leave the ministry.

b. Where there have been accidents or abuse, or any shock and trauma, the person has been taken off guard and protection is lowered and fear infirmities can take advantage of the situation.

After our 4th serious car accident where we nearly all died as a family, Becky, my daughter who was only 9 at the time, was filled with so much shock and trauma. It resulted in her almost being paralysed with fear every time we got in the car. We drove to another church which we were attending. It was about 25 miles away. Becky would sit grasping hold of her car seat so tense she almost turned herself white. We couldn't go over 30 mph.

While in the meeting the Spirit of God was moving. Becky received prayer and the spirit of fear left. When we were travelling home Becky called to me, "Dad, can't you go any faster?" This was a miracle. Before we had screams every time we got in the car. Now she wanted to go faster.

Praise God. This Jesus is alive and loves us so much. He has provided salvation and freedom at His own expense. We just need to appropriate it.

When we had the 5th accident, Becky now knew how to protect herself as she said, "Dad, that old Devil tried to give me back that spirit of fear and I told him that I am a winner!" It's one thing getting delivered, but it's another thing to walk it out as it requires discipline in our mind and behaviour.

***

This is a basic foundation on the gateways Satan tried to use to enter our lives – some principles I learnt over the years. **God doesn't deliver us from our friends – if we don't see sin as an enemy we don't get delivered.** It's desperate people who get delivered and at times we have to lose our dignity to get our deliverance. We can't be in control if we are to surrender to the Lordship of Jesus.

I heard Jackie Pullinger, who as a young girl of 22 worked with the triad gangs and prostitutes in the Wall City which was just outside Hong Kong. It was called the square mile of sin. She said, "Why do you think the rats are in the Walled City? It's because garbage is there. Remove the garbage and the rats (demons) will go. If we love our sin more than Jesus we won't get delivered".

I deliberately haven't over emphasised this topic today as there are so many books which will explain the whole revelation on how the demonic effects our lives on a daily basis.

There is too much fascination today, along with an unhealthy curiosity, which has created minds to be impressed with power demonstrated that is out of the ordinary. I can't stress enough... this is no game. We are living in a world of war against our health, our family, our finances and relationships. As you have read up to now, I have faced death on a number of occasions. It is so important to live focussed on the Lord, with a working knowledge of the spiritual realities and laws at work in our lives. **The Word of God is always our plumb line** to live by. Unfortunately for me, due to my ignorance, I have had to learn that lesson the hard way, with no books and only godly people watching over me. The Word of God is also a weapon Jesus used when he defeated Satan in the wilderness. It is interesting to know that all spiritual weapons are launched through the mouth.

Prayer

Dear Heavenly Father,

In the name of Jesus I renounce all involvement in the occult. I renounce .... (Specific involvement eg practising yoga, visiting spiritualists etc). I honour my father and mother and forgive them for any sins. I renounce the sins of my ancestors – fear, unbelief, doubt, blockages of mind, wrong doctrine (anything the Lord shows you). I believe it is through the blood of Jesus Christ that I have now been redeemed. I ask you Lord to cleanse my spirit from any defilement, and also to cleanse my conscious and sub-conscious and unconscious mind by your blood, Lord Jesus. I command any demonic intruder to leave. I ask you now to baptise me with the Holy Spirit and your fire Lord.

Thank you, in Jesus name,

Amen

Chapter 18

FACING UP TO THE TWO GIANTS

This season of seeing the incredible power of the Holy Spirit being manifest was thrilling to say the least. It seemed wherever we went, we kept walking into what appeared to be coincidences, or shall I say divine appointments.

One that does stand out was when I was asked to estimate a job in a small village, just outside the city. I approached the long driveway, which to me looked like a mini-mansion. There was so much land and various outhouses.

I knocked on the front door and as it opened there stood an architect I knew from working on the building sites. He must have been in his early sixties. Before I could put a zip over my mouth the words just came out, "You look terrible".

He replied, "Yes Pat, I have been suffering depression". His countenance was so dark. He was walking as if he had a hump on his back. He could hardly speak, he was so low.

He showed me to the kitchen. His wife then showed me some office furniture that needed welding. She explained he hadn't been out of the house for months. Nothing seemed to have shifted his depression. She was fairly bright but you could see she was struggling as it's not always easy living with someone who is depressed.

I explained it really wasn't practical to weld this office equipment. I then said to them both, that I knew someone who could help them and his name is Jesus. With that he seemed very angry and asked me to leave. We then made our way over to the back door. I said, "Do you mind if I just say a little prayer?" So as we prayed a very general prayer the power of God just came upon him and the next thing I knew he was on the floor. I thought, I hope he hasn't broken anything, as he was frail. You don't expect a 60-year-old to be on the floor, because of a divine intervention. I said, "Mate, I don't believe it's right for me to go, God is in the house and He wants to bring you into freedom". Looking still quite dazed, off we went to this very large kitchen, with so much glass, which opened up to such beautiful gardens.

We then prayed and I broke a generational curse off him and commanded this spirit of darkness to leave. With that CRASH, he was on the floor again and was so still. I didn't have the heart to move him. I thought, just let God continue to do what He knows best. I went around the island of cupboards and sat at a table overlooking this beautiful view, and engaged in conversation with his wife over a cup of tea. That solves everything, doesn't it? Her husband was still out for the count. I was beginning to see the funny side of this. We were talking normally with her husband out of sight behind the island on the kitchen floor. I was smiling on the inside thinking God, you are so unpredictable, as this man's face slowly appeared above the worktop, but there was a difference. The darkness that was over his face had left him. He looked so light and was smiling. Well, his wife nearly choked on her biscuits.

"I don't believe it! He hasn't smiled in months".

He then said, "I think I need some fresh air. I'll take the dog out for a walk". His wife explained he had been so bad he wouldn't even go out in the garden.

I was almost hysterical with joy on the inside of me. This is funnier than "You Have Been Framed" on the TV. It's a good job I don't have a film camera following me. People will think I am crazy. I really was just overwhelmed to see Jesus come to his people.

I returned to the house six months later to see how he was getting on. This time he came to the door standing upright, as if all those burdens he had been carrying that caused him to be bent over, had gone. Also, his countenance was glowing. "Hi Pat, great to see you again".

I said, "How are things?"

"Well", he said, "I took the wife abroad for a skiing holiday in June. We had a great time".

I came away thinking, if only we, as God's people, spent less time over who is right or wrong and just become a little more simple, like a child, perhaps we could see the Kingdom of God demonstrated.

"unless you change and become like little children, you will never enter the kingdom of heaven". (Matthew 18:3 NIV)

It seems to me that the politically correct spirit has married the religious spirit and has been robbing God's people. I never knew there was any power on the earth that would nullify God's word until I read:

"Thus you nullify the word of God by your tradition that you have handed down. And you do many things like that".
(Mark 7: 13 NIV)

Jesus is a living person and the DNA handed down isn't working in systems that seem to have replaced relationship with Jesus.

Watching God show up in people's lives was having a profound effect on me. I started to examine my own life and the tension that existed between Daph and myself. Although we loved each other we were still hurting each other. The loneliness of this walk with the Lord seemed to be taking its toll. It seemed when I shared these stories of freedom that Christians either didn't believe, or really weren't interested. It was getting to me. I was becoming frustrated with myself. I still hadn't any answer to my own mental condition where I couldn't seem to retain things, and also my mind, at times, kept going blank, and I kept getting my words back to front. I also was feeling the hardship of working by myself, not having a companion that understands, and all the weathers lying under cars, welding floors and chassis. The rain always stopped me. It was tough in wintertime welding outside. My dad had passed away. Pastor

Anthony was so much of a father to me, I realised for the first time in my life. I was looking at my circumstances and how little I had changed. I thought, I am seeing so many people blessed, yet I am struggling emotionally and mentally and everybody else is blessed. I felt I had slipped down a very large pit and no matter how hard I tried to climb out of it, I just couldn't find a way. I would pray, then feel guilty because I couldn't muster any faith. I would try and explain it away. Then I thought time would change things. But as each day went past the pit became darker as I seemed to be slipping downwards. I am not the sort to go to the doctors. I needed to prove God. I wouldn't take tablets. I knew God had the answer. He is the Creator and knows me. It's as if I had a watch and it needed repairing but there was no use giving it to me because I am a welder. Logic says, take it to the watchmaker to fix it. I started to feel a bit scared as I wasn't able to control this darkness I was in. I am a positive person, yet despite all my positivity, nothing changed.

I started to cry out to God. I felt I was going past the point of no return. I remember looking up from the deep pit and I saw a little round hole with some light at the top. I cried out from the depths of my spirit, "Please God. Help me like King David in Psalm 142:1". He poured out his heart to the Lord. This cry was so deep in the midst of my struggle, trying to find something on the sides of the pit for me to hold on to so I could start to go up. Everything was getting blacker. I was losing my vision, hopelessness seemed inevitable. The little hole of light was almost gone. I was almost at the point of giving up.

Then a divine intervention took place in the middle of my darkness in this black hole. An arm reached down to me and caught my hand. As I lifted my hand up, I was pulled out of this totally hopeless feeling which had filled me with despair. I came to the top. Light had, at this stage, become a stranger to me. As I embraced the love of my Heavenly Father whom I thought had forgotten and abandoned me, the cleansing power of God flooded my being as the grip of Hell left me.

That experience taught **me never to look on the inside of me, but to keep my inner focus on the Lord.** SELF PITY was the deepest and most devastating pit I have ever been in because I was utterly helpless. I vowed never to do that again, no matter how bad things got in my life. I learnt despite all the miracles I had seen, it's God's grace that comes to us. I know I can do nothing without Him. It's one thing saying it, but it's knowing in within your spirit. There are disciplines I must keep to keep me from allowing Satan to work in my life. It's so important today, with so much pressure that exists in modern life, to keep your spirit man light and buoyant. This is the normal position of your spirit. If it isn't, an evil spirit can be touching you. What a lesson to learn! Despite all the negativity I was thinking, my past and my weakness, I am accepted as I am, with my issues, and only Jesus can change me (Ephesians 1:6). Thank God. My identity isn't looking within myself or how other people see me, but I look to the Lord. This is my identity.

> *"But we all, with unveiled face, beholding as in a mirror the glory of the Lord, are being transformed into the same image from glory to glory, just as by the Spirit of the Lord".*
> (2 Corinthians 3:18 NKJV)

> *"They looked to Him and were radiant, And their faces were not ashamed".*
> (Psalm 34:5 NKJV)

I can't tell you how relieved I was coming out of that darkness. I realised how insensitive I had become to other people as I was so focussed on my own life. I think today we rush to get relief so quickly. If God doesn't come good after a few prayers we just give in.

Yet in Matthew 11:12 (NKJV):

> *"And from the days of John the Baptist until now the kingdom of heaven suffers violence, and the violent take it by force".*

Passivity is, I realise, the worst position of your spirit.

This experience was my own making. I had no idea that I had taken my inner focus off the Lord Jesus, and this would open me to the giant of SELF PITY. My own flesh gave the right for this giant to take advantage of me.

Second Giant

The next giant I was to face was one I had no idea about. I was deceived and I didn't know it. I have always said **deceived people don't know they are deceived**, which is why as true Christian believers we belong to the Body of Christ and know how important it is to listen to other members, and if we don't God can even use your boss, your neighbour or even the bus driver to reach you. God even used an ass to speak to Balaam the prophet who was to speak to Israel.

The pressure started to increase in the home as my work suddenly dried up. I had no phone calls. I had adverts in the local paper and the yellow pages, yet no work. No income, yet bills to pay.

Whenever I didn't have any work I used to go to the local park and walk around it and seek the face of God. It takes 2-3 hours. It has woods and just fields of grass. I couldn't bear being at home as the tension in Daph rose and those familiar words were released – "Why don't you get a proper job like other men?" It was hard to take as I knew God had told me to work for him.

My first port of call in my thinking was to start spiritual warfare against the enemy of my life (Satan) and bind his power, to be positive and start declaring God's word. I did this every day of the week for a week. The park was so big that nobody was ever around. I was in warfare mode. Yet nothing had changed.

I had always felt the welding business was like a barometer if something was wrong. God who controls the wind and the weather and rules as he is enthroned, and has never been dethroned because He is Sovereign, would show me. I just had to keep faithful and keep seeking Him. Yet I couldn't find Him. Yet another inspiration seemed to hit me – "I know my lovely wife Daph. He is exposing all her insecurities and fears", so I took great comfort with what appeared to be an important revelation.

I would continue to walk around the park, this time with an element of thanksgiving that at last I can endure this pressure from within the home. It wasn't long before the cold light of reality was hitting me. I lasted another week yet still nothing had changed. On the inside, I could feel the weight of responsibility – being a dad of 2 children and a husband that wasn't able to provide for my family. The desperation was causing a lot of my own fears and anxieties to rise. Once again Monday arrived. I was up the park again. I was now contemplating whether I should claim benefits as we were going to get into trouble financially. There was no light at the end of the tunnel. Nothing but blackness and pressure. I knew my previous experience of looking within me. I just couldn't do it. I had to keep focussed on the Lord despite the pressure of unanswered prayer. I just kept pushing through the negativity and darkness and kept in faith.

I was now more desperate. I was even up the park twice a day. By the end of another week listening to God's silence I kept in mind that **everything God does, works,** so it's no use just flogging a dead horse. I need to listen more.

It was the middle of June. I didn't know how to pray but was still living with the attitude of seeking Gods face, not just to give me more work to rescue me, but what was He saying to me? The darkness started to increase around me as the sun had gone down. No other cars were in the car park. I sat: a very lonely figure. The gates of the park were to close within the hour. All I could hear was the wind rustling the leaves of the trees. The birds were silenced. I had nowhere to go. I knew God had the answer but He appeared silent. I must have done something wrong. I was still believing... just! I decided to put a cassette tape on then as I didn't have any teaching tapes on CD at the time. It was called the Third Temptation by Derek Prince. I had heard the teaching and it was only the summing up I hadn't to listened to. As I listened to that teaching on pride, and how it was the very nature of Satan, that this would be used as a lever to deception and how Satan had become independent, the Holy Spirit just overwhelmed me, as I became so convicted.

The Lord spoke to me. The problem wasn't the enemy (Satan), nor was it my wife Daph. I was the problem. Tears welled up within me and I saw this ugly thing in the spirit called Pride. It was touching my spirit despite being a servant of the body of Christ and also to the world as I was looking after all their cars and machinery. I knew the theology about pride, that one must always start at the bottom to serve, and not self-promote, as Jesus illustrated about being a servant (Luke 22:27). The servant knows the masters will. It's not just about the works but the state of heart. All my works and information and doctrine hadn't changed me, but now this was a revelation. I couldn't stop weeping tears of repentance. I almost got locked in the car park overnight as it was now black everywhere. I felt so humbled and weak and awestruck that the God I knew, knows everything about me, yet still hadn't rejected me. He knew my weakness and failure and success yet still called me before time had started on earth, at the same time knowing I was a son of God and He is my Heavenly Father. He promised when I entered the wilderness He would correct me.

I said, "Father, why haven't you shown me before the work ended?"

He said, "Son, I had to reposition you to hear because you couldn't hear me".

The sin that is Satan's nature almost made me feel sick, as the last thing I ever wanted to have anything that identified me with Satan.

The repentance became so deep within me. It was something I just had to get over. To know I had been deceived all these years, despite the Pastor telling me. I was blinded. I knew what God had shown Job about Leviathan in Job 42:34 (NKJV): "*It looks down on all that are haughty; it is king over all that are proud"*.

I didn't want the king of pride ruling over me. I didn't want to be under his power any longer, but thank God for His grace to give me the gift of repentance and His grace to empower me to live free from this giant in my life that had remained hidden to me.

I shared with Daph my experience with the dealings of God in my life and after asking for forgiveness for judging her, I literally couldn't stop the work coming in. It felt as if there was an Almighty dam and now the dam was opened up, the river of God's goodness just flowed and flowed. It seemed everybody wanted me to do their welding jobs and so many were prepared to wait. I can't thank God enough. I am so glad He is so much bigger than our thoughts and ideas and has His ways of doing things. Because He is the Almighty God. OUR FATHER. Who is in heaven.

It is so easy to limit God with our impatience and ways.

It goes to show one can't really repent until God convicts us of our sin.

The following is just some of the ways we can identify the workings of pride:

1. Difficulty in recognising one is wrong and saying sorry.

2. Pride finds it difficult to ask for help and receive help.

3. Pride can manifest as hardness – like a wall around emotions.

4. Pride promotes self and loves position.

5. Pride is always in the right.

6. Pride thinks it is entitled to more than others.

7. Pride thinks of himself more highly than others just as we see in Luke 18:9-14 when the Pharisees look down on the sinner and think – I am glad I am not like him.

8. Whenever, as an individual or a church fellowship, they think they are better than the others. Then pride has touched their heart.

9. Pride masks the true condition of the heart.

10. Pride causes one to view themselves as a victim.

11. Pride provokes the wrath of God.

12. Pride is the lever to deception. God said in His word, He will resist the proud and give grace to the humble.

13. Pride thinks it knows more than others.

14. Pride hardens the heart and keeps you from dealing with the truth (Hebrews 3:13).

15. Humility and brokenness are 2 major keys to draw near to God and release the fragrance of His presence.

Fasting is what God sees as an act of humility as we are afflicting our souls as the word translated is "to humble". In Psalm 35:13 (NIV) David wrote, "*Yet when they were ill, I put on sackcloth and humbled myself with fasting*" and in Isaiah 58 which is known as the great fasting chapter verses 3-5 describe the kind of fast not acceptable to God. Then from verses 6-12 describes the fast that is pleasing to God. In Matthew 6:16 (NIV) Jesus said to the disciples "*When you fast*" and explains how to go about it. Fasting isn't an option. It is part of our walk with God.

Fasting brings our body and soul under subjection to the Spirit of God. Paul in 1 Corinthians 9:27 highlights the position of our body and soul. When our body cries out for food our spirit man says no, you can't have it. Fasting not only brings one into a place of humility as we cannot act as Satan does, independently from God, but we come in faith recognising God sees we are in an attitude of humility. Fasting isn't going on a hunger strike and coming to God demanding he answer our prayers, but positions us to listen to Him as He does know already what we need.

Fasting certainly tunes one's spirit up. Like a radio, you have to tune in to hear the station of your choice.

To be honest, I never felt the need to fast while I was asking God to bless all that I did. But this wilderness experience of having to depend on God for everything in life caused me to fast to seek His face and to listen to His voice. **No longer did I want a religion with me in charge**. I want to follow Jesus and fasting is God's way of recognising our humility. It's advisable to obey God. I know Satan got kicked out of heaven because pride was found in his heart. I know for sure God is not having pride back, and we, the Body of Christ, are called the Bride and need to prepare for when we see Him face to face.

> *"Let us rejoice and be glad*
> *and give him glory!*
> *For the wedding of the Lamb has come,*
> *and his bride has made herself ready".*
>
> (Revelation 19:7 NIV)

One thing that struck me from that verse is that the bride got herself ready. **There is no culture in the world where the bridegroom gets the bride ready.** It is our own personal responsibility to be prepared to meet the Lord face to face. I have always felt living on earth we should be preparing ourselves for eternity as the bride. I know there are some wonderful pictures of this as Esther in the Old Testament prepares to marry the King.

The Fear of God makes me aware of two things in life that are imposters – success and failure. It's important not to let either touch your spirit as both have the potential to destroy you. Jesus did so many miracles and when the disciples came back so full of their success Jesus warned them:

> *" "Then the seventy returned with joy, saying, "Lord, even the demons are subject to us in Your name."*
>
> *And He said to them, "I saw Satan fall like lightning from heaven. Behold, I give you the authority to trample on serpents and scorpions, and over all the power of the enemy, and nothing shall by any means hurt you. Nevertheless do not rejoice in this, that the spirits are subject to you, but rather rejoice because your names are written in heaven." "*
>
> (Luke 10:17-20 NKJV)

We have got to be more than the Pharisees who read the scriptures, prayed and fasted and gave their tithes to the Lord. I was convicted. This is what I was like. Alright on the outside but pride had deceived me. This brokenness opened me up to humility. I thank God He treats us all as his children, even when we are blind. He leads us into all truth and still does not reject us.

Chapter 19

FATHERS HIDDEN MANNA

The provision of God for our family was amazing. I particularly noticed this as we entered the winter season. That year we had so much snow. We found it difficult to drive out of our private road where we lived. Let alone go out and start welding other people's vehicles and machinery. The snow was now becoming heavier by the day. As soon as I swept the path by the side of our house it seemed to have another 4 inches! The main road was becoming blocked and the weather forecast was predicting a long spell of snow.

I turned to Daph and said, "Well, love. There is nothing I can do about this. I really can't see me working in this". I had almost settled the situation within me. That this is it. I really need to keep my head down now. Life could get difficult if I was in the house all day.

Then out of the blue, I had a phone call. Would I be interested in welding some scaffold pipes in a garden nursery, about half an hour's journey from home, as each joint had cracked and was leaking water? Well. Just praise God. I didn't even have to ask Him this time or go into warfare. It's like, before you call I will answer. I took the job on. The main roads by now were just about drivable and I welded over 1000 joints. It took just over a month to complete. All the time the snow was on the ground. For me, I just felt provided for. I was paid really well and they became a good customer for many years. They were pleased with my work.

Experiences like this, when everything looks so impossible in the natural realm, were so precious. My Heavenly Father knew where we were and saw our hearts. He knew that we had chosen to live a life of trusting Him, irrespective of our circumstances. This reminded me of Paul's statement when he said that whatever state I find myself in, I will be content. I had a few experiences like this when God's provision for us in this wilderness was beyond anything we could imagine or control. It felt so awesome. Here we were wandering about in a wilderness experience and our Heavenly Father demonstrated His goodness to us time and time again. It certainly is one thing saying we have a Heavenly Father but another thing knowing He is being a Father, not just in name. But His nature is to be a father and now I knew He was watching over us.

"I will be a Father to you, and you shall be My sons and daughters, says the Lord Almighty".

(2 Corinthians 6:18 NKJV)

This was so new to me. Coming from so much abuse in my early years growing up the Lord had brought spiritual fathers like Pastor Anthony and the Rev John Barr, but now I was in a wilderness experience with no-one. It's no wonder Father God sent His only Son to show us His Father. As I was born again, I too, like millions of others, have His seed of eternal life within me. **It could only take a Son to really reveal what a Father is like.** The prophets of the old covenant couldn't, it had to be Jesus, the Son of God.

> *"And I have declared to them Your name, and will declare it, that the love with which You loved Me may be in them, and I in them."*
>
> (John 17:26 NKJV)

And that was all I needed to know, that I was being obedient to Father. I didn't want to be a son in a wilderness of rebellion doing my own thing, like the prodigal son or the elder son in the father's household, working away and not knowing the Father (Luke 15).

We met some lovely people called Ann and John Smith. It felt as the cloud of His presence moved so did we. Now we were meeting with friends going through similar experiences in their farmhouse about half an hour from our home. We had some great times. We would spend all day there just sharing our lives together.

On one occasion we went out to a local restaurant to have a fellowship meal. I was the last to go in. Just as I got to the entrance I remember looking up to a clear blue sky. It was a lovely evening: the stillness of the surroundings, of those beautiful old cottages, was so picturesque. Within my heart I just cried to the Lord. Please let this year be the end of what seems like eternity going round the mountain and not knowing where we are going. We seemed to have been living with uncertainty for so long with little goals and ambition.

As far as my makeup is concerned I am the sort of person that enjoys projects and goals. This motivates me. Yet as my flesh was now learning really the only motivation was to do the will of the Father and follow His leading. Once again words from the past started to have more relevance and meaning to me, like my baptismal text in Psalm 32:8 (NKJV):

> *"I will instruct you and teach you in the way you should go; I will guide you with My eye".*

Little did I know there were a few more years to go. I knew Moses had 40 years and Israel 40 years in the wilderness. But what could I do? My heart is always to know God is with me. My hopes became raised after a visit to see our dear friends Bill and Molly. They had a word from the Lord for me – that I should study God's word. I was at the time already meditating on the verse found in 2 Timothy 3:16-17 (NIV):

> *"All Scripture is God-breathed and is useful for teaching, rebuking, correcting and training in righteousness, so that the servant of God may be thoroughly equipped for every good work".*

As soon as they spoke the word my spirit leapt within me from one side of my body to the other: totally unexpected. I had never felt anything like that in my life. The word that struck me was:

"Study to shew thyself approved unto God".

(2 Timothy 2:15 KJV)

Daph and I decided to go for an interview at a bible college in Birmingham. We had the interview with a number of the tutors. Everything was very formal. They went away for a few hours and called us back to say I had been accepted. Yet somehow, I knew this wasn't right. I had no witness but plenty of doubts. I replied to them thanking them for their time, but wouldn't accept the offer.

Years seemed to fly past. I decided to do a correspondence course called 'The Foundation Series' by Derek Prince. He was one person I related to. I felt I needed to know what the Bible (The Word of God) teaches. I am not interested in commentaries or people's opinions, I just need to know the truth. Work was busy and I seemed to be getting increasingly involved with various people who had issues in their lives.

On the inside I was becoming very weary in my spirit, as disillusionment with church world was setting in. At that time, it felt I was living alone in a desert with no supply of water. I was becoming dry and needed to connect again with the life source. God seemed to have moved and was not hearing my prayers, but I had the determination still, despite all my circumstances saying the opposite. God is the source of life... it's like you are in the desert and somewhere you just know there is water around. There is a little evidence of life, even in the desert. All the things of life were bringing me only a temporary satisfaction. I wouldn't give up. I had given up on church world and the thought of endless meetings, for what? I was really feeling I had lost my way. I didn't fit in anywhere. I was getting fed up with the sense of a swollen cheek and lip due to the severed nerve in the car accident we had years ago. It's like coming out of the dentist with that numb feeling and waiting for it to wear off, but I knew this wouldn't because my nerve was severed. Something was changing on the inside of me. I suppose it was more the workings of brokenness and a deprogramming of what I felt I was, having been in full time ministry for God. With my past I always thought it had to do with church world or pulpits. Now, all I could see – I was in a desert experience, lost. Feeling hopeless having given up on church I thought, has God abandoned me? I had had popularity, position, everything one could want in life. Now it felt I had nothing to offer anyone anymore. I knew I couldn't look inwards as I couldn't bear to face that giant of self-pity again. I remember the consequences. I didn't know at this time I was seated on the seat of judgement. All I knew I was I needed God to be at the centre otherwise what's the point? I don't just want my social needs met, or to be committed to good Christianity. I am committed to the reality of the Kingdom of God being manifest among us. I look at Jesus and this was visible, this Kingdom. Wherever He went people just knew. I like what Paul said in 1 Corinthians 2:3 (NIV):

> *"I came to you in weakness with great fear and trembling. My message and my preaching were not with wise and persuasive words, but with a demonstration of the Spirit's power, so that your faith might not rest on human wisdom, but on God's power".*

I was lonely. I could not face all those doctrinal arguments of why it can't happen today, or you have taken this all out of context. I would rather keep my head down. I had seen it, being self-employed, meeting people who knew little about the Bible being changed in all sorts of places, whether it be in bus stations, in the middle of the High Street, on planes or in their homes. But this still wasn't enough to sustain me. I need that source of life for me now. Seven years had passed since God called me to study. Then I heard of a lady called Jean Darnell, a prophetic evangelist. She was American. I heard that she had raised her mother from the dead when she was a young girl, and she and her husband Elmer were holding a number of Tent Meetings in a place called Fellowship House which was near where we lived.

Something within me started to create a desire to go. In the end I said to my friend who had mentioned it, I will go and take the family for just one meeting. ….can't do any harm I thought. We sat near the front in the tent that was pitched on the lawn. There must have been over 150 people there. The worship was very simple with the focus being on the Lord Jesus. I started to sense God was in this place. Jean's appearance was what I would call very old fashioned with her hairstyle and dress. She started to speak on the parable of the 5 loaves and 2 fishes, and she was saying, "**Whatever you have you must give it away for God to multiply it**".

I was wriggling on my seat feeling a bit grumpy thinking, I don't want to hear this. Yet, deep within my spirit I just knew God was speaking to me, even though I was trying to turn a deaf ear. I just couldn't stop those words penetrating all my defences. "You must give what you have away, no matter how small and insignificant you think it is". I just knew God was convicting me. Then after Jean finished her message, just being still, no hype, she then gave a prophetic word and it involved the anointing of God on my life, and about a way not to go to the left, nor to the right. Keep going straight and follow My leading. The power of God's voice was strong. **This word became my life source for me.** It just flooded my being, as if I was being refreshed and cleaned up in this desert experience.

Nobody knew where I was in this experience, or what was going on on the inside of me. Only my Heavenly Father. Then we stood up to worship. As we were singing this dear little lady, in the world's value might not look like much, but with the authority of God she said, "The Power of God is on this row". The row where myself and family and friends were sitting. Then this power went from the top of my head to my feet. I felt I was in heaven. I remember thinking, my ears, my ears, I can hear so clearly. I knew I had damaged them when I used to work for my company as there were no health and safety regulations in those days. I knew something had imparted to my spirit that day. No wonder Jesus said, *"Man shall not live by bread alone, but by every word that proceeds from the mouth of God"* (Matthew 4:4 NKJV). This wasn't swallowing a bible verse. The word God was speaking to me connected with my spirit and fed me and gave life to my spirit (the engine room of who I am).

Jesus himself said in John 4:34 (NIV) " *"My food," said Jesus, "is to do the will of him who sent me and to finish his work""*. It is no wonder Jesus, when he taught the disciples to pray said give us this day our daily bread, and in John 6:33 (NIV) " *For the bread of God is the bread that comes down from heaven and gives life to the world"*. And earlier in John 4:32 (NIV) Jesus said to the disciples *"I have food to eat that you know nothing about."* In Matthew 4:4 (NIV) *"Man shall not live on bread alone, but on every word that comes from the mouth of God"* and in Revelation 2:17 (NKJV): *"He who has an ear, let him hear what the Spirit says to the churches. To him who overcomes I will give some of the hidden manna to eat."*

I went up to Jean after the service to thank her for the prophetic word and prophecy. Before I had a chance to finish my sentence she said "that was for you!" Feeling so humbled that Almighty God had spoken at the ninth hour when I was about to cave in, I just had to repent on the inside of me, of so much, knowing no matter in life how difficult things become, God knows. Never give up.

There is a verse which is often quoted in times like this, but I don't think we appreciate all of it:

> *"And we know that all things work together for good to those who love God, to those who are the called according to His purpose."*   (Romans 8:28)

While we are still living to our plans and purposes, we can't really claim this as a promise. We are then not following the Lord, as God doesn't bless Christian rebels.

At that tent meeting, I heard that Jean and Elmer were running a college in London called Christian Life College. They really wanted to teach about life and what wasn't being taught at Bible College. It was a 2-year course. For part-time students who had to work for a living it was 3 evenings a week. But when I heard this I was quickened in my spirit as I could relate to this. I don't know if I wasted the 7 previous years and gave up too early because of my sin of judging the church. I haven't the answer for that.

While I was on the driveway listening to a recording called "Discipled by God" by Derek Prince, he explained that David and Moses and others had to go through the wilderness to be trained.

I felt God speaking to me that he needed me to be balanced as he had trained me in the ways of the Spirit, but I now needed to study the Word.

Also, at that time I was still conscious that there was a cloud of darkness between myself and the church I had to leave, and I needed to address that and remove the cloud.

The new minister had left and his associate was in charge. Daph and I had a time together with the Elders of the church and were accepted into fellowship again.

Now I couldn't believe it. I was doing two things I hadn't really believed I ever would do! I had gone back to church world and was also going to college to study. God certainly has a good sense of humour.

All I knew was, I had to trust him, because I still couldn't see the end. It was just another step of faith, no matter how reluctant I felt.

I started college feeling humiliated as most of the students were quite young and I was in my forties, but it was good for my pride. The Lord gave me instructions that I was there to study and not try to fix everyone's problems. Yet in church world the opposite would happen. I was asked to minister to the people of the church and help them come into more freedom in Christ. I would do this every Friday in a small prayer room behind the main meeting. Isn't it amazing how God turned things around? We were called the family of rebellion while in the wilderness and yet here I was, having to minister to the congregation and my son Patrick was leading the youth into evangelism on the streets.

I certainly wouldn't have orchestrated this.

While in church world I also had instruction from the Lord to keep quiet, irrespective of what I could see was going on. This certainly was a discipline.

For the first few months of attending college, I found it hard. I could almost feel myself becoming a bit depressed with it all, but as I pushed through I eventually came to enjoy it. Being bonded as a student family despite our age or experiences seemed good. It was great being among people who were so eager to learn more about God and His ways.

I passed my exams and achieved a diploma from the college, and we would then all go away for a weekend at Herne Bay Court, now that college was finishing.

We had an ex-student called Clive Corfield who now had a ministry of his own particularly in equipping the church to live in the Kingdom of God. After he spoke the power of God would come and it seemed all the students, about 50 of us, needed help. There was a lot of noise and manifestation. I could see he really needed a hand as it was the final time we would all be together. I decided to come out of the woodwork and help Clive to minister to the students. We just connected. We had the same heart and vision to see the church mobilised in the power of the Holy Spirit. We became good friends.

Meanwhile, about the same time in church world, I was attending a meeting with quite a few hundred people as there was a famous Bible teacher coming to speak to us. The meeting began at full pelt. It was becoming very hyped: everyone talking about revival. There came a time of open prayer and worship. At this point I was doing my best to keep restrained, but the Spirit of God was rising up within me until I could no longer keep to my seat. I just had to pray and intercede to the Lord from the depth of my heart as it felt like I was crying on the inside of me. I said, *"Please Lord, forgive us expecting you to come in revival when we cannot even live by your word"*.

I sat down, not realising the atmosphere had changed. I was feeling broken inside. I noticed a deafening silence had swept over the congregation.

This tall, well-built former preacher slowly rose to the platform, not looking like any ray of sunshine. All eyes were fixed on him except my wife who had been in this position before and wanted to walk out. Then with a very strong, stern voice, looking at me he said, "I don't know if you are a good one or a bad one", and then carried on with his message.

I knew then that my time was now up. I had obeyed God as much as I knew and it was once again time to move on. We had ministered to lots of people and we saw God change many lives. Some of these people had gone into the ministry, others had been realigned to fulfil God's purpose in their lives. I am always so grateful for the foundation that was built up in me in those early days by Pastor Anthony.

Looking back, I can see I had to bring my past to a conclusion in order to move on.

Obedience brings blessing. This was certainly a reality to me. Those acts of obedience and just trusting God opened up so many doors of opportunity. I was now a very different person.

The dealings of God aren't always very comfortable, but necessary for our growth. To hear and obey the voice of God gives us a substantiality and faith, but as Moses and Israel needed manna every day, so we too cannot really grow without this hidden manna, that is invisible but contains the life of God. These are realities that go beyond natural reasoning, which I believe is Satan's greatest tactic is to separate and break the connection between God and His people.

"For *without Me you can do nothing*" (John 15:5 NKJV), Jesus said. How many times do we read in the bible, especially in Kings, that they sought the face of God, and God was with them?

> "*I am the vine, you are the branches. He who abides in Me, and I in him, bears much fruit; for without Me you can do nothing*". (John 13 NKJV)

Chapter 20

FATHER INTRODUCES THE BASE LINE

Jesus is more than a concept or someone to reference to from the past. He is alive today, seated at the right hand of the Father and is with us today by the power of the Holy Spirit, which is why Jesus had to ascend to heaven from the confines of an earthly body. He is here today, living through His new Body, "The Body of Christ", people who are born again believers. He said to his disciples in John 14:18 (NKJV):

"I will not leave you orphans; I will come to you".

Wow! What a promise. No matter where we are in our experience, whether we are in a desert place, or in the midst of a storm, suddenly out of work, or a broken relationship, in the middle of sickness, or even on top of the mountain, **God sees all. He can see no other way.** That is a comfort to some, to others committing their favourite sin, perhaps not.

I love it when Jesus turns up in the most unexpected places; even when Jesus was raised from the dead nobody believed that would happen. Yet we find Jesus appears to Mary Magdalene while she was crying outside the tomb. Jesus spoke to her as we see in John 20:17 (NIV):

> *"Jesus said, "Do not hold on to me, for I have not yet ascended to the Father. Go instead to my brothers and tell them, 'I am ascending to my Father and your Father, to my God and your God'".*

"WOW!" What a revelation! This is the first time he could say and declare to the world, that WE have a Father in Heaven, that we have been adopted as His sons. Even the believers before ascension were orphans. Now they had a Father, not just in name, but who will father us in life and never forsake us.

> *"I will never leave you nor forsake you".*
> Hebrews 13:5 (NKJV)

That truth in itself is enough to bring security in a world system which is all around us and is under judgement. Our whole mental health would improve if we could but face these eternal truths that God has revealed in His word and is communicating to us today.

While on our summer holidays in Mallorca, visiting a friend

from the Bible College I went to, she invited us as a family on the Sunday morning to a meeting of her local Salvation Army.

All the family went: Daph, Patrick, Becky and myself. My friend Nicky sat beside me on these long wooden bench seats which didn't do your bottom any favours. The local officer in charge of this church was away on holiday and the General for the whole of Spain was taking the service (for those who don't know these dear people not only have a uniform but like an army have ranks such as an Officer).

The General guy spoke and asked who would like to share an up to date testimony. A hush seemed to fill the room so you could hear a pin drop. In this hush, there was an elbow digging in my side and a look that I should share something. It's a look you don't really want to refuse. After thinking about whether to go up or not, a thought came "tell them about the man with the shoulder condition." The stillness was soon disturbed as I found my way up to the platform, then going up some steps. It was a bit high for my liking. I shared a little testimony and the story of a man who had a shoulder condition and how Jesus came and healed him, then sat down. Well, that wasn't too bad. My family could sigh a sense of relief as everything was still normal. That might have appeared so, but I have noticed God doesn't always work to our normal.

After the service we all went down to the basement for some refreshment. It seemed full of young people. Quite a few were holiday makers, just like us. While drinking my tea, a mother and daughter appeared and said God had spoken as my testimony had spoken to them. She explained the daughter has a shoulder condition like the one I described, so would I pray for her? I was thinking, I'm not sure they'll be prepared if God shows up. I replied, the church doesn't know me here and I cannot go against their authority, so you would have to ask the General and get permission, otherwise I will pray for your daughter on the streets outside.

The mother now had the bit between her teeth and went and got permission. This was a young girl, very slim, probably late teens, early twenties. I asked her a few questions. Well, she started to tell me about her shoulder, the break in her ankles, the back problem. She just went on and on. I could feel my faith just disappearing out of the window as it was just too much. It really was overpowering. It turns out she was a dancer and was on holiday and came all the way from Venezuela, in South America. I prayed what I had faith for. She had one leg a lot shorter than the other. As I prayed her legs started moving until they became even. At this time, we had a whole crowd around us. The mother was in the corner of the room praying. The power of the Lord was present to heal. The young girl fell over backwards so I just let her slide down to a chair so we could continue praying. It appeared a lot of this started from a broken relationship with her boyfriend. There were some sin issues. Also, I prayed into some generational witchcraft. With that the mother in the corner let out an almighty scream, and was in floods of tears. Now we had the daughter crying and the mother crying all at the same time. The crowd seemed a bit amused. I was still conscious we were on holiday and my family were waiting for me, so I just wrapped everything up. There was a buzz in the air so I just left and continued the holiday. I didn't think much more about it. I was just amazed at how God could send someone all the way from Venezuela to heal them.

Approaching Christmas I had a letter from the mother. She

was so grateful to God and wanted me to know her daughter was now dancing in a worship group for the Lord. Praise God! But then I thought, how did she get my address? I found out that she wrote to the Salvation Army who then contacted my friend, Nicky, who was now in London. Nicky then passed my address back to Mallorca and they passed it on to Venezuela. Only God could set this up! The timing was perfect.

One cannot help wondering about the importance of closing those doorways of sin and curses that bring judgements. It's important to recognise that in our universe we live in a legal system that is governed by laws and principles that are in place as a loving gift from God.

Can you imagine what it would be like if there was no Law of Gravity? It would be catastrophic! People would be going up and down all the time. There would be people injuring themselves, people dying without reason. We see natural laws that work within the earth. For example, an architect is governed by architectural laws as they design bridges or tower blocks which have to withstand stresses and strains.

There are mechanical laws that are used in engineering. The mechanic knows he needs engines, fuel or a power source otherwise nothing is going to work.

The pilot has faith when flying the plane that the aerodynamic laws have been taken into consideration when the plane was built and how he must obey those laws to keep the passengers safe. How would you feel if, being a passenger on the plane, the pilot announced, "Today I am doing my own thing"? If the passengers knew that before boarding the plane how many would go?

There are invisible laws of life such as we need to eat and

need time to sleep to keep us healthy. Also, within the universe God has given us moral and ethical laws, like the Ten Commandments and the Sermon on the Mount.

This whole universe has been created with order, with thought and responsibility.

Our freedom isn't a license to disobey these laws and do what we please, as there are consequences.

When we look at the beginning of time everything was in God's order, which is perfect.

> *"The law of the Lord is perfect,*
> *refreshing the soul.*
> *The statutes of the Lord are trustworthy,*
> *making wise the simple.*
> *The precepts of the Lord are right,*
> *giving joy to the heart.*
> *The commands of the Lord are radiant,*
> *giving light to the eyes.*
> *The fear of the Lord is pure,*
> *enduring forever.*
> *The decrees of the Lord are firm,*
> *and all of them are righteous.*
> *They are more precious than gold,*
> *than much pure gold;*
> *they are sweeter than honey,*
> *than honey from the honeycomb.*
> *By them your servant is warned;*
> *in keeping them there is great reward".*
>
> (Psalm 19:7-11 NIV)

I love these verses in Psalm 97:1-2 (NIV):

"The Lord reigns, let the earth be glad;
  let the distant shores rejoice.
Clouds and thick darkness surround him;
  righteousness and justice are the foundation of his throne"

What a picture! Righteousness and justice. What a combination! It is the foundation from which God operates.

Today it seems that we are far from the definitions of sin and righteousness that God explains in His Word. We can say sin is described with various words in the bible. It can mean we can fall into error or miss the mark.

Transgression is a breaking of God's laws.

Trespass speaks for itself. e.g. It can mean we go into an unholy place that is defiled like Stonehenge, witchcraft museums and temples that are defiled by false gods.

Disobedience to God's laws e.g. to gossip or to judge wrongly, so we have been used to rob someone of their honour.

Rebellion is really deliberately disobeying the authority of God's word.

Iniquity is the weakness that we inherited from Adam and our ancestors, like alcoholism, addictions, perverseness, sexual sins and even grief (1 John 3:4 NKJV).

Then, as most of you know, there came into our earth an intervention of sin and disobedience to the laws of God. This irreversible force was released in the earth and all creation suffered. It was a disease that affected not only Adam and Eve, but the whole of creation. A slave system was set up that would have dominion over those under its power. In Romans 7 the law of sin and death is described as invisible and now controls the very nature of mankind, no matter how much we struggle, no matter what attempts to change. To attempt to change this law is futile. There is the penalty of the law – sickness, pain and disease. Separation now from God exists as the nature of the one called Lucifer who came to earth. His nature was pride and rebellion is now within humanity. He wanted to be a god, in charge, and we see it in those systems 1 Samuel 15:23 (NKJV), pride and stubbornness are like twin sisters:

> *"For rebellion is as the sin of witchcraft, and stubbornness is as iniquity and idolatry".*

Mankind is now independent from God, living in an alien environment that has been infected. Corruption has set in to everything now on the earth and is subject to decay. How do we know that sin exists? Because of the penalty. That shows that it does. When somebody commits abortion the law of life has been violated. Murder has taken place, and the highlight of breaking the law believe it or not, is guilt. It controls the consciousness. The conscience becomes harder so one doesn't even think it is sin to continue in unrighteousness. We read in Psalm 74:17 (NIV):

> *"It was you (God) who set all the boundaries of the earth; you made both summer and winter".*

The final sting of sin is death. Death to the environment, death to the emotions, mind, body, then eventually the spirit, just like a bee. Touch sin, and it's not long before you discover it has a sting.

The law of sowing and reaping was a wonderful gift to mankind, so that we could find an increase. It was designed to be a blessing, before sin came to the earth. Now as mankind continues to sin the increase of it is found in this invisible law which applies – if we sow bitterness or unforgiveness, it's not long before it multiplies in our lives.

> *"Do not be deceived: God cannot be mocked. A man reaps what he sows. Whoever sows to please their flesh, from the flesh will reap destruction; whoever sows to please the Spirit, from the Spirit will reap eternal life".*
>
> (Galatians 6:7-8 NIV)

Praise God our Heavenly Father, who sent His son Jesus to die on the cross and be resurrected from the dead. He who became sin for us and took the penalty of our sin at the cross.

> *"having cancelled the charge of our legal indebtedness, which stood against us and condemned us; he has taken it away, nailing it to the cross".* (Colossians 2:14 NIV)

The full legal demand of the law was completed by the finished work of the cross.

> *"Much more then, having now been justified by His blood, we shall be saved from wrath through Him".*
>
> (Romans 5:9 NKJV)

We have been acquitted as if we were on trial. We have the pronouncement – "NOT GUILTY" and now we have been reckoned righteous. This is good news. We read in Matthew 5:18 (NIV):

> *"For truly I tell you, until heaven and earth disappear, not the smallest letter, not the least stroke of a pen, will by any means disappear from the Law until everything is accomplished".*

As we can see, heaven and earth are still here. Jesus goes on to say:

> *"For I tell you that unless your righteousness surpasses that of the Pharisees and the teachers of the law, you will certainly not enter the kingdom of heaven".*
>
> (Matthew 5:20)

We are made righteous and we are acquitted and justified because of the blood of Jesus.

A higher law has come into mankind through the death and resurrection of Jesus, which is the law of the Spirit of Life which gives life to our mortal bodies through His Spirit living in us.

> *"And if the Spirit of him who raised Jesus from the dead is living in you, he who raised Christ from the dead will also give life to your mortal bodies because of his Spirit who lives in you".*
>
> (Romans 8:11 NIV)

That was some power that raised Jesus from the dead. Yet that same power, the Spirit of Life, contains no death. It has life and health... Wow! That's amazing!

Yet as we look around us, both in believers and non-believers we see mental illness, we see physical illness. There is shame, guilt, anger, unforgiveness, premature death, confusion, envy, and strife at work, for example. In the Christian world there is the doctrine of grace, but in recent days it has been misunderstood. In Ephesians 2:8 (NIV):

> *"For it is by grace you have been saved, through faith—and this is not from yourselves, it is the gift of God".*

In Hebrews 12:28 (NKJV):

> *"Therefore, since we are receiving a kingdom which cannot be shaken, let us have grace, by which we may serve God acceptably with reverence and godly fear"*

And in 2 Corinthians 12:9 (NKJV):

> *"My grace is sufficient for you, for My strength is made perfect in weakness. Therefore most gladly I will rather boast in my infirmities, that the power of Christ may rest upon me".*

Grace is a means of empowering and enabling us to overcome. Trying to be a Christian and keeping the law of God doesn't work. It's like trying to be human – you already are!

This higher law of the Spirit of Life has come by confession which leads to salvation (Romans 10:9-10). If we throw a ball up in the air, gravity brings it down. But if I put my hand in the way I have introduced a higher law and caught the ball. Yet gravity still exists. The consequence of sin has an effect on our lives and our bodies and our families. The outworking of the glorious salvation can be appropriated which is such a key. But only by faith, as the Lord brings the searchlight of the Holy Spirit into those dark areas of our lives by our confession. This isn't automatic.

> *"Therefore confess your sins to each other and pray for each other so that you may be healed".*   (James 5:16 NIV)

What we don't uncover we cannot expect God to cover. It is only confessed sin that is covered.

> *"He who covers his sins will not prosper, But whoever confesses and forsakes them will have mercy".*
> (Proverbs 28:13 NKJV)

If you read Psalm 38 and you can see what problems King David encounters. He was the other side of the cross, yet by his confession (verse 18) of his iniquity and sin, he finds mercy. This revelation will open us up to faith and a new way of living. The dominion of sin has now been broken over our will which leads us to a new freedom to choose: to serve sin and become a slave or choose righteousness, which is imputed to us by the Son of God. By choosing righteousness we are choosing life over the outworking of death. Wow! This is such good news, to wake up every day free of guilt.

This is such good news as the law and principles of God outwork and the consequences take effect over time. Yet there is an ABSOLUTENESS of the higher law of life, the law of the spirit, the law of forgiveness. We can have faith in God's word that we can appropriate and undo the consequences of sin because Jesus paid the price. The power of the cross is the place of exchange as by faith we come to him and confess our needs to him, rather than put up with what the enemy of our souls has used to take advantage. How exciting is that? God has no favourites and no second-class citizens – these laws work for and against everyone.

It's important that we understand this gospel message of good news. We have to have a base line to work from and this is it. If we think we can break God's law and get away with it without appropriating what Jesus accomplished on the cross, we will have trouble.

If we look at the story of Balaam in Numbers 22 we see that Balaam was a prophet and Balak was a heathen king who approached Balaam to find a way to curse God's people. As God's people are blessed, Balaam could not curse God's people, for they are in covenant with Him. But Balaam taught Balak how to get the people to sin so they would come under judgement. He did that by tempting the boys with the girls in his country (2 Peter 2:15, Jude 11). By committing sexual immorality and worshipping pagan idols, the legal ground was established, curse and judgement followed and 24,000 of God's people died in a plague that came as a result of sin.

> *"But I have a few things against you, because you have there those who hold the doctrine of Balaam, who taught Balak to put a stumbling block before the children of Israel, to eat things sacrificed to idols, and to commit sexual immorality."*
> (Revelation 2:14 NKJV)

Beware today of the doctrine of Balaam, a doctrine that says there will be no consequences if you break God's laws because you are a covenant believer.

As we look, for example, at the law of forgiveness in John 20:23 (NKJV) *"If you forgive the sins of any, they are forgiven them; if you retain the sins of any, they are retained"*, we see the consequences of holding unforgiveness (See Mark 11:25-26, Matthew 18:34 and Matthew 5:23-25). If there is unforgiveness in the heart it prevents you from approaching the throne of grace. Satan wants to take you to court so you can be judged. The legal system in the universe exists. There is a court room in heaven as we see in Job 1 and Daniel 7. If we trespass into sin the full penalty of the law starts to take effect. We cannot bypass the penalty of sin without confession. *"If we confess our sins, He is faithful and just to forgive us our sins and to cleanse us from all unrighteousness"* (1 John 1:9 NKJV).

In Psalm 97:1-2 we have already seen that the foundation of the throne of God is righteousness and justice. Thank God we have an advocate in the courtroom of heaven that intercedes for us (1 John 2:1). It's best to live with short accounts. I suppose we often only think of sin to be what we consider very serious like the occult, but self-hatred, jealousy, gossiping, envy, speaking words of death over yourself, anger, backbiting and fear are still sins. We who are believers live in a war against the kingdom of darkness. Satan is doing all he can to destroy the life of the Son of God within us by trying to bring us under curse and judgement. We cannot become complacent around the issue of sin, which is also a lie of Satan, or mute. A lot today don't talk about sin; it's all about grace. We need a balance. Jesus said blessed are the peacemakers, not the peacekeepers.

Thank God for the work of the cross. The total provision for humanity if it is appropriated. Understanding the covenant of God and the base of the law will give us a foundation in helping us all to come into freedom and being conformed into the image of the Son of God. It is having faith in Jesus and His Word. So often we cannot see our sin, which is why our Father sends the Holy Spirit to help us, as He reveals what needs to be done in the work of salvation within us. Jesus Christ paid such a price by becoming sin for us and taking the full penalty of the law. His pain, his life, is almost beyond comprehension. But boy, what a cost!

The justice of God was satisfied as Jesus paid the price for us.

> *"But as many as received Him, to them He gave the right to become children of God, to those who believe in His name".*
> (John 1:12 NKJV)

The cross wasn't the cross of man, but the cross of God, as a gateway to a union back to God which is now open for us to walk through. It's not by man's efforts – it's all about what God has given us.

In today's society it seems our definition of sin and righteousness is very different to what the bible teaches.

One of the battles that exists today is the battle for truth, which is why we need Jesus who is not only the way to the Father, but is also the embodiment of truth. The Holy Spirit is sent to lead us into all truth if we listen and obey the Lord as He conveys His Word and Will that he has put on the inside of us. But the consequence of allowing the seed of sin in our own lives can be so devastating. This seed can even come into our own lives through people sinning against us as we respond to that hurt and pain. An indication that something is wrong on the inside of us is when we react as someone has pressed a button that has outmanoeuvred our defence mechanism.

We saw this in a young lady in her early twenties who was sexually abused when she was a teenager. The effect was devastating emotionally and mentally, yet it wasn't her fault. She was sinned against. Her sleep was invaded by nightmares. Fears became apparent that she couldn't control. The medication she had been on for years didn't seem to be having any effect. She got to the point where holding down a job was more difficult.

Patricia, who was a member of my team, sat with me. Patricia carried so much love in her. The room that day was filled with love and the presence of God. One couldn't help but feel accepted and not judged in any way. This young lady was living under such a cloak of shame and in a cave of darkness in her soul. As the Holy Spirit came in such gentleness, the fear and shame tightened its grip and she couldn't even speak. This seemed to go on for such a long time and no breakthrough was to be seen on the horizon. Then suddenly the intensity of the love and presence of God increased. A mighty scream was let loose as the demonic knew its days of occupation were numbered. As this young lady faced the pain and forgave those that had sinned against her, pure light flooded her whole being. She forgave the abusers. All the false guilt she carried left too, as often happens in sexual abuse. The enemy of our souls lies and whispers, "You asked for this", "It's your fault". The imprint of the abuser was taken off the young lady's face – the devil likes to leave his mark. In this case the generational victim spirit had to leave too. No longer would she be set up for an abusing spirit to seek her out.

Today she is free from medication which had been a prop for a time, but it was only masking her issues as she had had to learn to manage them to manage life. Thank God for His grace that opens us up to apply the finished work of the cross, where Jesus took her abuse and gave her acceptance and healing, so she can now live as an overcomer, and not a survivor. The darkness left her countenance and the glory of God filled her soul and radiated from her.

Silence in the abuse scenario is never golden. Facing ones pain and sharing with others is a major key to freedom (James 5:16). The devil loves secrecy and that keeps us in the darkness where he has authority still. It was the reactions that she used to experience that highlighted that there was an unresolved issue that she needed to face.

Chapter 21

A SEASON WITH A DIFFERENCE

I had thought so many times in the wilderness that surely there must be others experiencing what we are and seeing the Lord Jesus come and change people's lives. It seemed crazy that wherever we went people were still talking and praying and singing about God coming to His people as if Jesus was still in the past.

The pain of loneliness was beyond anything I had ever thought or imagined it would be. It seemed to be this way for so many years going round this mountain. The loneliness is not that I didn't see people as I took the family around different churches, but if you shared, there seemed no connection. It seemed to be just verbal communication, despite the wonderful gifts we saw

God give to people, and His power manifested. I could understand that must have been what Elijah felt after the victory over Jezebel and the false prophets. Yet it was in the stillness God let him know there were 7,000 others that God had reserved, which we read about in Romans 11.

Meeting Clive at the college weekend was a divine appointment for me. I became part of Sovereign Ministries which led me to join up with Ellel Ministries. We all seemed to have the same heart and vision of how we saw the ministry of Jesus. In Luke 9:11 (NIV):

> *"He welcomed them and spoke to them about the kingdom*
> *of God, and healed those who needed healing".*

These keys of welcoming and loving people, accepting them whoever they are, teaching them, then demonstrating the Kingdom of God, was so fundamental to me. It was so encouraging as the Gospel of the Kingdom was where it all started for me, and to be working with others was such a blessing. I didn't feel out of place any longer.

Going to various places in the UK and abroad was what I had been trained for and to be among people who had varied experiences, we could all share and minister in different ways. We weren't expected for example, to do things the Ellel way, as it was the fruit that mattered – that people's lives were being changed because they met God and not just some philosophy. I had been trained in the School of the Spirit, the Wilderness of Loneliness and knew not to put on King Saul's armour, just like David tried when facing Goliath the giant. David had found when offered, it didn't fit him and it didn't work for him so he couldn't function effectively (1 Samuel 17:38-39). The revelation God had given to me was proven and I was comfortable operating in what God had given me, which is why I cannot be an echo of somebody else's revelation. That might work for them, but it doesn't for me, which is why I love the uniqueness of the body of Christ with so many parts looking and functioning differently as we are living stones, not bricks, that are being built together. As we are knit together in love, we are not independent from each other and we all supply something to the whole (Ephesians 4:3-6 and Colossians 3:14) as we are built for a dwelling place for God.

There are some strongholds in people's lives that need a corporate anointing to break. Trying to bring unity by bringing people only into a verbal agreement isn't unity. Within the body of Christ there is so much diversity yet united under one head, our Lord Jesus Christ, who is head of the church. The Cross of Jesus Christ is where we can all meet, it is the leveller, where there is no status, no position, just submission in humility, honour, love and respect in the Fear of God. This picture of the body of Christ is a wonderful picture of uniformity and not conformity. Conformity is controlled by the law that leads to witchcraft to enforce it. To see hearts united respecting our difference was for me, something new. I was so used to having my guard up, so I didn't offend people.

Watching the corporate anointing outplayed was incredible when we visited a Baptist Church in Northampton. These were people on a journey. They found the faith doctrine still had limitations to them, and were hungry to learn more. We loved the people. Clive taught them on Friday and Saturday, then on Saturday evening it was like an explosion as the light of the word of God revealed the darkness in people's lives. Over 100 people were doing all sorts of crazy things: crying, falling over and making loud noises. It was like a nursery – noise everywhere. So different from a cemetery where nothing changes. The Sunday morning was so beautiful as we took communion. The air waves were cleaned out. So many people were receiving revelation prophecy. The Holiness of God felt almost tangible as Satan's kingdom was exposed, with all the defilements it brings to a human life. The gentle breeze of the Lamb of God seemed to be impregnating the atmosphere.

I was to be a part of these type of meetings in so many countries in the entire world.

While in Poland we met with over 1,000 Catholics. I watched hundreds giving their lives to Jesus and being filled with the Holy Spirit. What was preached was the principle of idolatry from the scripture and the devastating consequences. When the issue of generational sin was preached I had a young couple, a brother and sister in their mid-twenties, come to me and say, "We hate the Jews, yet to be honest, they have done nothing wrong to us, but we know our father and his father also hated them". This lovely brother and sister confessed their ancestral sin, the power of God came upon them and they both fell to the floor and started manifesting as their faces appeared to change. They were coughing and wriggling a lot but praise God, the joy on their faces was beautiful. This cycle has now been stopped in their family, so future generations would not be having that anti-semetic spirit in their DNA.

This is what I am used to. I am not crazy. I have seen these things happen in the wilderness with people who didn't even know Jesus, then coming into a relationship with the Living

Jesus, rather than a doctrine or a religious Jesus. I was not alone. But I couldn't help thinking, how many people are still sitting in church week after week struggling in life with a smile on their faces to hide everything. Alternatively being taken down the success route, working for God, slaving away trying to do the right thing but not knowing the principle of freedom to enjoy the adventure of living with Jesus – putting up with things or burying their heads in the sand, just like the elder son in the story of the prodigal son. Effort isn't the key to the Christian life. The key is a relationship with God.

On one of my visits to the Ukraine, I was just part of a small team of 4. We went into Kiev. Then took a 24-hour train journey down the Crimea where we would change trains to go to our destination. The train must have been going around 40mph. It was the slowest, nosiest train I have ever been on. The toilet was a hole in the floor of the train behind a little door. We slept on very hard bench-type bunks. After the change of trains, Roger the leader had been praying about our visit to the very large Charismatic type church of almost 1500 people. We also had to go to a bible school for four days and teach them. Roger, quite casually, turned to me and said, "Pat, I believe you should preach on Sunday morning at the service". My heart went into overdrive and the anxiety hit me as nobody knew I struggle with some sort of mental condition which sometimes causes my words to come out of my mouth as the opposite of what I am thinking. If I say forward the word would come out backwards. Other times the blackboard of my mind would be blank with nothing on it. Despite prayer, nothing has shifted this. But I knew I could trust God, and that this is something I would have to push through.

I stood with my translator next to me, with my favourite prayer on my lips, "HELP!" As I opened my mouth the clarity of the Holy Spirit just came as I preached about the presence of God and how King David tried to bring the Ark of His Presence back to Jerusalem, not respecting the ways of God. For me as a person, I am constantly amazed time and time again how, despite our weakness, God keeps on showing up. On this occasion, there was a big response.

I came off the platform and was walking among the people. I came to an elderly lady who looked as if butter wouldn't melt in her mouth. She spoke no English. Then suddenly her face changed and she snarled at me and said: "Get back to England you old goat". It wasn't long before that demonic spirit left.

I just loved Eastern Europe. The people are so full of appreciation and just loved us.

While in a Romanian Pastor's home, the wife shared with us about how deaf she was in one ear. The leader asked a few questions and it turned out that when her brother died, she leant over and kissed him. At that precise moment, the brother expelled some breath and she realised since then she had been deaf in that ear. A familiar spirit had transferred from the brother and attached itself to her. It was so interesting to see the freedom of healing coming to her life and to so many people in so many ways.

While in Hungary there were over 1000 Hungarians. Some had walked for days to come to the conference. Those of us on the mission provided lunch for them all as at that time poverty was a real issue. One of my tasks was to make salami rolls. The sheer smell I think has put me off salami for the rest of my life.

As we were ministering to the Hungarians there were so few

translators. I was praying for a lady whose countenance was so dark you could see the evil in her eyes. She followed the instructions from the translator on the platform. I started to break the power of evil and darkness that had been there for years. She didn't speak English. The lady with me didn't speak much Hungarian, but we know the Holy Spirit isn't English. I shall never forget her countenance as she looked at me. It was like the sun started to come up and the shadow started to disappear. Her face gradually became lighter and lighter until every part of her face shone with the glory of God. Only God could do this. We cannot get into someone else's skin, let alone their soul, yet to watch God change this lady in front of my eyes was so beautiful to watch. This has such a high value to God as Jesus died to give us this gift of freedom. To us in the west, so much is measured by what is seen, such as how much you do for God in acts of service, rather than what is unseen to others but of infinite value to God. It's like God has given us this amazing gift, and because it is not outwardly visible to others, it is not so valuable to us. I have leant that the most important thing is to focus on what matters most to God, rather than what matters most to man. No wonder Jesus said you can do nothing without me. These are the works I want to be involved in, the works of the Holy Spirit.

Thank God, the miracle-working power of Jesus Christ isn't confined to certain countries.

A friend from the north of England had booked in one Thursday for ministry. In between time his new wife was 14 weeks pregnant. She had just had a scan to discover her baby had died. Needless to say, the agenda for the day changed. When my friend arrived, he was so upset and in pieces. He had a Greek background and I knew that in their bloodline there is a lot of ancestral worship. We had had a few holidays there and had heard lots of their stories. We spent some time ministering, breaking off a number of curses. As we walked out onto the drive, it was a bright sunny day, something had changed in my friend. He looked so much lighter now the glory of God was all over him. He said, "Can we pray for the baby?" We agreed in the Spirit. Somehow God just released faith. It wasn't hope, but **faith that leads to hope.** We just knew the baby was going to come alive. We prayed and thanked God. My friend's wife who at the time wasn't a Christian, was booked in to the hospital to have what is commonly called a 'clear out'. My friend went to the hospital on the Monday and insisted on another scan as he believed God had touched his baby. When they took another scan, to everyone's amazement they found a heartbeat, and this little boy is alive today having been resurrected by the Living Power of Jesus Christ.

I loved this. To me, it gave the Devil a kick in the teeth for taking my son. We were able to hit the target as the Lord showed us, the legal ground that Satan can have in our lives through these open doors that haven't been closed through repentance and confession. This gave me encouragement as we were discovering the spiritual laws and principles we were ignorant of for years, that Paul in 2 Corinthians 2:11 (NKJV) talks about, *"lest Satan should take advantage of us; for we are not ignorant of his devices"*, and Peter also warns us in 1 Peter 5:8 (NKJV) *"Be sober, be vigilant; because your adversary the devil walks about like a roaring lion, seeking whom he may devour"*.

Paul and Peter were writing to the Christians warning them not to be ignorant and to keep vigilant as the devil is looking for those doors in our lives that are opened and not closed. I had read this so many times but hadn't believed it as a reality. It seemed a false doctrine as I was so legalistic blinding me to the truth. It was only through my brokenness that I started to journey to find out the truth of how Satan could get the advantage over me, let alone try to destroy me.

This new season was accelerating with me ministering to so many people. The Lord spoke to me about beginning a ministry to minister to individuals on a one to one basis, called Freedom in Christ Support Ministries. I knew I couldn't help people just by myself. God started leading me to a number of people who needed ministry themselves. They were the best people to minister to others as they had received themselves and were currently experiencing the freedom of living in a new way with Jesus.

The verse of scripture that became a foundational principle before we ministered to others is in 1 Timothy 4:16 (NKJV):

> *"Take heed to yourself and to the doctrine. Continue in them, for in doing this you will save both yourself and those who hear you".*

Such an important sequence we find in scripture. A wonderful principle. It's like a spiritual check for us that we know we are right with God, that our past is up to date. Doctrine was secondary to the first principle of taking heed to yourself and the result would be salvation. Brilliant!

When the International Bible Version (NIV) came out and was used more in church world it really affected me as we treated the King James Version as a Holy Bible. The NIV easily became an ordinary book because as far as I understand the NKJV is the most accurate word for word translation, whereas the NIV gives more of the meaning but so many truths are missed out with this and other versions.

Now as a small ministry we set up newsletters which reached over 500 people I knew personally, so I suppose with friends and family we were reaching over 1000 people.

I felt a lot like Moses with so many people now in the wilderness that weren't settled in church but still loved God, yet hated religion and didn't know what was going on. It was an incredible season of God's people journeying to discover truth and freedom.

As we ministered to people from so many different cultures and backgrounds we realised even more how much more we still had to learn.

One person we saw lived in the city. A young girl, I suppose, late teens to early twenties. She suffered from a problem of self-harming. She would go to her house group with so many cuts on both arms that she couldn't wear short sleeves. We listened to her story of how she had cancer at the age of 6 months. When she reached the age of 10 her dad came home from work one day and just said to her "I think you have had enough attention". Those words impregnated and marked the spirit of this little girl. This soon was highlighted by the Spirit of God as to the cause of her behaviour.

She judged her dad and felt he had rejected her, hence she started rejecting herself as she felt unworthy to be loved or even live.

This is one of the major principles taught in God's Word. It is a Spiritual Law, that we don't have the right to judge another person. (In Matthew 7 Jesus warns us about not being a hypocrite through judging others). This law outworked in her life. Her Dad might have had a bad day at work, yet he had loved her and cared for her for 10 years, yet in one moment of time one phrase was to blind her to the truth and create her own reality. This is where we make judgements about what we believe about a person or group and then a new reality takes place within our thinking that isn't really the truth. No matter what her dad did or said from that day she could only see rejection, which led to her behaviour changing towards him. That would have confused her Dad, then eventually his responses would have changed. She could not see his heart as the judgements blinded her to the truth. I was reminded of this when I saw the film Beauty and the Beast. How the judgements made were based so much on external behaviour and not seeing that there is actually a prince underneath all that exterior.

This judgement law, when applied to our parents breaks the 4th Commandment in Deuteronomy 5:16 (NIV):

> *"Honour your father and your mother, as the Lord your God has commanded you, so that you may live long and that it may go well with you in the land the Lord your God is giving you".*

It doesn't say honour them if they are perfect. Our parents gave us life. The areas we don't honour them and judge them instead are the areas where it will not go well for us.

This dear lady was healed that day as I stood in proxy for her Dad and asked her to forgive me, and she responded by asking me to forgive her of her judgements. The Lord also spoke about washing her feet. A good thing she didn't have tights on! My friend Patricia filled up a bowl of water. I knelt on my knees. We looked at each other and tears started to well up as all the buried emotion that was alive with the pain in her heart came to the surface. The Holiness of God filled the room and revelation took place within herself, as well as in the Spirit with her Father, Father God. The beauty of repentance and forgiveness and the cleansing of soul and spirit is just so beautiful.

When we live in separation from ourselves and from others and from God, there is nothing but pain and breakdown in so many ways.

We see in Romans the power of breaking this law has far outreaching consequences.

> *"You, therefore, have no excuse, you who pass judgment on someone else, for at whatever point you judge another, you are condemning yourself, because you who pass judgment do the same things".* (Romans 2:1 NIV)

We will do the very same things that we have judged. I felt this so much when bringing up our two children. I kept thinking, "I am shouting just like my dad". I said I never wanted to be like him, yet I see it's impossible to stop this cycle of behaviour. It doesn't matter how good our intentions are, they don't change the law, but provision is made once again, by repentance and confession.

Unfortunately, the longer we hold a judgement, that seed of death multiplies as what is sown will also be reaped. The law of increase through sowing and reaping comes into play as we read in Galatians 6:7 (NIV):

"Do not be deceived: God cannot be mocked. A man reaps what he sows".

God's laws were in place before sin came into the world as His heart was for us to experience His love, yet we will reap depending on what we sow.

We found out how the laws of judgement and sowing and reaping work when one of our team members developed some lumps in her breast. Her mum had had breast cancer and had a full mastectomy while she was growing up. Our team member prayed and bound the devil's power yet nothing changed. I have always said, everything that God does works. When she confessed that she had judged her mother as always being weak, overnight, the lumps disappeared! Learning the hard way isn't always easy but it certainly changes you.

These Spiritual laws, like natural laws, are for our freedom and left unchecked will multiply.

The following are just a few examples of the type of judgements we make on our parents which affects how we see them, but we can become blind to the truth and they will outwork in relationships close to us:

If a wife judges her father for example, of being critical, judgemental, not trusting, too busy, too cold and distant, they will outwork this in the wife's life. If left unchecked it will manifest in her relationships. Particularly with the husband. He may become critical, cold or distant, etc.

You might judge your mother for being controlling, inattentive, strong, always knowing it all. I know of a National Leader's wife who felt she had a sign on her back saying "Why do all the women in the church try to control me?" It was only as she released her mother that she came into freedom and a new relationship with her mother and also those in the church.

I also know of a husband who judged his mother for not showing him enough affection. This outworked after a number of years in his marriage that the normally affectionate wife slowly became like the judgements he had on his mother.

One could go on, "My dad is drunk". "My mother never listens". "They have both committed adultery". All the negative ways you see your parents, even if they are true statements. Underneath the factual statements are the hidden meanings of what they represent to you.

Judgement creates your own reality.

Every action in life must reap a result. No law of God is inert. These laws will outwork, believe in them or not, they will outwork in your life.

To be free from the laws of judgement on our parents we need to confess them specifically – a blanket prayer will not suffice. It is important to be true to ourselves and humble ourselves to be honest before God and apply the law of appropriation. Then our expectancy will change as we deal with these issues. Time and time again Christians always want to do the right thing and rattle off a load of prayers and move on. That's only a religious exercise. As we allow the Holy Spirit to convict us and get in touch with what is going on on the inside of us, can we really begin to move in reality and confess and experience the freedom in this wonderful salvation Jesus purchased for us.

A principle I have learnt is **never look in as you build your own prison.** As you gain more freedom in Christ you will find it will cost others more than you, but it gives everyone the opportunity to accept you and not go into the sin of offence, which is just another way Satan wants to cause division. The word for offence in Luke 17:1 (NKJV) *"It is impossible that no offences should come, but woe to him through whom they do come!"* The Greek word for offence is SKANDALON. It's the bait which is attached like a mouse trap. The offence acts as a bait to cause division and bring the power of sin to bear which brings the consequences of sin which leads to death of relationship. It's a tool of Satan. A weapon he uses against us. Understandably these laws and principles enable us not only to hit the target in prayer, but causes us to grow up into sonship and move away from thinking and doing as we please, expecting no consequences. I personally had to ask myself the question of what is the difference between discernment and judgements? The judgements made bring separation, discernment will always be seeking good and motivates one with compassion to pray.

As we see in 1 Corinthians 11:29-30 (NKJV) it talks about discerning the body so we can take communion together and it shows us the consequences if we don't.

Prayer

Father God,

I know I have messed up and have been hurt and held unforgiveness in my heart. I now confess my sins of resentment, accusation, hatred and slander against (name the persons specifically).

Father I release (name the persons) for (specific instances). Forgive me now Father, for all the judgements and slander and gossip, and the punishments I wanted them to have. I tear up today all the I.O.U's. I ask you now Lord to cleanse me from all the defilement and the consequences that these sins have brought. I release myself from any guilt and I choose to accept myself and (name person) in the name of Jesus. I ask you Lord, to heal my heart and any other damage to me.

Amen

Testimony

Dear Pat,

Enclosed is my testimony as promised. I'm sorry it's taken me so long! I can hardly believe how much Jesus has changed my life. When I think back and remember how I was, it blows me away. There is nothing better than Him.

Thank you so much for bringing me to Jesus so that He could do this.

God bless you.

"I came to Freedom in Christ Support Ministries in a desperate state. For many years I'd felt a deep sadness and depression. I hated myself and my life and often felt that I wanted to die because it was too painful to be alive. I felt like I was in a blackness which I couldn't get out of. I was tormented by painful memories and I frequently had thoughts of wanting to die or harm myself. Often I would cut myself with razors as the pain was so overwhelming. I felt that there was no way out, that things could never be different and that God was far away. Through the ministry I feel a joy and happiness to be alive. The blackness and feelings of wanting to die have completely gone and it doesn't hurt any more. I have found relationship with God as my Father and I know that He loves me and will never leave me. This transformation and the freedom I have now is incredible. My life has totally changed. Praise God!"

Chapter 22

WEAPONS OF MASS DESTRUCTION

Everywhere I went and listening to various ministries there was reference to an organisation called Freemasonry. This kept coming up in people's lives, no matter how much I tried, I couldn't ignore this any longer. I had learnt in the past only to go into battles that the Lord leads me in for people's lives. I didn't need extra hassle in life.

When one is advancing in the Kingdom of God, particularly exposing the demonic kingdom, there is an ongoing invisible war to bring as much disruption to life through any means the enemy finds open to him. Even Jesus had to rebuke Satan in Peter the Apostle in Mark 8:33 (NIV) *"He rebuked Peter, saying, "Get behind Me, Satan! For you are not mindful of the things of God, but the things of men*". It is possible Satan can use even those closest to us if there is an open door in that person's life. I was soon to discover that Freemasonry was not just an organisation, but a religion with an altar and a priesthood. They take communion and worship and embrace all religions and many false gods. The only name forbidden in the Lodge is Jesus. It is an anti-Christ religion which has invisible strongmen of Jezebel, Death and Hell and Baphomet. It is totally incompatible with Christianity and our faith in the Lord Jesus Christ.

There are many signs and symbols used, along with many rituals that each member is expected to go through, commencing at what is known as the Ceremony of Initiation for the Entered Apprentice. You progress from this degree through various ceremonies and rituals. Each degree is an oath to the 33rd degree and beyond.

Scripture tells us how important taking a vow or oath is to God as oaths will lock you in to the terms and conditions of that oath, which is why we had better not take them. These can become a curse and the demonic are the agents sent to fulfil them. The taking of oaths would also include inner vows that we make to ourselves inside.

This all seemed at first very complex, but no matter how I avoided confronting this, I kept coming up against it.

A couple came to see us. They were in their late fifties or early sixties. His wife became a Christian 30 years previously and her husband had said the same prayer as his wife. He too had this desire to become a Christian. Yet nothing changed in him. The wife was so in love with Jesus. She was really born again, but the husband was still feeling empty and had no experience of God, only information. He had carried on going to church for a little while, really to keep his wife happy, and had then given up. **Whatever you do by law and duty is just a religious experience and is dead.**

I asked him the question, "Do you still want to know Jesus?" "Yes", he said, "but it doesn't work for me. I have tried it and nothing has worked". At least he was honest, I thought. Then I said to him, "Is Freemasonry in your line?" "Yes", he replied, "I think my grandfather was involved a bit."Then I said, "Would you like to follow me in a prayer to renounce Freemasonry and give your life to Jesus Christ?" He agreed. As I led this gentleman in a prayer the Lord spoke to me and said to dismiss the Knights Templar as they were acting like invisible guards around his spirit. I did this. Well...the power of God just hit him like a tornado. He went to the floor like a rocket. His wife went to the floor in the other direction. She was laughing and he was manifesting and doing strange things on the floor. When he eventually regained his composure, his face was as if he had just come out of an over-heated sauna, he was so red. I then said with such joy, "Today you have met this Jesus who is alive and has risen from the dead, and you have now connected with him". He was so radiant. He met the person, Jesus. The wife, bless her, was so overjoyed. The tears of joy just trickled down her cheeks. I was very moved, but once again I had to ask the question. My engineering mind again was asking, "Why was this such a power encounter?" I felt the Lord say that the wife had been praying for 30 years. **It only took a small key to unlock the prison door of his heart.** I have seen him since in church just enjoying Jesus.

I really needed now to look into this teaching of vows and oaths in the word of God.

"If anyone thoughtlessly takes an oath to do anything, whether good or evil (in any matter one might carelessly swear about) even though they are unaware of it, but then they learn of it and realize their guilt".

(Leviticus 5:4 NIV)

"It is a trap to dedicate something rashly and only later to consider one's vows".

(Proverbs 20:25 NIV)

"When a man makes a vow to the Lord or takes an oath to obligate himself by a pledge, he must not break his word but must do everything he said".

(Numbers 30:2 NIV)

"You boast, "We have entered into a covenant with death, with the realm of the dead we have made an agreement. When an overwhelming scourge sweeps by, it cannot touch us, for we have made a lie our refuge and falsehood our hiding place".

(Isaiah 18:13 NIV)

"Again, you have heard that it was said to the people long ago, 'Do not break your oath, but fulfill to the Lord the vows you have made.' But I tell you, do not swear an oath at all: either by heaven, for it is God's throne; or by the earth, for it is his footstool; or by Jerusalem, for it is the

*city of the Great King. And do not swear by your head,
for you cannot make even one hair white or black. All you
need to say is simply 'Yes' or 'No'; anything beyond this
comes from the evil one".*

(Matthew 5:33-37 NIV)

I looked at the story in Judges 11 about Jephthah. He was the head and commander of God's people Israel. They were at war against the Ammonites:

*"And Jephthah made a vow to the Lord: "If you give the
Ammonites into my hands, whatever comes out of the door
of my house to meet me when I return in triumph from
the Ammonites will be the Lord's, and I will sacrifice it as
a burnt offering".*

(Judges 11:30-31 NIV)

The Lord helped Jepthah win the battle. The problem with the secrecy of the vow was that he didn't tell anyone his vow. His only child, his daughter, was so full of joy on his return that she came through the door and was dancing and playing the tambourine. In Judges 30:35 (NIV) we read about his response:

*"When he saw her, he tore his clothes and cried, "Oh no,
my daughter! You have brought me down and I am devastated. I have made a vow to the Lord that I cannot break".*

What a sad story, but it shows what a God-fearing family they were and how they respected God's principle. The daughter agreed that the vow must be carried out and asked for two months to get herself ready. She was a virgin. Now she would never marry and have children. She respected her dad and the principle about oaths. Today you can imagine a daughter's response, which would go something like this – "On your bike dad, stuff the principle".

Thank God we are living this side of the cross and provision is made through grace to repent.

There are families today who have no idea about all the oaths and vows made in their bloodline. How deceptive is that? We can be living in the consequences of these from generations back as unless they are rescinded they remain in place. A family name is placed in the Book of the Lodge, which really is the Book of the Dead, and is shut. But God has a book called the Book of Life.

> *"He who overcomes shall be clothed in white garments, and I will not blot out his name from the Book of Life; but I will confess his name before My Father and before His angels".*
> (Revelation 3:5 NKJV)

And to those that overcome is a promise that our name will not be taken out of the Book of Life. When a book is sealed on earth, like the Masonic book, it is not opened again. It's possible in our generational history that our family name is under that seal of death only broken by the blood of Jesus.

Usually, when a person leaves the lodge these oaths and vows become a deadly weapon that can be activated by Satan, especially when a person dies. For the Christian believer, who has inheritance like a gold mine, these curses come into play and act like toxic waste and dilute what has been promised. This explains why in some families the blessings are not overtaking them. I don't know many Christian families where this is a reality. I notice these weapons Satan has. He seems to distribute them to various members of the family. Some have physical problems, others financial problems, others have unexplained deaths.

The following are just some of the consequences of the curses that come from Freemasonry:

1. It defiles your spirit.

2. There is a restriction placed on the flow of life.

3. It's a covenant of death that affects you spiritually and also your physical, emotional and mental health.

4. It brings divorce and separation.

5. It can bring a coldness to the emotions as it is a secret society, although many now have become Christians and brought exposure.

6. It can bring financial ruin.

7. All sorts of fears and nervous disorders.

8. Heart and throat problems are quite common.

9. Premature death or deformity in babies.

10. Poverty.

11. Schemes set up in the bloodline. It can bring about a scenario like false trials with a judge. A false trial is when false accusations, whether at work or in the family or any other relationship, one becomes the judge and the others the accusers.

12. It becomes difficult for a person to carry on being a

Christian with so much doubt and unbelief.

13. There is the third eye of freemasonry. It is the eye of Horus and opens you up to the occult ability to see into the spiritual realm (you can see the pyramid eye on the American dollar which is masonic).

14. Migraines, cancers, accidents, shoulder issues, emotional hardness… one can go on. The consequences of taking these hidden oaths is death to the family.

It is a real hinderance in being able to understand things by spiritual revelation, as Hermes is the false god of logic and reasoning, which is outworking in Freemasonry.

Offices and Mantles:

There are Masonic Offices and Mantles used within this religion. I know people who have been carrying a false mantle in the spirit which was put in place by an oath and passed down through generations. One of the signs would be that they can't help fighting life in the natural way by sheer will power and their own strength rather than allowing God to flow through their weakness in faith. At times they can even become aggressive in their spirit. This would be a false warrior spirit operating.

In the natural you can see a person change when holding an office in church life, or when a mantle of authority is passed down and placed upon them. It seems to empower them to do the job at hand, but what happens is they inherit an office or mantle, either from headship in church world or from the family lines, and the Masonic can still be there but not completely dealt with, which brings me to the point of mixture.

I have often wondered why the Spirit of Christ isn't always manifested in myself and others. Is it possibly in our spiritual pneumgenetics (Spiritual DNA)? This would mean we have inherited this mixture.

I understand the continuation of the sins and iniquities of the generations and the curses involved. I have seen too much evidence of people breaking free from all this, but why, for example, are some people carrying the spirit of the bull, or anti-christ spirit or kundalini spirit, when they are Christians? Baal is another false god worshipped. We often use the phrase, 'acting like a bull in a china shop', or it feels 'like being bitten by a serpent' and I wonder why we suffer so much back pain. I really had to look into this. In Hebrews 7:9-10 (NKJV) we read:

> *"Even Levi, who receives tithes, paid tithes through Abraham, so to speak, for he was still in the loins of his father when Melchizedek met him".*

How is that possible when Jacob was the father of Levi and Isaac was the great grandfather of Levi? Yet the scripture is saying Levi was in the body of Abraham in spirit form, all those generations ago. Jeremiah was known before he was formed in the womb and held the office of prophet to the nations:

> *"Before I formed you in the womb I knew you;*
> *Before you were born I sanctified you;*
> *I ordained you a prophet to the nations".*
>
> (Jeremiah 1:5 NKJV)

We know in the New Testament that God has given the offices of Apostles, Prophets and Evangelists, Pastors and Teachers as gifts from Christ to the church. People hold this office and the mantle to equip the church and build up the body of Christ, which is so important. There is a divine authority in what they are and what they carry that doesn't come from a man appointed position. But what happens in the spiritual DNA if what has been placed upon them is the inheritance of a false priesthood and a false warrior and a false mantle and given an office in the church to function? We have in the spirit realm, a mixture operating, which helps me to understand the confusion that exists in the Body of Christ. Then there can be a mixture of false signs and wonders that appear in a wrong spirit.

The gifts and the calling of God are without repentance.

There was an African guy I met who had raised 10 people from the dead (impressive) but to be honest, I just didn't like his spirit. He came to a meeting not far from where I lived and I heard later that he died at the age of 50 on the platform.

I sat in another meeting where so many people were on the floor under some sort of power. The guy appeared a nice chap but I left feeling as if I was being crushed. I was becoming heavy in my spirit and it felt like an anvil was on my head. Other times I have listened to apostles who have planted many churches. I understand they are the front line ministry sent out and usually strong people, but some have had such a hardness in their spirit. It's not what they have said that is wrong; it quite often is the truth, but I have felt really abused. It is as if something is trying to rape my identity. Other times there can be a spirit of divination operating when false prophetic words are given. You often find it's the Masonic in their bloodline or there will still be some occult influence. Other times I have witnessed friends of mine giving large sums of money in response to the preacher. We can see, once again, witchcraft can be at work which Paul spoke of to the church of Galatia. He wasn't speaking to an individual so it is possible for large groups to come under some sort of mind control, which explains why Hitler was used to convince the Nazis they were superior and we see that still today in some quarters where this has come down the family line.

In 1 John 4:1 (NIV) we read "*Dear friends, do not believe every spirit, but test the spirits to see whether they are from God*". It doesn't say to test the doctrine. None of us are a pure spirit and we all have some sort of mixture which is why it is important to clean ourselves up as in 1 Corinthians 7:1. We can see a mixture in families as the children marry and become one. Differences become obvious over time within their spiritual make-up.

It was time, now, to start ministering to these dear people whose lives were under the influence and power of the Masonic on a one to one basis.

We would lead them in general prayers and renounce what we felt at the time was the basic structure of the Masonic with just about a dozen of the degrees. This opened my eyes as I met believers who didn't really believe it, but were struggling in their Christian walk with the Lord. We would lead them in prayers of renouncing each degree (renounce means to 'speak off'). When we got to one degree this one person's mouth just locked open. She couldn't speak. She couldn't close it. It really freaked her out. Trying to say the name of Jesus was impossible. We carried on persistent in prayer and with a sudden rush the name Jesus was spoken out and the demon left.

On another occasion I was to share at a group in London. It was a very cold night. We were meant to share a meal with my friends. As we approached the steps to the flat a young couple came flying out in quite a hurry apologising for leaving. They said "help yourselves. There is a microwave inside". The wife's face had seemed to change shape and she was in a lot of pain, the doctor had agreed to see her as an emergency. We got inside. It was freezing. The heating now had packed up. About 30 people started to arrive. We had only one electric fire with one heating element that was working. Nevertheless, we shared. The Glory of the Lord filled the room as we raised our hands in worship. Many people were set free that night. The couple explained after the meeting that the doctor had diagnosed the wife as having Bell's Palsy on that side of her face. It was just an attack like everything else to disrupt God's plan and purpose. We broke the power of the Masonic curse on her face and teeth and within a short while the pain had gone and her face returned to normal shape. Praise God.

More and more people needed to be free from this weapon of mass destruction that affects whole families and spreads through the generations.

We now had too many people wanting help. The word spread. We started having public meetings to bring them all together. It would take a day to renounce the vows. We would instruct the people how to move in faith and how to engage the enemy of their souls by moving out of the soulish realm to push through in the spirit. This would be a head-on confrontation with the Goliath of an enemy. We would prepare ourselves now as a small team of about 10 people. We would engage in a Daniel fast of at least 21 days with no meat or sweet foods with prayer and intercession. We learnt a lot in these meetings as we were engaging in this spiritual battle. Some people were doing yoga positions and didn't know they were doing them. Others were flat on the floor. I shall never forget one meeting we took. The evangelist argued with me the night before as we were preparing the people to engage in this invisible war. He didn't believe it at all. He was used to healing people on the streets. Yet when the day came, he was so humble and honest that God met him and he was on the floor for most of the day. In his own words, he said, "I had no idea all this stuff was in me and affecting me". He was just so grateful. Who needs arguments? Let God come and demonstrate the power of His Kingdom.

There are a number of associated orders of Freemasonry. The order of the Eastern Star which the ladies go to. The Royal Orange Order. The Buffalo Lodge and Mormonism started by Joseph Smith who was a Freemason and the Jehovah's Witness Movement which was started by Charles Russell, also a Freemason.

One of our team members, now with the Lord, was a millionaire. In the 80's that was a lot of money. Then her husband owned jewellery shops. They also had a Rolls Royce and an Aston Martin, a swimming pool and tennis courts. A really lovely lifestyle. They were both Christians and decided to buy the Swan pub in Exeter, Devon. Everything was going so well. However in the middle of doing the place up the insurance wasn't in place. Her husband was only 42 when the pub caught fire with him and the son inside. The son managed to escape but her husband died in the fire. Within a year she went bankrupt. The police also accused her of starting the fire. Now poverty loomed at the door. Fortunately, the banks couldn't get their hold on her semi-detached property near where I live. It turns out a schizophrenic had started the fire. The Lord brought her into our path and it turned out that her father belonged to the Buffalo Lodge which is like a poor man's freemason.

The curses we see operating here are:

- Accidental death
- Death by Fire
- Financial Ruin
- And Humiliation

These are the consequences of the specific vows related to the Buffalo Lodge.

All of which this lovely lady had lived through. How tragic is that? All that loss and robbery. The pain was enough after losing her husband, let alone being judged and condemned as being guilty. There were specific oaths and vows that needed to be renounced and broken free from specifically. I counted it an honour to baptise her in water and for her to be free from the buffalo curses. Her testimony was that despite having all that wealth she now had a new and lasting happiness in her relationship with the Lord. She is now in heaven and is one of those precious jewels of God. There was so much of the love of God just flowing from just being in her presence. She became part of our team, reaching so many people who just like her had lived with a hidden agenda in their lives that the enemy of our souls had in place.

There are many signs and symbols and regalia used in the involvement, from covenant rings to blindfolds, to cords around the neck, shoulder, and stomach with a breastplate and a veil of mourning, crossed swords, pyramids, and special handshakes. One could go on. As these prophetically are put on, they need to be taken off prophetically.

Thank God that although Satan has deadly weapons that are used through deception, **God has an atomic bomb and it is called the Blood of Jesus.** Jesus who is our true High Priest who became a living sacrifice on the cross of Calvary where His blood fulfilled the justice of God by becoming sin for us.

> *"In Him we have redemption through His blood, the for-giveness of sins, according to the riches of His grace".*
>
> (Ephesians 1:7 NKJV)

And in Revelation 12:11 (NKJV):

> *"And they overcame him (Satan) by the blood of the Lamb and by the word of their testimony, and they did not love their lives to the death".*

This is spiritual warfare.

As we apply the blood by our confession it is speaking on our behalf in Heaven, as it continually cleanses us from all sin. The condition to overcome is we love not our life to the death. Whatever we hold on to will weaken us.

God designed families to be like an orchestra, all different looks, different abilities, yet to flow in harmony like His family – Father, Son and Holy Spirit – so it is a touch of heaven on earth. How precious is that? How important is it today that we not only renounce the oaths and vows taken by our ancestors to remove our families from the consequences of having taken those oaths, not only for ourselves, but for our children too. What oaths do they take by joining various clubs and organisations? Ever thought how legally binding they are to God, and what does it lock our children into?

After serving on a jury for the Crown Court it really brought home to me not only the importance of taking an oath, but how the point of law had to be the governing factor on which our whole legal system is based. Time and time again we, as the jury, had to come out of the Crown Court while a point of law was clarified. Satan doesn't need it to be clarified. He knows whether he has legal rights to our life, whether given to him by our ancestors or ourselves. What a privilege today, that we can stop his weapon of mass destruction outworking in our lives and also for future generations in our families. All because of Jesus.

How we desperately need to keep growing in revelation that will open us up to more freedom in Christ not forgetting that the authority of scripture is always paramount above anything else.

> *"Where there is no revelation, the people cast off restraint; But happy is he who keeps the law".*
> (Proverbs 29:18 NKJV)

The true interpretation means where there is no ongoing revelation. We can't afford to be complacent today as God has an agenda for us to be conformed to the image of His Son.

To begin to grow in this revelation was a quantum leap for me. I was struggling with moving not only in deliverance, but to spiritual warfare. I would rather know the truth and not remain blinded by ignorance or prejudice, because there must be fruit, even though I only knew a minority of God's people operating and living in this revelation.

Where there are friends or people you know who belong to the Masonic Lodge, or people where you can see it is evident they are operating in mixture, we must remember, **people are never our enemies**. We should treat all with love and respect. We are called to walk in the light and have fellowship one with another (1 John 1:7 NKJV) . As we do the consequence of fulfilling this is the Blood of Jesus cleanses us from all sin. If we fail to walk in the light and not have fellowship, we cannot expect the Blood of Jesus to cleanse us. And as we have learnt, nothing is automatic. We must meet the condition to see the protection and cleansing.

Prayer:

"Father God, Creator of Heaven and Earth, I come to you in the name of Jesus Christ Your Son. I come as a sinner seeking forgiveness and cleansing from all sins committed against You, and others made in Your image. I honour my earthly father and mother and all of my ancestors, but I utterly turn away from and renounce all their sins. I forgive my ancestors for the effects of their sins on me and my children. I renounce all of my own sins which have Masonry at their root. I renounce and rebuke Satan and all his works, and every spiritual force of his affecting me or my family. I renounce every involvement in Freemasonry or any other lodge or craft by my ancestors. I renounce witchcraft, the principle spirit behind Freemasonry. I now break its power over my life and family. I ask you Lord to lead me through this maze of deception. I am prepared to follow your leading.

In Jesus Name, Amen.

Chapter 23

FACING CANCER
AND DEATH

After the amazing time we had in Bedford in bringing the people to engage in Spiritual Warfare for themselves and their families, seeing the glory of God in the Sunday morning service as we looked across the congregation of hundreds on those that came and had been cleaned up from curses and defilements, unknown to me at the time, there was a plague outworking in my body. In October the previous year, I had noticed my stools had blood in them every time I visited the loo. Like most men, I just ignored it hoping it would just go away. Eventually, I spoke to Daph who is a Palliative Care Nurse. She soon made me go to the GP and within 2 weeks, I was sitting in hospital seeing the Registrar, still not really concerned. Ignorance at that time was bliss. He attempted to put a camera up my rear end, but was unable to do so as I was sore. Another appointment, then another appointment.

We had now completed the mission at Bedford helping the people to engage in Spiritual Warfare, by moving out of the soul realm into the spirit realm. Still really ignorant at the seriousness of the situation in my body I decided now, in July, to ask the question to the doctor. What if this is serious as I have been bleeding now for 9 months? This was the beginning of their change in attitude and thinking. Within a few weeks, I was admitted to hospital to have a procedure when a camera would be put up me. I started to feel a little nervous now – "What if they find something like a cancer?"

We had already booked a holiday in a holiday camp in the south of England and it would be there that we would be informed by telephone of the results.

When we got there the room was dark, small and very dingy. I just knew I couldn't spend a week there in this dark place. I had enough conflict going on in the inside of me that the environment was going to add to the situation. After my family persuaded the holiday camp I got an upgrade. The weather was bright but very windy most days.

We eventually heard from the hospital as Daph received the call. The results had shown from the examination they had found cancer in my rectum.

No matter how much one can prepare for such news, just knowing that this was the reality, that I had been living with cancer in my body all this time and it had only just been discovered. 9 months had gone by. The news just sent invisible waves of fear into my emotions which caused me to feel a bit like jelly wobbling all over the place on the inside of me. I couldn't think straight at first as the shock hit me like a bullet.

At least being on holiday gave me time to process this news and bring my spirit back to its rightful place. Despite my mind and emotions being all over the place there was an inner rest that I knew no matter what, **my Heavenly Father knows and He is never caught by surprise.** I was concerned as I was self-employed. Although I had some savings, things in life could become difficult. If I didn't work, I didn't earn anything. Meeting with the consultant who explained all that was going to happen and the possibility that I could be left living with an ileostomy bag for the rest of my life, I somehow felt that this was wrong. I explained I was a Christian and if there was a 50:50 percent chance I would like them to lean towards me living without the ileostomy bag. He explained that might not be possible as there wasn't much left of the rectum. I said I would pray. He wasn't a believer.

Within 2 weeks, Daph and I arrived on Sunday 23rdAugust early in the morning, to begin to prepare for the operation the next day. Daph looked distraught. I felt, after processing the situation, God was with me and I wasn't conscious of any fear and anxiety. The Lord had given me Psalm 91:14-16. I felt encouraged and supported by all the prayers and love shown to me. I was given Picolax to clean me out, but I was still able to go on a walkabout and meet some of the other patients. I met one guy who was 57. A self-employed taxi driver. His cancer was in a similar place to mine in the rectum. He had had chemo and radiotherapy since May and his bowels were still not working properly. He was fed by a drip. It was then that a cloud of negativity tried to land on me. I knew I had to maintain my disciplines and not allow fear to land, yet something changed and my blood pressure went up. I thought I would go back to my little room and keep there now. The stories were not doing me any favours.

Thinking about home, seeing Daph look like she was really struggling, especially with all that knowledge of cancer, and Becky who was 6 months pregnant at the time, and Patrick and family down in London... It was tough lying there – even more so when they changed my mattress to one that moves all the time.

I was first on the list Monday morning to go to theatre. I sat in the pre op room with 7-8 people all around me. I knew I had to prepare spiritually before the operation. Part of my preparation was that I would bind up any forces which would seek to take advantage of my vulnerability while being operated on. As soon as I did this within me, I couldn't say it out loud as people would think I would be talking about them, the guy behind me collapsed on the floor. I thought, not a good sign, as I drifted off to sleep as the epidural was administered in my back and the anaesthetic started to work.

Six and a half hours later I started to come round in the recovery room. I was as sick as a dog as I am allergic to anaesthetic. I felt really ill. The epidural would last about three days which would be my pain relief. I just knew on this unknown part of my journey that the Lord was with me and faithful, despite a growing sense of darkness around me. The following day my left leg felt like it was numb. There was no feeling right down to my foot.

The consultant who I was under had gone on holiday so another consultant who assisted with the operation was going to look after me. It was like I had two teams of people coming to see me on their rounds every morning. The problem to me was it was a bit confusing as for example, one team would encourage me to eat, the other team didn't mention it. But I was still feeling sick and dizzy and just had to keep lying down.

The first evening approached and I put my hand down the side of my body to feel the ileostomy bag and liquid was flowing down to my right leg and the smell was choking me. The bag had burst. So I had to have it changed, and all the sheets too. It was in the middle of the change-over of staff so I was left unattended. I had lost three pints of blood and seemed to have tubes in every part of my body. Drainage bags, catheters, oxygen, cannulas, which I kept knocking off frequently. What I called the wave machine that I was laying on was making me dizzier. I just couldn't sleep.

By Thursday the anaesthetic started to wear off. My left leg was still numb, and they said it was possible I could be suffering some nerve damage. My rectum had been taken out which is like a holding device in your body. I now had an ileostomy bag. My drain bag was taken out and I was deemed ready to go home. All the tubes were off ready for me to be released on the Friday. My blood pressure was still up at 196 over 106, for those who know about these things, and I had to have an ECG exam.

Unfortunately, it was August Bank Holiday weekend and I would now have to stay in until Tuesday. This was highly disappointing when I thought I would be home. They had to put my catheter back. I was highly emotional with the thought of having to stay in another three days until Tuesday.

That evening I started to experience a level of pain that I

have never experienced before. It felt like a continuous electric shock in the abdomen area. I was given some oromorph that didn't do much and wasn't strong enough pain relief. I would go just a few hours and it would start again. This went on over the weekend until I just couldn't bear it any longer and was then administered a big injection of morphine (which derives its name from the god, Morpheus, the god of dreams). I would be lying near to the nurses' station so they could watch me. A problem was now added to my discomfort in that a light was on all night, which just added to the problem that I just couldn't sleep. Every 3-4 hours it was like someone had flicked a switch and without warning my pain was unbearable. I would toss and turn trying not to cry out and not always being able to get the nurses'attention. I didn't know whether to scream or shout. All I did was continually groan. Louder and louder. I would press the call buzzer but get no relief. The morphine increased. I can only describe it as that I was in my unconscious state it felt that I was levitating and looking down from a very high position in the sky. I knew this was against God's commands and I bound up that spirit and immediately I was dropped only to be picked up by some weird people who whisked me through a load of underground tunnels travelling at what felt like 100mph. I then came across an altar with a false bronze statue of false god with people on their knees worshipping. I said to myself in my semi-conscious state, "Have I entered Hell? Have I died?" This was terrifying. It seemed as if it had been hours that I was in this state before I came round with sweat and my body shaken as I tried to keep my spirit in charge and not panic. The problem it caused was more anxiety – when was this going to happen again? And it's a bank holiday with no-one around! No help.

No relief. I kept crying out to the Lord for help, but it appeared Heaven had gone silent on me. The bank holiday finished and the consultant came round on Tuesday morning and suggested that they put the drain bag back in place.

I felt so sorry for my family who visited me every day. To see them so distraught and worried. Patrick came down from London and was so looking forward to good news, but there wasn't any.

I told Daph about what happened in the anaesthetic room with the guy collapsing after I had bound up all the demonic activity. She was concerned I was again engaging in invisible warfare. She said, "Let other people do this. There are other people praying everywhere. You don't have to fight now". I was thinking, "This is my life here". I now knew this was more serious than I first thought. I had to engage as well in the battle for my life. I have never experienced such pain as in this darkness and yet God didn't seem to be around. I wondered what would happen if people sent up soulish prayers? By that, I mean prayers that are given in little faith that originate in the soul and not in the spirit. They can act like curses. In Proverbs 28:9 (NKJV):

> *"One who turns away his ear from hearing the law, Even his prayer is an abomination".*

It is through the spirit of God and dependence on His leadings in our weakness that we pray. As in Romans 8:26-27 (NKJV):

> *"Likewise the Spirit also helps in our weaknesses. For we do not know what we should pray for as we ought, but*

the Spirit Himself makes intercession for us with groanings which cannot be uttered. Now He who searches the hearts knows what the mind of the Spirit is, because He makes intercession for the saints according to the will of God".

Praying soulish prayers in agreement is a very powerful force which can do much damage.

I could not afford to be passive. I knew passivity was the worst condition of a person's spirit which leaves them totally open. I had to engage in the battle to fight to live. I was aware it wasn't the doctors or nurses that were operating against me. The Devil wanted to take me out.

My drain bag was back and it wasn't long before another series of pain started. It was like we got through one issue and there was another one. Different, but still pain. I would now watch my stomach start to expand as if I was in a rapid pregnancy state. Before my eyes it kept growing till it could hold no more. I would then vomit 500mls of black bile a day filling up the cardboard hat they give you to be sick in. I would start to dread this as every vomit would pull all the stitches on the inside of me and I would be in agony. The nurse quickly pulled the curtains around me so as not to cause the other patients concern. Unfortunately, I can't vomit quietly. This went on for 2 weeks. I worked out the frequency. It took about 8 hours before the next big vomit which would last 15 minutes. Anxiety built up every day as I knew what to expect. While this was going on there were five attempts to put what is known as an NG tube into my nose, through my throat, down into my stomach to drain the bile. It started from the lowest rank nurse, right through to doctors and then I had to wait for a specialist another

3-4 days from another hospital who would then anaesthetise my throat to stop me gagging, but that didn't work. It was now decided that I would have to go under anaesthetic again to have an NG tube put in me.

Laying on a trolley in the pre-op room, I bound every invisible force in there. Suddenly the lady to my left who was carrying the tray with all the sterilized equipment on jumped and all the equipment fell to the floor clanging and banging. As I was drifting off, I thought, "Here we go again, I am in Your hands".

I woke up in my bed with the tube I could now feel at the back of my throat, only to discover my throat was so sore, I could hardly swallow. One of the doctors came over to me and apologised that while I was under and before they had correctly connected the NG tube to my stomach I had had a massive vomit where I discharged 1.5 litres of bile which was about to go down my airways. They had to quickly suction me and in the panic of the situation scarred the back of my throat.

I couldn't believe it. What else could go wrong? I was almost weeping with despair. At least I was alive. All I kept hearing from the Consultants in the morning was the phrase, "I think we have turned the corner now". Once again I was thinking, "I don't know what or whose notes, mate, you are looking at, but now would you like to swap places and say that?"

On one of Becky's visits (she was working as an intensive care nurse), urine was seen in my drain bag. Becky pointed out that it should be tested. The Consultant came round the next day and didn't really believe it, as it looked like during my first operation they cut my urethra tube by mistake, which is why the urine was in my system and why I felt such a degree of pain. The Consultant said, "I have never done this in 25 years working as a Consultant!" I thought, I am not interested in your past or pride but something is wrong.

After more CT scans, X Rays and MRI scans it turned out that Becky was right. This was what had happened and I would need a stent put in place to take the urine back to where it should be.

I kept hearing about mistake after mistake and I was becoming weaker and weaker, not only physically but every part of me. I kept crying out to God, "Where are you?" I have served you faithfully all my life. I have gone through so much pain and rejection, all because I love you more than I do myself. I have sought to obey you without counting the cost. **I believe if you ever have to count the cost you haven't paid the price.** I had said after Matthew died, and resigned from position and authority. I give You everything. This isn't fair!

I could feel I was getting angry with God. It was a stage I went through to be honest. I felt humiliated. I was having to be washed by nurses. I couldn't even sit myself up in bed. I had no energy. I had to ask anyone who was passing by to bring my little table with my little clock from home. For some reason I cherished it as it reminded me I had a home. I needed my table to be near me as at times it got moved when cleaned and I couldn't even reach it to bring it back. I had books I couldn't read, let alone write a journal. I was too dizzy and ill to do anything.

I was then told this Friday I would see the specialist to have the stent put in my back which would lower the pain. Friday came round. The morning came and went. Friday afternoon came. About 3pm I decided to ask one of the staff nurses when I would be taken down to have my stent fitted.

Looking rather embarrassed, he said, "I'm really sorry. There has been some trouble in communication and we thought it had been done, so it won't be today now".

I could feel the anticipation of hope just collapse within me and I was filled with despair. I now had to be very watchful as **I knew that the worse death of all is the death of hope.** My soul was weakened by another blow. Trying to be positive, at least the weekend had arrived, with nobody hauling me about or putting me on these pat slides. At least I could rest and see if it could be done on Monday.

Monday morning arrived along with a parade of white coats and the sound of busyness and curtains being pulled back. I asked the question when my curtains were pulled around me and I lay there trying to hold back my tears of desperation, "When is my stent going to be put in?"

Sheepishly came back the reply, "We are really sorry but the specialist who is meant to put your stent in has gone on holiday for 2 weeks which means you will have to wait until he returns".

I replied, "Surely in a hospital of this size there is more than one person who can do this procedure?"

"The other specialists have looked at your notes and feels yours is so complex it's best you wait until the top man comes back", was the reply.

Talk about filling you with confidence. I was almost at the point that nothing surprised me anymore, as on every single stage of this journey, I seemed to have a battle. I had no control over my life. I have never felt so vulnerable as having to trust those who are supposed to care for me. I felt worthless and that I had little value to them. I just felt so alone. I cried to God again, "I am only human. I don't know how much longer emotionally and spiritually, let alone physically, I can cope with this." The assault of darkness just never let up on my spirit. I was now having dreams about my own funeral. I could see the coffin go through the curtain and my friends and family were crying. I was so sleep-deprived. I asked to be moved away from the nurses' station. I felt I hadn't slept for weeks. I even begged for a sleeping pill which I would never normally take. I asked to borrow Patrick's sunglasses because of the light at night above the centre of room. I just had to keep my spirit in charge and refuse to be controlled by the circumstances and keep my inner focus on the Lord, despite all my mind being tormented and all over the place over which I seemed to have little control.

It was 3 weeks before the specialist saw me to have my stent put in. I asked him before he started how long would this procedure take. He said anything from 10 minutes to an hour. I laid on my side facing half a dozen TV monitors. He started to weave this stent in the base of my back. The pain hit me like a thunderbolt. I shouted out, "It's hurting mate!" The anaesthetic where he had injected me had worn off. He gave me another injection and then I finally had my stent in, which would at last give me some relief from the pain and discomfort.

It was great seeing so many friends and leaders come to visit me. It helps when you are laid there for so many weeks, now turning into months. I heard years later that people thought I was dying, even Daph said that and she has seen so many deaths as I looked so grey and thin and looked like I was dying. The Consultant even wrote to my GP and said this was a battle, and he wasn't a Christian.

The drama didn't stop. I was now not eating and was watching my muscles wasting away. I was now fed with a central line put in my neck which would give me enough nutrition to keep me alive. I knew I was slipping away. My faith went down to rock bottom. I had to say to myself, what are the pillars of my faith, and to this I stand.

1. I know God is good and He is my Heavenly Father.

2. I know that Jesus died on the cross for me and lives today.

3. I know the word of God is true.

4. I know God loves me and is sovereign as I am forgiven.

5. I tried repeating a prayer for overcomers that I taught Becks years ago. Even that felt like a ritual. I had so little faith. Daph and Becks on their visits noticed I didn't have any pain relief. They had forgotten to give me my little button which when pressed releases a little morphine when you need it. The guy opposite had his curtain pulled round in the middle of that night and then I saw him wheeled away. He had died.

I now had taken a turn for the worse. Becks contacted her boss in ITU and he got permission to look at my notes. I was starting to think this was becoming more serious. Becks spoke to the doctors and said, "If something isn't done we will have to go privately as something is wrong". I can't remember much – I think I must have blacked out. I knew there were people interceding for me. The next thing I knew I was being rushed to theatre as a blood clot had been discovered. Everyone seemed a bit panicky. I was then operated on. More anaesthetic. When I woke up and looked under the sheets and saw a number of bright metal clips, it looked like I had been cut in half right through my stomach muscles. I now had a very lumpy front stomach held together by metal clips that were holding me together. It felt as if I had been mutilated in the spirit. That I had been put on the altar, cut open and blood shed, but thank God I have the breath of life on the inside of me, given to me by God. Then I got the answer to the torment in my dreams, when I saw my funeral. It was a cremation and all my family know I don't want to be burnt. I want to be buried like the saints and the prophets of old. So Satan had lied to me. It wasn't my funeral. Those dreams stopped then.

After having so many operations I was so dizzy I couldn't even move my head. I had to keep perfectly still as I had got labyrinthitis. Once again, the surgeon was baffled. They sent for another specialist from another hospital. I had a CT scan on my head and was given medication to settle that.

On the eighth week, the consultant came round with his entourage and was so angry, almost shouting, to the white coat people, "Get it out, get it out!!" meaning the central line in my neck that was feeding me as I had had it in too long. While all this noise was going on, I heard a conversation in the spirit world. The demons were talking. "We can't kill him. We can't kill him". I remember saying in the spirit, "I will only go when God calls me, not when you try and take me".

I knew that if I came into agreement with death I would be dead. I can see, to be honest, when you are that weak, it is so easy to cross over, but I refused. I knew I had more to do on earth. I needed to keep my will in a position of agreement with God as death at this stage would be wrong.

"Again, truly I tell you that if two of you on earth agree

about anything they ask for, it will be done for them by
my Father in heaven. For where two or three gather in my
name, there am I with them".

(Matthew 18:19-20 NIV)

On one occasion I was asked to pray for a guy in hospital. I thought, "What's the point? He has had lots of prayer already?" I felt the Lord say to me to ask him a question, which I did when I visited him. I said to him, "Have you completed God's call on your life now? If so, you can die, but if you haven't, you need to start to align your will with God and stand." You could see he had given up on life. He thought about it and it wasn't long before he recovered and was out of the hospital serving God now all over the world.

I am careful what I come into agreement with, as it can work negatively as well as positively. The secret is in Matthew as above. The disciples had been gathered together in the name of Jesus – no other name but Jesus. We see the contrast in Genesis 11:1-9 when agreement was made to build the Tower of Babel, and also wrong agreements with Jewish people when they shouted in Matthew 27:25 (NIV), *"His blood is on us and on our children!"* bringing a generational curse that exists and operates today.

After being tested when the central line was taken out, it was discovered I had an infection. I had to wait another week before they could treat me and for the infection to clear up. I knew there were strongmen called Death and Hell who are mentioned in Revelation 6:8. I wondered if this was who I had been fighting?

After 9 weeks, it felt as if I had faced death and hell and the enemy finally gave up. I sat in a wheelchair in the entrance to the hospital waiting for a car to arrive to take me home. I had lost 3 stone in weight and looked like death warmed up. I had little colour, just a grey complexion. While I sat there this cloud of fear descended upon me, a voice saying, "It's not safe at home. Now what if something goes wrong? You don't have the expertise at home, nor any equipment". I was shaken on the inside of me as all my nerves were filled with anxiety with everything that had gone wrong. I now battled the thought. I had been almost institutionalised.

When I got home, my dear wife Daph had had the hall and bedroom decorated. I could feel my body was still in trauma as everything seemed to be moving on the inside of me. I tried to put pen to paper. I was shaking so much I couldn't write. I saw my little garden. It looked so beautiful. A whole new appreciation of life itself just overwhelmed me. Everything seemed to have colour and was filled with so much peace.

I still struggled to walk up the stairs but I knew they wouldn't have let me leave hospital until I could manage them. I literally pushed these little legs of mine that had wasted away up to the top. Yes. It was difficult but at least I was out of hospital.

I had this ileostomy bag for another 9 months. I went into hospital in August. Now it was November and my daughter Becks had given birth to a baby girl, Esther.

Visiting my son Patrick and his family in London for Christmas time turned out for me to be a wave of unexpected emotion. Being with everyone was so lovely, until my dear granddaughter Abigail jumped on my lap and the ileostomy bag came away from my body. The humiliation I felt was something I just couldn't control. I quickly made my way to the bathroom and my dear wife came and cleaned me up. Unfortunately, I had forgotten to bring a spare bag with me which is a lesson I would never forget.

After 9 months, I was admitted to hospital for a week to have the ileostomy bag taken off. As I am allergic to anaesthetic the effect didn't wear off for four days. I now had a hole in the side of me that you could drop a golf ball in and just about see it!

When my body started to work again, which it hadn't for about a year, the pain shot through me like a knife. I was walking like John Wayne – slowly, with very wide steps. I was back in hospital dealing with infection and pain control so many times. Eventually, something had to give. Daph took me to see the GP, crying herself which is just not like her, and pleaded for them to increase the dose of amitriptyline (a nerve pain drug) which really knocked me out. I just wasn't myself. It took me about 2 years to recover. I had lots of prayer ministry which helped me to come off the drugs. I was told not to lift anything now, due to the number of operations I had had. I have an incisional hernia which means I'm not allowed to lift any heavy equipment. The season of being a self-employed welder had now come to an end.

Losing so much in such a short period of time makes one think. As usual I would start asking the question, Why????

Interestingly, as we walk with God, the Spirit of God does impregnate us with knowing the truth. Our minds can come up with all sorts of arguments, but I knew deep down there was a strategy operating that Satan had set up and part of that was that my Father had had a deep relationship with a lady who was not his wife which was a generational sin I had in my DNA. Also, I had given a legal right by crossing a line in a relationship many years previously. I developed an ungodly join in my heart which was hurting with so much rejection that I had gone through. I know in Proverbs 4:20-23 (NIV) it says:

> *"My son, pay attention to what I say;*
>   *turn your ear to my words.*
> *Do not let them out of your sight,*
>   *keep them within your heart;*
> *for they are life to those who find them*
>   *and health to one's whole body.*
> *Above all else, guard your heart,*
>   *for everything you do flows from it."*

I have always said your heart is like a safe. You don't give the key to many people. Whatever is in your heart will win at the end of the day. I found intimacy in a relationship which was ungodly. I knew it wasn't possible for me to commit physical adultery, but there is what is known as spiritual adultery, and it exposes you to a takeover spirit. Yet the most possessed man in the bible, Legion, who was in the graveyard, tied with chains which broke when Jesus came, still had enough of his will left intact to come to Jesus. I could see that despite the experience in the hospital, death couldn't touch my will. Temptation and sin are nice, which is why we are tempted. The only way out is to share what you are going through which was where I found the beginning of freedom, when I shared with my wife Daph. The invisible sin of pride was thinking I could handle this. There are powers that are invisible that we have to wrestle against. An enemy who is scheming and looking for ways to rob us of our health; whether it is physical or mental, he wants to destroy us. I leant a new lesson the hard way as this was something I had never been exposed to before, but also it goes to show when different pressures come to us we really don't know our hearts. We read the progression and the outworking of being disobedient to the principles and laws of God in James 1:13-16 (NKJV):

> *"Let no one say when he is tempted, "I am tempted by God"; for God cannot be tempted by evil, nor does He Himself tempt anyone. But each one is tempted when he is drawn away by his own desires and enticed. Then, when desire has conceived, it gives birth to sin; and sin, when it is full-grown, brings forth death. Do not be deceived, my beloved brethren".*

It is like when a baby is being born there is a birth of life, but here there is a birth of death. It opens us up to a spirit of death which affects every part of our spirit, soul and body. When you are under that power you can see that unless you bring it to the light your will may be taken over to the degree that you can lose sight of reality. It costs us to expose our hearts, as pride wants to hide these failings.

I think the reason God has to speak clearly about not being deceived is that we all have blind spots. **Deceived people don't know they are deceived.**

It was years ago I walked through that experience, a long time before I was ill, and I have lived in the spirit of repentance. I didn't appreciate the significance of God's love gift – His spiritual laws. What I had allowed to be sown was reaping death in me and lay there growing. I thank God for his grace and mercy. Years after God has shown me my problem was the guilt of not being able to forgive myself for what I had done. By not doing so, I was limiting the power of the Blood of Jesus.

I have talked to leaders and others who are struggling and tried to warn them. **Be careful how far you go into sin. You can get forgiven but you might not be able to change the consequences.** Like Esau when he gave his birthright away just for a bowl of soup, he couldn't find a place for repentance.

> *"for he found no place for repentance, though he sought it diligently with tears".*
>
> (Hebrews 12:17 NKJV)

Thank God for His grace! In today's world we need to come off the seat of judgement because nobody knows how they would be under certain pressures that exist in life. Never underestimate the power of Satan. I know God is far greater than anything against us.

> *"You are of God, little children, and have overcome them, because He who is in you is greater than he who is in the world".* (1 John 4:4 NKJV)

Chapter 24

HAVE WE MISSED THE POINT?

I heard Jamie Buckingham, a famous writer, say in a meeting that "God has been kicking the hell out of me". After all that I have been through in life I can relate to that statement. God exposed my heart and dealt with me. He knew when I was ignorant, full of pride and my own strength, when I thought I could overcome anything.

I was to discover my greatest obstacle in life was myself, being independent and self-sufficient. I now thank God for the wilderness training which caused my life to be totally dependent on God for everything – being stripped away from my church family and financial security. Living with my dear wife Daph, who is opposite to me in almost everything, was used mightily by God bringing change to me. Daph is what I call my 'gracelet'.

Brokenness is such a major key to deal with the soul and opens one up to the release of the Spirit of God. When one knows you can do nothing without the Lord Jesus, beyond words and doctrine, but that through your brokenness experience you can become vessels that can bring life.

The mental issue I grew up with today is known as dyslexia. I didn't know this was a disability as in my earlier years people weren't diagnosed, so we just got on with life. If that's all you have ever known you tend to think it is normal. Yet isn't it amazing that this weakness became a strength as I had to rely on my spiritual intuition more than most. My spirit would just know things but my mind wanted to understand. My spirit grew as my mind didn't always have the capacity to understand. It was a blessing not having a label in some ways, because it is possible to live under the power of a label put on oneself.

The imperative need today is to distinguish what is operating in us and around us, whether it is a mixture of Spirits, or the hidden power of the soul being manifest. I am a welding specialist. I know, for example, if you have to weld 2 pieces of metal together it is possible to have the join with air holes and what is known in the trade as 'slag trap impurities'. These weaken the joint and when subject to certain pressures, can cause fractures and break.

Dealing with the mixture in life is so important as what we carry can block the flow of life of God flowing within us, if we are to be led by the Spirit and not by circumstances, or by our own common sense. God is a supernatural God. We can be like the welded joint in life, but when subject to certain pressures, this can cause a fracture in our life and sometimes a breakage can occur.

Prevention is better than a cure when the searchlight of the Holy Spirit comes and exposes the mixture within us through the trials and testings of life. We can deal with this mixture of spirits that exist in our makeup by following the strategy of the Lord as we give Him permission to clean us and bring us to wholeness; body, soul and spirit. One of the greatest enemies in our time is being driven and being busy. It's no wonder Jesus drew himself away from the pressure of the crowd to spend time in prayer. It's so easy to be just caught up in good works that might be dead works if they are not the Will of God. They can be just like hay, wood and stubble which is found in large quantities but burned up when the Fire of God comes. God has ordained and prepared works for us to enter into. They will be like precious jewels, found in smaller quantities yet stand the testing of the Lord in the Day of Judgement.

Depression, discouragement and unrealised dreams, broken relationships and unanswered prayers with the loss of hope and feeling trapped in an invisible prison, are like those air holes and slag traps within us. This isn't God's will for our life, which is why **we need to bring our past to conclusion and get cleaned up spiritually so when the unexpected and invisible pressures hit us we won't fracture or break.**

God's love for us is stronger than death itself and has our best interests at heart. He is calling us to a higher ground in life that we may be able to see as He sees and hear as He hears so we can discern what is happening behind the circumstances of life, otherwise we can misinterpret what's really going on in the invisible world. Instead of sheep being led astray and just wasting our life with no real purpose, we are those with experience, becoming a voice and not just following circumstance or any personality.

In my training in the wilderness the Lord was teaching me this new way of living, being led by the Spirit of God and looking beyond what is happening in the natural realm.

We parked our little caravan at the Christian camp in Suffolk which was a family camp led by the Evangelist Don Double. There must have been about 1,000 people there. We were part of a group of about 100 people. After the evening meeting, we would have some hot chocolate and a chat. A young man came up to me. I suppose he was about 21 or 22 and said he had a problem. I said to him, "What's that, mate?" "This uniform I wear. At times it seems to come between me and God. Can you pray?" My first thought was, I haven't a clue what to pray. "Let's ask the Lord," I said. The first thought that came to me was – it's the spirit of the anti-Christ. The second thought, which is usually me was – that's a bit strong, isn't it? But I decided to step out in faith and come against this spirit. This young man was thrown to the ground and started making noises and was all over the place. He started ripping up handfuls of grass like a mad-man. It all looked and sounded quite scary because of all the commotion. A couple of leaders came out and said, "We will go and get John Barr", who is one of the main leaders in the UK on Deliverance Ministry. Well, I know John. He was one of my mentors. I said, "He won't be very happy if you wake him up at 11pm at night". 10-15 minutes later I was still struggling to remove this spirit and John's head popped up between the tents and said, "It's only Pat" and left! I thought – now you are here you might have helped me! Eventually, the young man came into freedom as this spirit left. He came into the awning and as we were talking the Holy Spirit came again and he was baptised in the Holy Spirit and started speaking in tongues. Also, that week he was baptised in water.

Once again, I asked the question why did a Strong Man called Anti-Christ have anything to do with wearing a uniform? Then as the weeks passed by I was seeking God and I listened to a teaching by Derek Prince on the Enemies We Face. **One of those enemies was Anti-Christ, and this spirit is not only opposed to Christ, but comes in place of Christ.** That's not to say that for anyone who wears a uniform it comes in place of Christ, but to him, it had.

This really opened me up as I started to understand how today so much has come in place of Christ in our lives, which leads me back to what we looked at earlier when we looked at the world and its meaning. If the world's way of thinking, which God has already placed judgement on along with its values and way of doing things, if it hasn't a subordinate place in our hearts the spirit of this world is actually Anti-Christ – its ultimate goal being the zenith of it all – then the outworking of this world system is to create an environment to receive the full manifestation of the man of Anti-Christ, who will operate in false signs and wonders. Minds and wills are already being seduced slowly as so much is coming in place of Christ. He is even after our Worship. As the hidden power of the soul, often generated through music which produces such a feel-good factor, takes place of worshipping God in Spirit and Truth we can now see there is a practice of **worshipping the worship.** The focus has become the music and our feelings, which isn't God. **Power without presence is dangerous.** God inhabits our praises.

Our worship must be from our hearts with the focus on the Lord Jesus, and if the worshippers are not cleaned up from, for example, from a rock music background, the mixture of spirits is released which is becoming a takeover spirit. It is so subtle.

Bringing our soul under subjection to the Spirit of God within is essential which comes about through prayer and fasting. This isn't an option. **How different would our worship be today if we saw the Lord standing in the midst of us?**

On another occasion I had a pastor ring me up from London. Would I see this apostolic guy who had such a deep problem with anger that no matter how much counselling and prayer he received, he still has this problem? He was no longer in ministry as this mixture of spirits was affecting the people he spoke to.

I spent a number of hours with him and found I really couldn't reach him. I rang the pastor up and said he needed 6 months of the preparation of the Holy Spirit.

Well… 6 months went by. I had a call to say he was now ready. In some ways, my heart sank. I knew I didn't have the answer and felt helpless. Then the pastor asked if he could come down as well. Talk about anxiety wanting to kick in.

They both arrived. He was a big strapping sort of guy. They both sat down to the left of me. We had a cup of tea – that helps us to relax and break the ice, or so we are told. I was really hoping by now God would have given me some keys, yet despite all my preparation, I sat there not having a clue. I said, "Let's just start this time in prayer." I was still feeling nervous as I knew he was desperate and had been to bigger ministries, yet all I am is a welder with a heart for God. As we prayed, the Holy Spirit quickened my prayer and as I looked across the room, I could see the Holy Spirit was all over this guy. Without any words I got out of my seat, walked over to him and started to minister to him as the Lord directed. The major key that unlocked his prison was when I came against the Beast of the Age and the Anger of the Beast. I had never prayed that before. I just knew it was in Revelation 13:2 (NIV):

"The dragon gave the beast his power and his throne and great authority".

The Holy Spirit just kept pouring in His revelation and power. The whole room was now filled with such glory it was almost tangible. After ministering, I noticed that the pastor had the Holy Spirit all over him, so we just had to just follow what God was doing as I just ministered to them both.

I came to this meeting, helpless in my own understanding, but I trusted God. I felt this was another divine appointment. Once again, I could now see how events in the Book of Revelation are now happening on the earth before the Lord comes back. We can also see the rise of the spirit of Jezebel in our midst who operates in illegitimate authority. This spirit loves power and will try to bring as many people under its influence as possible, and will seek to take you over eventually.

Six months later, I was asked to go to a meeting with a lot of leaders coming together in London. It was there that the wife of the apostle guy came up to me with such a lovely smile. She was so thankful to God. She said, "I have been married to my husband for over 20 years. I can honestly say I have a new husband. He is a changed man".

For me, once again, this is the reality of the new covenant, **living with a resurrected Christ not a historical Christ.** Watching our God come to His people by the power of the Holy Spirit. This is the point – Jesus is alive and working now through ordinary people, the nameless and the faceless, who just live in the flow of life that comes from our Lord Jesus – today.

Our Heavenly Father is the life source of us all. We are family, not an institution or an organisation. Jesus is our elder brother. **Jesus himself calls us brothers because Father God calls us sons.**

Our God is bringing us out of thinking and acting the same as the world. We are different and distinctive, which is why we don't feel at home in this worldly environment.

We were ministering to an unmarried mother and I was explaining about the Gospel Jesus preached, that it wasn't just the Gospel of Salvation, but the Gospel of the Kingdom. As she was repenting and confessing her sins, she found it so difficult to talk. Her voice became broken, tears flowed from her just running down her face. Her little girl was also in the room and was so affected by it all as she gazed at her mum. Eventually, through her broken voice, she finished, and the Lord showed us how to continue to minister to her. After we had finished, she explained what was going on. She had felt the Lord's presence so strongly – He was standing in front of her – and the reason she had a job to talk was that His holiness just overwhelmed her.

Our Lord Jesus is moving through His body, this living organism that we call church today, and He wants to do so much more. **The lady came the prescribed way through repentance and confession which is our lifestyle.**

Our Lord Jesus learnt obedience through suffering himself. Jesus Himself took on the baptism of suffering in Luke 12:50 and Mark 10:38. If we follow Jesus the Spirit of God will lead us through this baptism if we want reality and truth as God has His divine purpose in creation that He shall have many children. In Romans 8:19 (NKJV):

"For the earnest expectation of the creation eagerly waits for the revealing of the sons of God".

Also in Hebrews 2:10:

"For it was fitting for Him, for whom are all things and by whom are all things, in bringing many sons to glory, to make the captain of their salvation perfect through sufferings".

That's not suffering for sufferings sake. But our Lord has a purpose. For us to grow from just being born again to becoming a true son, to identify the hallmark of being a son as in Romans 8:14 (NKJV):

"For as many as are led by the Spirit of God, these are sons of God."

This suggests movement. It also shows us that the sons of God have their souls in subjection to Father God just like Jesus who by his subjection has dominion. Authority was given by the Father as Jesus obeyed the Father. Jesus lives in relationship with the Father. As sons on earth, developing our relationship with our Heavenly Father who loves us intensely is the highest priority in life. I've always thought it was so sad that the elder son in the parable of the prodigal son had only a relationship with his father based on works. He lived with a slave mentality and didn't really know the Father's heart. Yet he had lived in his Father's household all those years. Having just a biblical knowledge of Jesus and our Heavenly Father without experience is lifeless. It prevents us from realising the fullness of this glorious relationship because of the new covenant which has been established by both parties. It brings us to a lifestyle of expectancy and spontaneity as we follow the leading of the Holy Spirit and seeing the manifestation of His Presence and Glory and Power. Didn't Paul the apostle say, he came not in word only, but in the power and demonstration of the Spirit of Life (1 Corinthians 2:4)?

When we look at the description of the one who lives within us in Colossians 2:9 (NKJV):

"For in Him dwells all the fullness of the Godhead bodily; and you are complete in Him, who is the head of all principality and power".

Wow! What does that mean? We can have access to His nature, His Love, His Authority, His Grace, His Power and Truth? That **we can live on a daily basis being Christ conscious, and not self-conscious.** We can live with the unpredictability of our God as it becomes so natural when we just abide in His presence. Yes. This is normal Christianity.

I have said many times to people who work with me, when the Lord shows up and just ministers to the hopeless, the discouraged, the depressed and those in all sorts of prisons, Jesus comes and brings release. The prophets of old looked forward to this day of the new covenant when the veil of Jesus, his flesh and the temple veil was removed. The presence of Jesus becomes a reality. It is so much better than just reading stories about Jesus and living in concepts that don't produce life. In Galatians 2:20 (NKJV),

> *"I have been crucified with Christ; it is no longer I who live, but Christ lives in me; and the life which I now live in the flesh I live by faith in the Son of God, who loved me and gave Himself for me".*

When you think about it, you cannot crucify yourself in the future. Our old man (nature) was crucified in the past at the cross with Christ. How exciting is that?

Satan, all through life, will always try to destroy the life of Christ within us.

We then become life-givers, like Jesus in this world of need. We would change our heritage into a legacy, which will go on forever as the life we carry is eternal. God's best for our lives isn't visitation although revival is great, but habitation in us so that the purpose of God can be fulfilled. There has been in recent years such a turning away from the Living Christ into managing our problems by embracing many philosophies. Paul warns us (Colossians 2:8 NIV):

> *"See to it that no one takes you captive through hollow and deceptive philosophy, which depends on human tradition and the elemental spiritual forces of this world rather than on Christ."*

It cost the Father with His extravagant love to make provision for all the needs of humanity by the finished work of the cross. How sad it is that we are turning to anything but the

Living Jesus and obeying Him. Today, particularly in the West, we have so many resources or means to manage our problems, but I would encourage you that there is another way of living, and not just to accept the historical fact that Jesus died on the cross. He has purchased full salvation, body, soul and spirit. The provision for all our needs is found because of the completed works of Jesus at the cross of Calvary. These wonderful promises are given to us because Jesus is alive today.

When you think of God's people under the leadership of Joshua in the Old Testament, when they came to the River Jordan and could see the Promised Land, their inheritance as God's people, they did not just look at it and say, "How wonderful. This is a land with so much provision that can meet all our needs. This looks so different from living under those taskmasters who took so much from us and gave us so much fear and anxiety. It's almost too good to be true, that this is our promised land," and then just camped there looking at it. If we apply the truth of this today, we know we have the land of promises because of Jesus, but to talk again and again of yesterday and about what Jesus did for His people in the bible is good, but the reality is that He is here by the Spirit of God to lead us to the full provision of His promises today by listening and obeying Him. We find in Exodus 23:20-33 God's battle plan for deliverance, gaining ground little by little.

It was theirs as they began this journey of life and hope under the Commander Jesus Christ and took hold of this wonderful provision by trusting, by believing and then acting on the faith God had already given them. How often do you hear, "I haven't the faith"? In Romans 12:3 God has given each of us a measure of faith. The problem is we use it to believe our doubts and struggles and strive to obtain more. There is a rest in faith. Nothing is going to be handed on a plate to us. **It's been a lie of the Devil that we don't have to engage in the invisible war against him who wants to keep us with the mentality of slavery. You never win war on the defensive.** It's too easy today to just live by sight, but we are called to live by faith to become overcomers. **You can't have a victory unless you have a battle.** People are never our enemies. The war is against the Life of the Son of God on the inside of you. The Devil wants to kill that life and seeks our agreement through weakening and breaking, and bringing in substitutes to replace the Living Christ, so our relationship eventually leads us into death. Like so many marriages today when other things come between, eventually, there is a separation.

We are the Bride of Christ joined to Him by the Spirit of God. As we engage in the trials and battle of life, we will grow into becoming full, mature sons of God. In doing so, we will be a voice because we have walked with the Lord in our life. Our experience of the Knowledge of God creates a message within us and what eventually happens is we **no longer just speak the message, we become the message.** A voice, not an echo of something we read or have heard. Jesus called John the Baptist the greatest prophet yet. There is no recorded prophecy that he gave. He was that voice in the wilderness, living and speaking the message God had given him. No wonder. He wasn't afraid of death. He had a faith within him that gave him hope for the future.

There are so many tensions in the body of Christ that exist as we are all in different places on this journey of life. The following are some of those that still exist. Perhaps you can ask

God and identify where you are and how you operate.

1. World (system of thinking)   *Kingdom of God*

2. Natural Life   *Spiritual Life*

3. Visible   *Invisible*

4. Soulish   *Spiritual*

5. Law   *Grace*

6. Doctrine   *Life*

7. Bondage   *Freedom*

8. Restriction   *Health*

9. Religion   *Intimate relationship*

10. Lies   *Truth*

11. Information   *Revelation*

12. Being an echo   *Being a voice*

13. Concept of Jesus   *Reality*

And one that has been used for decades and hasn't changed – the term is old and new school. Have you ever thought of what is of real value to God Himself? Look in 2 Timothy 2:20-21 (NKJV) – it does shed some light on this.

This is a journey of transition. If we embrace it we will find our options become less as we will have entered the narrow way.

> *"Enter through the narrow gate. For wide is the gate and broad is the road that leads to destruction, and many enter*

through it. But small is the gate and narrow the road that leads to life, and only a few find it." (Matthew 7:13 NIV)

As we embrace the love of the Father, our motivating force will be one of being led, not driven. The Father has given us His map (His Word) and the Spirit of God as our guide. Together, as His Body, we recognise all these different tensions in the Body of Christ. As we learn to love and accept each other with the empowering work of Grace in our life, we will mature as Sons of God, living in freedom and as carriers of life. No doubt we will make many mistakes that are part of growing up, but we learn to become overcomers as in Revelation 21:7 (NKJV),

"He who overcomes shall inherit all things, and I will be his God and he shall be My son."

If we are going to inherit all things, we must have to overcome. **We never have a victory unless we have a battle to overcome.**

It's not us indulging in false guilt, which is often used as an argument to hinder us even trying.

We are faced with choices every day of our life and this wonderful living saviour Jesus Christ, can be with us, not historically, not in concept, not in word only, but in person.

How many of us would not get in an aircraft today if the pilot mentioned to everyone "Oh, by the way, this is my first flight. I have read all the books. I have been to many meetings, but I have never flown before". I don't think he would have many takers. **Knowledge isn't enough.** We must have experience and we will only have that by God given permission, and ourselves embracing the journey by being true to oneself, so then **you will**

no longer be an echo, but a voice, part of the living organism of the Body of Christ. Living by Faith, not by sight.

> *"When the Son of Man comes, will He really find faith on the earth?"* (Luke 18:8 NKJV)

When we look at those on the other side of the cross in the Old Covenant and how they lived and died:

> *"These all died in faith, not having received the promises, but having seen them afar off were assured of them, embraced them and confessed that they were strangers and pilgrims on the earth".* (Hebrews 11:13 NKJV)

These are historical examples that demonstrate the outworking of faith and hope and love in life today. There is an extravagant love that our Heavenly Father has for us, His people. There is a love that surpasses all knowledge. We can know and be filled with the resources of the One who upholds the universe.

As we yield to the progressive discipline of the Spirit of God in life it will lead to the formation of Christ within us by the Spirit.

> *"My dear children, for whom I am again in the pains of childbirth until Christ is formed in you".* (Galatians 4:19 NIV)

From our lives we can impart life, no longer be tossed to and fro by every wave of negativity. We can live consistently, walking together with our God.

Today we face a choice the moment we get out of bed and

put our feet on the ground. We can choose to obey the life of Christ within us, or choose to come under those negative lies about ourselves and our future. Quite often we are at our most vulnerable coming out of sleep as the unseen battle continues.

To abide in Christ is to live with a conscious reality of living and trusting Christ within and agreeing to follow the Life of God, just as Jesus did when he said in John 5:19 (NIV),

> *"Very truly I tell you, the Son can do nothing by himself; he can do only what he sees his Father doing, because whatever the Father does the Son also does".*

To be able to be conscious of that one must be following the thread of the Holy Spirit in life. This is so empowering, even when our circumstances say the contrary. But following the Lord leads us to revelation which is to equip His children and increase our light and authority.

We can fall behind in a time zone created by disobedience and just keep dancing around past altars of revelation instead of allowing them to become building blocks in our experience in order to become fully mature sons of God. God has His timetable and has appointed times as we have seen. When Jesus came to the earth it was the appointed time, but if we are 20-30 years behind we might find it difficult to catch up as God is always moving forward to bring fulfilment to His plans and purposes. Today, let's not fight all our circumstances. It could be that God has something to say in order to being us into alignment with His will. Let us come back to simplicity, become like a child and follow the life of the Son within and not follow the knowledge from the tree that God calls forbidden in the Garden of Eden where it brought nothing but death. Even though it looked good it didn't bring life. **God has a way in life, and Jesus is that Way.**

One of Satan's major objectives is to kill the life of the Son of God in those that are born again of the Spirit of God, stemming the growth of that eternal life by dysfunction, deception and substitution, along with compromise and our religious DNA which belongs to our past, and even our fleshy desires, so that we lose the life source from our Lord God and live by good fruit from that tree of knowledge and information. This does not bring transformation. Jesus even confronted this issue to the religious people of the day in John 5:39 (NKJV):

> *"You search the Scriptures, for in them you think you have eternal life; and these are they which testify of Me. But you are not willing to come to Me that you may have life".*

It's no wonder the apostle Paul in 2 Corinthians (1:8-9) could praise God in circumstances of great pressure which was beyond his ability to endure. He felt the sentence of death yet knew this was so he would not rely on himself but on God. He knew the body of Christ has one law, the law of the Spirit of Life. As we see in Psalm 133, the anointing oil flows down and not up, as it is on Christ first, and then flows down to the Body of Christ. We cannot make it flow up.

Our individuality is lost as we live and operate not in independence, but as a part of the Body of Christ, subject to the authority of the Father and those who have a greater authority in God than ourselves. Being accountable in a relationship does not require us to relinquish our wills to another person. It is only to strengthen our relationship with God. We will recognise and know the principle of life because there is no control in this relationship.

God will never cause us to go against the principles of His Word which brings light and freedom.

In these times now there is becoming a silent divorce between the Word of God and the Spirit. This unseen battle that is raging is changing our culture and world view away from the Word and heart of God. How much more should we love our Lord Jesus Christ with all our hearts, minds and strength and stand up and be distinctive and not ashamed of the gospel that Jesus paid the price for with His shed blood at Calvary.

I heard R T Kendall speaking recently on TBN saying "Why is Hell everlasting?" and the answer he gave was "It's only the blood of Jesus that satisfies the justice of God".

How true that is. The love it cost the Father to send his only Son to "save us in every way", just like Rose said to Jack in the film Titanic.

Any parent knows what love for their child is, multiply that and there you will see the extravagant love ongoing day by day that God has for us. Also, how that love is continuously calling us to Himself with the vision of us becoming mature sons of God in this world of darkness. May we as His children align ourselves with His will in this season now and stay within the boundaries of God's love, so that God can bless us (Jude 21 NKJV).

> *"Arise, shine; For your light has come! And the glory of the Lord is risen upon you. For behold, the darkness shall cover the earth, And deep darkness the people; But the Lord will arise over you, And His glory will be seen upon you"*
>
> (Isaiah 60:1)

Sources and Additional Information

Song:
Alleluia, Alleluia *by Terry MacAlmon* on Youtube

Books:
Exit the Devil *by Trevor Deering with Dan Wooding* ISBN 090515603X

My Utmost for His Highest *by Oswald Chambers* ISBN 1572937718

Disciple *by Juan Carlos Ortiz* ISBN 9780551005860

Love Not the World *by Watchman Nee* ISBN 085476114.4

Spiritual Man *by Watchman Nee* ISBN 0-935008-39-X

Restoring the Christian Family *by John and Paula Sandford*
    ISBN 0-932081-12-6

The Transformation of the Inner Man *by John and Paula Sandford*
    ISBN 0-932081-13-4

Foundations for Righteous Living *by Derek Prince* ISBN 1-90114405.4

Blessing or Curse *by Derek Prince* ISBN 190114405.4

Unbroken Curses *by Rebecca Brown MD* ISBN 0-88368-372-5

The Dangers of Alternative Ways to Healing *by David Cross and
    John Berry* ISBN 9281852405373

**A More Excellent Way: Spiritual Roots of Disease – Pathways to
    Wholeness** *by Henry Wright* ISBN 9781603741019

Death to the Family *by Yvonne Kitchen* ISBN 0-646-34807-8